REVELATION: A LINE BY LINE BREAKDOWN

2nd Edition

By: Patrick Muldowney

Copyright © 2024 Patrick Muldowney

All rights reserved. This includes the right to reproduce any portion of this book.

ISBN: 9798334258426

Revelation: A Line by Line Breakdown

Table of Contents

INTRODUCTION:	4
HOW TO STUDY THE SCRIPTURES	13
PRETERISM THEOLOGY:	17
REPLACEMENT THEOLOGY:	18
WHAT ABOUT ISRAEL?	22
REVELATION CHAPTER 1	30
REVELATION CHAPTER 2	38
TO THE CHURCH IN EPHESUS	39
TO THE CHURCH IN SMYRNA	42
TO THE CHURCH IN PERGAMUM	44
TO THE CHURCH IN THYATIRA	46
REVELATION CHAPTER 3	49
TO THE CHURCH IN SARDIS	49
TO THE CHURCH IN PHILADELPHIA	52
TO THE CHURCH IN LAODICEA	54
SUMMARY OF THE LETTERS TO THE SEVEN CHURCHES	55
THE RAPTURE	57
SUMMARY OF WHAT THE SCRIPTURES TEACH ABOUT THE RAPTURE:	64
HOW LONG WILL THE TRIBULATION LAST?	65
REVELATION CHAPTER 4	69
REVELATION CHAPTER 5	74
REVELATION CHAPTER 6	78
REVELATION CHAPTER 7	83
REVELATION CHAPTER 8	88
REVELATION CHAPTER 9	91
REVELATION CHAPTER 10	95
REVELATION CHAPTER 11	100
REVELATION CHAPTER 12	107

Revelation: A Line by Line Breakdown

REVELATION CHAPTER 13 112
- SOME OF THE CHARACTERISTICS OF THE ANTICHRIST: 121
- IS PRESIDENT TRUMP THE ANTICHRIST? 125
- THE FALSE PROPHET 126
- HOW CAN BELIEVERS RECOGNIZE A FALSE PROPHET? 128

REVELATION CHAPTER 14 129

REVELATION CHAPTER 15 134

REVELATION CHAPTER 16 137

REVIEW OF THE TRIBULATION JUDGMENTS 142

REVELATION CHAPTER 17 143

REVELATION CHAPTER 18 154

REVELATION CHAPTER 19 158

A 75-DAY TRANSITIONAL PERIOD 166

REVELATION CHAPTER 20 167
- WHAT WILL THE MILLENNIUM BE LIKE? 169

REVELATION CHAPTER 21 193

REVELATION CHAPTER 22 197

CONCLUSION: BE READY 202

BONUS STUDY ON THE MOUNT OF OLIVES DISCLOSURE 214

INTRODUCTION TO THE MOUNT OF OLIVES DISCLOSURE 214

THE MOUNT OF OLIVES DISCLOSURE - MATTHEW 24 223

DISCIPLES THREE QUESTIONS 225
- QUESTION 1: WHAT WILL BE THE SIGN OF THE END OF THE AGE? ... 225
- QUESTION 2: WHAT WILL BE THE SIGN OF YOUR COMING? 231
- QUESTION 3: WHEN SHALL THESE THINGS BE? 232

THE MOUNT OF OLIVES DISCLOSURE CONTINUES: 232

PARABLE OF THE FIG TREE 242

MATTHEW CHAPTER 25 THE MOUNT OF OLIVES DISCLOSURE CONTINUES 247

PARABLE OF THE TEN VIRGINS 247

Revelation: A Line by Line Breakdown

THE PARABLE OF THE TALENTS 251
THE PARABLE OF THE SHEEP AND GOATS 255
CONCLUSION FOR THE OLIVET DISCOURSE 256
FURTHER READING AND SOURCES 263

NOTE – ALL BIBLE QUOTES FROM THE ENGLISH STANDARD VERSION (ESV)

Revelation: A Line by Line Breakdown

Introduction:

This in-depth study of the Book of Revelation will assist those wanting to explore the Word of God about the *End Times*. Revelation is a book of the Bible about **PROPHECY AND HOPE**. It advises us about the future era called the *End Times*. The *Book of Revelation* is a prophecy concerning God's wrath on an unbelieving world called the Tribulation, the Second Coming of Jesus, to establish His *Millennial Kingdom*. This study is not a complete *eschatology* (end-times theology) study but predominantly about the *Book of Revelation*.

Revelation was written around AD 95, as most biblical scholars and interpreters date the book. Documents by the early church fathers all fix the date as the mid-90s, in the latter part of Emperor Domitian's reign (81-96). The unanimous teachings of early church fathers, like Polycarp, Irenaeus, Clement of Alexandria, Origen, Victorinus, Jerome, and Eusebius, all fix the date as the mid-90s.

Many say that Revelation is too hard to read and much less studied. Many who read and try to study Revelation stop due to the figurative language used. A point to remember is that the reason for the symbolism is that the predictions in the book were made by a first-century man (John) viewing events way in the future, at least 2000 years in the future. The understanding and language of John's Day couldn't adequately convey the message or what was seen. So, John, using his first-century knowledge and writing in Greek (the *lingua franca* of the New Testament), had to use symbols and symbolic writing. However, remember that Jesus promised He would send the Holy Spirit to guide us so we can understand the Bible, including the prophetic passages. Moreover, Revelation is written so that the meaning will unfold as the events get closer. Try to take a literal interpretation as you study this prophecy.

The Bible has volumes of *End Times* prophecy in both the Old and New Testament, but we are discussing only one, the Book of Revelation. We will look at Revelation's prophetic passages so we can mature in God's Word. We will analyze His Word, endeavoring to comprehend the passages with the help of the Holy Spirit. As you study, take a literal analysis of the Scripture, giving a clearer understanding of this prophecy. Be honest with yourself as you study.

"But the anointing that you received from him abides in you, and you do not need that anyone should teach you. But as his anointing teaches you about everything, and is true, and is no lie—just as it has taught you, abide in him." (1 John 2:27)

After studying prophecy for over forty years, this study will clarify Revelation based on my understanding of it. It started when I first read *Late Great Planet Earth (1970),* by Hal Lindsey, a book about *End Times* prophecy. I read it while in High School in the early 1970s. Since then, I have hungered to understand end-time prophecy, reading and studying everything I could on eschatology, and I am open to the Holy Spirit guiding me. I've taken several classes and read several study guides and books by several Bible prophecy scholars. You are to consider this analysis. I've spent over four years putting this study together, reviewing dozens of books, papers, and lectures. I was checking and rechecking every verse by several prophecy scholars such as Hal Lindsey, John Hagee, Tim LaHaye, Randy Alcorn, and others, too many. I take writing this very seriously since now I have taken on the role of a teacher.

"Not many of you should become teachers, my brothers, for you know that we who teach will be judged with greater strictness." (James 3:1).

So why study prophecy? To know what God wants us to know about future events. Jesus came to fulfill prophecy; He is the Messiah foretold throughout the Bible. John was told in Revelation

19:10 by an angel that *"...Jesus is the spirit of prophecy."* This means that Jesus has been the core of all prophecies since time began. Throughout Jesus' life, many biblical scholars accept that Jesus fulfilled over three hundred prophecies. However, many people believe that Jesus is not the Almighty God. This **FALSE** understanding of Scripture leads many astray. However, this study is about *The Book of Revelation*, not apologetics for Christ. This study assumes that Jesus is Almighty God, the Messiah, the only true Son of God, the Alpha and Omega, Lord of Lords and King of Kings.

It was written that Jesus came to us as a human (Genesis: 3:15), being born of a virgin (Isaiah: 7:14). He is a descendant of Abraham, Isaac, and Jacob, from the tribe of Judah (Genesis: 22:18). He would appear after the time of Babylonian captivity and Jerusalem's rebuilding (Dan 9:25). He would be born in a town called Bethlehem (Micah: 5:2) and be called out of Egypt, where his earthly father Joseph had taken him (Hosea: 11:1). He would be a light unto the Gentiles in Galilee (Isaiah: 9:1-2). A forerunner (John the Baptist) would precede His ministry (Isaiah: 40:3-4). He would teach in parables (Psalm 78:2), and miracles, signs, and wonders would confirm His Word (Isaiah: 35:4-6). He would be humble and meek (Isaiah: 42:2-3) and ride into Jerusalem on a donkey (Zech.9:9). He would be called the Son of God (Isaiah: 9:6-7) by those who followed Him, yet He would be rejected by those who mocked Him (Isaiah: 531-4; Dan. 9:24-26) and despised by those who opposed Him (Psalm: 2:1-12).

Over the three days of His trial, crucifixion, and resurrection, Jesus Christ fulfilled over thirty prophecies. The odds of one person satisfying that many prophecies in three days are less than one in one trillion (1:1,000,000,000,000). Isaiah Chapter 53, written over 800 years before the birth of Jesus, perfectly describes Him. It tells how He came to establish a new relationship between God and His people. I suggest you read it if you don't know it.

By studying Bible prophecy, we can acquire critical evidence about approaching prophetic events, such as *The End Times*. Revelation is about the Tribulation on an unbelieving world, Jesus' second coming, His judgment of man, and the setup of His Millennial Kingdom on the new earth. Moreover, the Bible would be hopeless if these prophecies were not in the Bible. The first ray of light and hope to come to the world was immediately after the fall of man in the Garden of Eden. God gave man the promise of a Redeemer in Genesis Chapter Three. This first prediction is the most crucial prophecy in the entire Word of God.

WHY STUDY REVELATION?

The primary reason is that Jesus assured us that he would return. Those who want to know about His return must also study The Book of Revelation with the Mount of Olives Disclosure. It also gives believers in Christ hope for the coming End Times and familiarity with the *Tribulation* and His *Millennial Kingdom*.

"For whatever was written in former days was written for our instruction, that through endurance and the encouragement of the Scriptures, we might have hope." (Romans 15:4 ESV)

Many fear *The Book of Revelation* needlessly. Many confuse the wrath poured out by God on those who reject Christ will also be the same wrath believers in Christ will have to endure—this is **FALSE. GOD ALWAYS PROTECTS HIS PEOPLE**. God will protect his people in the End Times with the Rapture before the Tribulation.

The Book of Revelation and *The Mount of Olives Disclosure* should be taken literally of things to come, the End Times. The critical point of *The Book of Revelation* is that Jesus Christ is returning to set up his Kingdom on earth; unbelievers will be judged. His return has nothing to do with anyone having faith in Him. Jesus will return because it is a sovereign act of God. No matter if you believe in God and His written Word or not. If you think the *Mount of Olives Disclosure* and the *Book of Revelation* are history or prophecy. If you believe in the Rapture or not. **THESE THINGS WILL HAPPEN** because these are sovereign acts of God, not dependent on faith.

A Gallup Survey on religion showed that more than 62% of Americans believe that Jesus Christ will return literally to the earth. Furthermore, this same percentage believes in Christ's unique deity. What makes this statistic so amazing is that the same survey showed that only 40% of Americans profess to have accepted Christ as their savior. In other words, 22% more Americans believe in Christ's second coming than are ready to meet him.

Revelation is the only book of the Bible that states that one should read it and receive a blessing. It also says that Revelation is a prophecy right in the opening.

³ Blessed is the one who reads aloud <u>the words of this prophecy</u>, and <u>blessed are those</u> who hear, and <u>who keep what is written in it</u>, for the time is near. (Revelation 1:3).

Remember that Jesus said we are to become like little children when studying Revelation. This is due to children's brilliance in their simplicity and trust. Likewise, children always take a literal view of everything. A child incarnates this reality.

² And calling to him a child, he put him in the midst of them ³ and said "Truly, I say to you, unless you turn and become like children, you will never enter the kingdom of heaven. ⁴ Whoever humbles himself like this child is the greatest in the kingdom of heaven. ⁵Whoever receives one such child in my name receives me," (Matthew 18:2-5).

The scriptures proclaim, *"...the Son of Man is coming at an hour when you do not expect Him"* (Matthew 24:44). So, what hour are we on the clock of history? Jesus Himself warns us seven times in Matthew 24 about the coming End Times. He tells us that there will be deceivers, false Christs, false teachers, and false prophets in the later days. This is a crucial reason why we should study this prophetic word.

We can know God's great plan for His followers and those who are not. Revelation offers hope and a warning. Jesus' second coming is not going to be in Independence, Missouri. What did Jesus have to say about his return?

²⁷ For as the lightning comes from the east and shines as far as the west, so will be the coming of the Son of Man. ²⁸ Wherever the corpse is, there the vultures will gather. The Coming of the Son of Man ²⁹ Immediately after the tribulation of those days the sun will be darkened, and the moon will not give its light, and the stars will fall from heaven, and the powers of the heavens will be shaken. ³⁰ Then will appear in heaven the sign of the Son of Man, and then all the tribes of the earth will mourn, and they will see the Son of Man coming on the clouds of heaven with power and great glory. ³¹ And he will send out his angels with a loud trumpet call, and they will gather his elect from the four winds, from one end of heaven to the other. (Matthew 24:27-31)

Preterism theology is a school of thought, which says all this prophecy has already happened in the first century. Allegedly, Jesus came in the clouds for the WHOLE WORLD to see and mourn Him for the crucifixion. It's hard for them to explain it; history does not record it, but they say it occurred. Christ warns of deceivers.

⁶ And you will hear of wars and rumors of wars. See that you are not alarmed, for this must take place, but the end is not yet. ⁷ For nation will rise against nation, and kingdom against kingdom,

Revelation: A Line by Line Breakdown

and there will be famines and earthquakes in various places. ⁸ All these are but the beginning of the birth pains. ⁹"Then they will deliver you up to tribulation and put you to death, and you will be hated by all nations for my name's sake. ¹⁰ And then many will fall away and betray one another and hate one another. ¹¹ And many false prophets will arise and lead many astray. ¹² And because lawlessness will be increased, the love of many will grow cold. (Matthew 24:6-12)

God chose the Apostle John to receive and write everything he saw in *The Book of Revelation.* He wrote this while in exile on the island of Patmos in the Aegean Sea around AD 95. John received this prophecy of the future for all of mankind from God. Revelation speaks to the Church and the Jews about the *End Times.* Jesus stated this is a literal prophecy, which John was to record so everyone may hear. Jesus told John to write of His resurrected glorified person. John was to record all the essentials for the churches. All the things which will take place through a time known as the Tribulation to *'the end of the world.'* Finally, John was told to tell of what would take place after Jesus returned about the *Final Judgment* and His *Millennial Kingdom.*

While John did not comprehend numerous things he saw, he faithfully recorded everything. He was told to tell of everything he saw as he watched the future happenings transpire from the very throne of God. At the time John wrote Revelation, he was an old man. God's revelations spanned from the first century to the end of the age, even to the time of a new earth and a new heaven. That was over 2000 years ago. John received this prophecy directly from God the Father, Jesus, and the angels.

¹ The revelation of Jesus Christ, <u>which God gave him</u> to show to his servants the things that must soon take place. <u>He made it known by sending his angel</u> to his servant John, ² who bore witness to <u>the word of God</u> and <u>the testimony of Jesus Christ</u>, even to all that he *saw. ³ Blessed is the one who reads aloud <u>the words of this prophecy</u>, and blessed are those who hear, and who keep what is written in it, for the time is near.* (Revelation 1:1-3)

Many feel terrified of what Revelation has to say. The purpose of this study is to uplift and give hope to everyone. Revelation discloses God's plan for the last days or end times, Christ's Second Coming, and His Millennial Kingdom. Revelation is not to frighten anyone but to inform and give confidence in future events. Fear comes from not knowing. God knows all things past, present, and future. God knows all things in advance. He is in control and has a plan that started with Adam and Eve.

God sent specific warnings of all things coming so we would not fear the *End Times* but embrace them. We must accept the fact that God's plan has His grace. It is a plan for salvation for all who are willing to listen. There is hope in understanding what is coming. There is hope in getting spiritually prepared for all future events. We all need to trust God's plan is fair and just. Everything is in His hands.

The understanding of end times prophecy, which Revelation is, will get clearer as the end times approach. Jesus called these events to come, just before the Tribulation, *"birth pains"* and *"signs of the times."* Are we entering that time? Many say YES. One of these signs is recorded in 2 Timothy 3:1-8.

¹ But understand, that in the last days there will come times of difficulty. ² For people will be lovers of self, lovers of money, proud, arrogant, abusive, disobedient to their parents, ungrateful, unholy, ³ heartless, unappeasable, slanderous, without self-control, brutal, not loving good, ⁴ treacherous, reckless, swollen with conceit, lovers of pleasure rather than lovers of God, ⁵ having the appearance of godliness, but denying its power. Avoid such people. ⁶ For among them are those who creep into households and capture weak women, burdened with

sins and led astray by various passions, ⁷ always learning and never able to arrive at a knowledge of the truth. ⁸ Just as Jannes and Jambres opposed Moses, so these men also oppose the truth, men corrupted in mind and disqualified regarding the faith.
(2 Timothy 3:1-8)

Look around. Is this what's going on now? Is this prophecy of the last days being fulfilled? Are we seeing signs of the times and birth pains? Be honest with yourself and compare what's happening in our time with what is said in 2 Timothy 3.

This study of Revelation is a line-by-line breakdown of the *Book of Revelation*, not phrases; there is no text out of context. You can read the exact text. By the time you finish this study, you will have read all of *The Book of Revelation*.

"Blessed is the one who reads aloud <u>the words of this prophecy,</u> and <u>blessed are those who hear, and who keep what is written</u> in it, for the time is near."(Revelation 1:3)

As you study Revelation, be honest with yourself about it. The Book of Revelation can be divided into three sections. The beginning is about humanity ruining Christ's Church. The next part is about the Tribulation and the earth ruled by Satan's antichrist. The last part is about Christ Jesus' glorious return to establish His Kingdom, His judgment of man, and the creation of the new earth.

Study the Word of God, and let the Holy Spirit lead you. Remember that *The Book of Revelation* should be taken as a literal meaning of things to come. The key point is Jesus Christ is returning. Also, it's a warning of the *End Times* and God's judgments on an unbelieving world. His judgment is for those who do not have Christ in their life. No one should ever fear the *End Times* if Christ is in their life by being **Born Again**. That is the HOPE for anyone who cares to listen. If you do not know Jesus and are a seeker, I pray you find Him. Study His WORD.

How To Study The Scriptures

When one studies the Scriptures (the Bible), one should use a few well-known techniques that Bible scholars have advised and used. In Scripture, God provides us with everything He wants us to know about Him and His plans. He spells out very clearly how to have salvation, about the coming future events, and how we can have a personal relationship with Him. God is the one who created the Bible. He speaks to us today, just as He spoke to His people in ancient times when His words were first given. As long as we read the Bible accurately and comprehend it correctly, we will never get lost in it or its teachings. The **First Thing:** every time you start to read Scripture, ask for guidance from the Holy Spirit.

9 But, as it is written, "What no eye has seen, nor ear heard, nor the heart of man imagined, what God has prepared for those who love him"- 10 these things God has revealed to us through the Spirit. For the Spirit searches everything, even the depths of God. 11 For who knows a person's thoughts except the spirit of that person, which is in him? So also no one comprehends the thoughts of God except the Spirit of God. 12 Now we have received not the spirit of the world, but the Spirit who is from God, that we might understand the things freely given us by God. 13 And we impart this in words not taught by human wisdom but taught by the Spirit, interpreting spiritual truths to those who are spiritual.
(1 Corinthians 2:9-13)

But the Helper, the Holy Spirit, whom the Father will send in my name, he will teach you all things and bring to your remembrance all that I have said to you. (John 14:26)

When reading prophecy, it is always best to take a literal approach. The word is *literal* comes from the Latin *sensus literalis*, which refers to seeking in a precise sense. This means taking the text as used, not in a nonliteral or allegorical sense. Another way to describe the literal meaning of Scripture is that it will hold to the everyday, common understanding of the terms. Words in Scripture should be given the meaning they usually have in everyday speech.

Remember, the Literal Method of Interruption Accepts Figures of Speech. For instance, when Jesus said in John 15: *[1] I am the true vine, and my Father is the vinedresser. [2] Every branch in me that does not bear fruit he takes away, and every branch that does bear fruit He prunes, that it may bear more fruit.* The literal system of interpretation does not take this as physically true. Reasonably, we know this is a figure of speech. Defining when a passage should or should not be taken literally may occasionally be challenging. However, there are definite guidelines on determining when a text should be taken figuratively.

- ❖ When it is obviously symbolic. As when Jesus said, He was a door in John 10:9: *"I am the door. If anyone enters by me, he will be saved and will go in and out and find pasture."*
- ❖ When the text itself authorizes the figurative sense. When Paul said he is using allegory in Galatians 4:24: *"Now this may be interpreted allegorically: these women are two covenants..."*
- ❖ When a literal interpretation contradicts other truths inside or outside the Bible. When the Bible speaks of the four corners of the earth, it is not saying the earth is flat. *"After this I saw four angels standing at the four corners of the earth..."* (Revelation 7:1)
- ❖ In short, always use the long-standing famous saying: *"When the literal sense makes good sense, seek no other sense lest the result is nonsense."*

The literal method of interruption does not eliminate the use of symbols. The Bible is filled with symbols; each symbol represents something literal. For example, the *Book of Revelation* is filled with symbols that represent literal things. Jesus stated in Revelation 1:20: ***"As for the mystery of the seven stars that you saw in my right hand, and the seven golden lampstands, the seven stars are the angels of the seven churches, and the seven lampstands are the seven churches."*** Each symbol represents something literal. Textual clues often point to the literal truth found in the symbol.

<u>The literal method of interruption does not eliminate the use of parables.</u> Jesus spoke in parables that are to be taken literally. He explains this in Matthew chapter 13. Parables convey a literal idea. Jesus wanted His parables to be transparent to anyone who listened to them.

He carefully interpreted two for the disciples, the *Parable of the Sower* (Matthew 13:1-9) and the *Parable of the Weeds* (Matthew 13:24-30). He did this so there would not be any doubt as to the correct meaning of His parables, plus how to interpret parables correctly. Jesus fully expected His believers to be able to follow His method and comprehend the literal meaning to which His parables pointed.

Reasons to use a Literal Approach. There are at least five reasons for adopting a literal interpretation of Scripture, including prophecy, which Revelation is.

- ❖ Most of the Bible makes sense when taken literally.
- ❖ It is the usual method of understanding.
- ❖ This method will allow for a symbolic or secondary meaning when it is essentially based on the situation.
- ❖ All allegorical or secondary meanings depend on the literal meaning.
- ❖ It is the only method of keeping with the nature of inspiration. Remember that all Scripture is God-given.

<u>Submit All Doctrinal Assumptions to Scripture.</u> Our opinions should not direct our interpretations of Scripture. Of course, our interpretations are influenced to some degree by personal, political, theological, and denominational prejudices. No one is without prejudices. Remember, our interpretations must agree with Scripture and be willing to change our understanding, as needed, based on Scripture.

Remember That One Passage May Apply To More Than One Event. Prophetic Scripture may refer to two events separated by a significant period in the same passage, such as the prophecy on the *Advent of Jesus*.

Look Up The History And Culture Of The Time. To study Scripture, as with history, one must get out of modern times and become as if in the time being studied. The Bible is primarily set in ancient Israel, with Jewish customs. Also, some Roman customs and laws must be known in the New Testament. Study those periods in history. What were the customs of the time? Learn about their marriages, burial rites, farming, and business practices. Learn about the system of government. Also, learn what a covenant is and how one is made and broken. Knowing these things makes interpreting the Bible correctly significantly easier.

Make A Correct Genre Association. The Bible contains a variety of genres. The main genres are law, history, wisdom, poetry, narrative, epistles, prophecy, and apocalyptic literature. Each type has peculiar characteristics that must be known to interpret the text correctly. An incorrect genre association will lead to misinterpretation. Revelation's genre is prophecy; it is not history, as some people want us to think.

Pay Close Attention To Context. Every word in the Bible is part of a sentence, every sentence is part of a paragraph, and every paragraph is part of a book. Books make up the Bible. Remember, when studying the Word of God, it is best to look at the line before and after a noted verse, read the whole paragraph, or read the book to understand the meaning entirely. This prevents misinterpretation based on text that is out of context, often used to cause a different meaning of a verse not intended by the Scripture.

While studying Revelation, be alert. Do not let those who teach Preterism or Replacement Theology try to sway you. Neither is based on any known Scripture or recorded history.

Preterism Theology:

Preterism comes from the Latin term *praeter*, meaning something is *passed* or *beyond*. Preterism Theology, also known as Dominion Theology, teaches that all the Biblical prophecies, including the Book of Revelation and Christ's Olivet Discourse (Matthew 24 and 25), have already occurred in the first century. This means both are history, **NOT PROPHECY**. This idea started around 1640 and is not grounded in any Scriptures, historical records, or literal interpretation of Bible prophecy. In the last chapter of Revelation, God cautions everyone not to modify the words of HIS Prophecy.

[18] I warn everyone who hears the words of the prophecy of this book: if anyone adds to them, God will add to him the plagues described in this book, [19] and if anyone takes away from the words of the book of this prophecy, God will take away his share in the tree of life and in the holy city, which are described in this book. (Revelation 22:18,19)

The key point of Preterism Theology is that everything Jesus says in *The Mount of Olives Disclosure* and the *Book of Revelation* happened in the first century. However, the Book of Revelation had to be written before AD 95 for this to be true. This is crucial for Preterism. So, they say Revelation was written before AD 70; however, history shows differently.

As most Biblical and historical scholars assumed, John wrote the Book of Revelation about AD 95. Even the unanimous teachings of early church fathers, like Polycarp, Ireneaeus, Clement of Alexandria, Origen, Victorinus, Jerome, and Eusebius, all fix the date as the mid-90s. The question to be asked is why John would write a book of prophecy over 25 years after the event. He wouldn't.

The early church was the primary source for the date of the Book of Revelation. John's spiritual grandson was Irenaeus. He was the disciple of Polycarp, a disciple of John himself. Irenaeus wrote about the origin of the *Book of Revelation*. He stated it was toward the end of Domitian's reign, AD 81-96.

Additionally, if John had been telling a historical story, he would have named the antichrist and false prophet. He would never have let those important names go unpublished, as he would in prophecy. Biblical history is how we have the great names from the Bible.

Replacement Theology:

Replacement Theology claims that the Church has replaced Israel in God's plan. The Church fulfills all the covenants God made with Israel. Replacement Theology is not based on or supported by any Scriptures or prophecy. The apostles never taught it in the first century. Supposedly, the Christian church has replaced Israel in God's plan for mankind because they rejected Jesus Christ as their Messiah.

This means Israel forfeited all covenants or Sovereign promises made to Abraham, Isaac, and Jacob called the *Abrahamic Covenants* (Genesis 12, 13, 15, 17). As well as all covenants made to Moses in the *Land Covenants* (Deuteronomy 29, 30). Israel also forfeited all covenants made to David in the *Davidic Covenants* (2 Samuel 7). And to all covenants made to Jeremiah in the *New Covenant* (Jeremiah 31). Thus, making most of the Old Testament invalid and useless, it demands God must be a liar, **WHICH HE CAN NEVER BE**.

[1]"Now the LORD said to Abram, Go from your country and your kindred and your father's house to the land that I will show you. [2]And I will make of you a great nation, and I will bless you and make your name great, so that you will be a blessing. [3] I will bless those who bless you, and him who dishonors you I will curse, and in you all the families of the earth shall be blessed."
(Genesis 12:1-3)

According to Replacement Theology's view, since Israel forfeited its place in God's plan, the Jews have no legitimate claim to the land of Israel or all covenants promised to them by God. Moreover, there can be no expectation. Jerusalem will not be the everlasting capital of Israel and the world as God promises. As Isaiah and Revelation foretell, Jesus Christ will not rule over the world from Jerusalem in a literal 1000-year kingdom from a rebuilt temple there.

[17]"For behold, I create new heavens and a new earth, and the former things shall not be remembered or come into mind. [18] But be glad and rejoice forever in that which I create; for behold, I create Jerusalem to be a joy, and her people to be a gladness.
(Isaiah 65:17,18)

[10] And he carried me away in the Spirit to a great, high mountain, and showed me the holy city Jerusalem coming down out of heaven from God, [11] having the glory of God, its radiance like a most rare jewel, like a jasper, clear as crystal. [12] It had a great, high wall, with twelve gates, and at the gates twelve angels, and on the gates the names of the twelve tribes of the sons of Israel were inscribed [13] on the east three gates, on the north three gates, on the south three gates, and on the west three gates. [14] And the wall of the city had twelve foundations, and on them were the twelve names of the twelve apostles of the Lamb."
(Revelation 21:10-14)

Rome destroyed Israel in AD 70, yet God brought it back as a nation in 1948. John, who wrote The Book of Revelation, knew that in God's plan, the Jews would return to the Promised Land as a nation. This makes the year 1948 significant from a prophetic understanding.

"And I will multiply people on you, the whole house of Israel, all of it. The cities shall be inhabited and the waste places rebuilt." (Ezekiel 36:10).

This prophecy was fulfilled in 1948. Ezekiel was written in 700 BC, and God knew that in AD 70, Israel would be destroyed and the people dispersed. Then, in 1948, Israel would become a nation again. Ezekiel speaks of a future redemption, a restored Jerusalem, and a worldwide acknowledgment of God and His Messiah. Due to God's faithfulness to His Word, through His covenants with Israel, He revived His people once more. He will protect them. Israel will overwhelm all the forces and powers arrayed against them. Replacement Theology denies this prophecy, calling God a liar. Ezekiel's prophecy was fulfilled when Israel was restored as a nation, plus they are now physically on the land God gave them at the time of Moses.

"Then he said to me, "Son of man, these bones are the whole house of Israel. Behold, they say, 'Our bones are dried up, and our hope is lost; we are indeed cut off." (Ezekiel 37:11)

When Ezekiel uses the term *"they say"* in this verse, it is comparable to what the Replacement Theology practitioners teach. They say or teach that the Nation of Israel was finished in AD 70 and had no future as a distinct people or nation. However, God identifies the bones in Ezekiel as representing *"the whole house of Israel."* This prophecy is factually predicting the restoration and spiritual rebirth of the whole nation of Israel. Don't believe those who say Israel is dead, such as those who believe in Replacement Theology. God knew there would be deceivers like them, trying to change His words and prophecies. Jesus Himself said:

17 Do not think that I have come to abolish the Law or the Prophets; I have not come to abolish them but to fulfill them. 18 For truly, I say to you, until heaven and earth pass away, not an iota, not a dot, will pass from the Law until all is accomplished. (Matthew 5:17-18)

I ask, then, has God rejected his people? By no means! For I myself am an Israelite, a descendant of Abraham, a member of the tribe of Benjamin. (Romans 11:1)

For the gifts and the calling of God (promises and covenants) ***are irrevocable.*** (Romans 11:29)

    The misguided thinking of those who believe the deception of Replacement Theology contends that the church has not actually replaced Israel but rather that the church is simply the True Israel. This way, they say they are not calling God a liar. All the promises made to Israel in the Old Testament were always intended by God to be fulfilled spiritually by the church rather than literally by the Jews. However, God made unconditional and eternal covenants with His people, Israel, which guaranteed they would experience material and spiritual blessings, have many descendants, and receive the land of Israel.

    The critical threat of Replacement Theology, or any theology that denies a future for the nation of Israel, is that historically, it has often fostered outright anti-Semitism. It was first proposed by Justin Martyr (AD 100-AD 165), known as Justin the Philosopher. He was an early Christian apologist and philosopher. However, Replacement Theology didn't gain much support until the fourth century when Augustine (AD 354-425) placed it into his allegorically based eschatology. Because of him, this became a doctrine that the Jews were labeled *"Christ Killers."*

Starting with the first crusade in 1095, tens of thousands of Jews were slaughtered. This was due to centuries of erroneous sermons about the Jews being guilty of Jesus' crucifixion. The crusades were supposedly about ridding the holy land of Muslims, but there were more calls for wiping out the *"Christ-killers."* The Crusaders were encouraged by anti-Jewish slogans and propaganda. They began to rid Europe of all Jews. Terrible massacres took place in town after town all over Europe, all the way to Jerusalem. The Jewish community of Jerusalem was obliterated in the name of Christianity.

This is also true of the Holocaust; Hitler quoted Replacement Theology in *Mein Kampf* as the reason for the *"Final Solution for the Jews."* Today, many supremacist movement groups want to continue Hitler's Final Solution. This is not to say that any given individual who embraces Replacement Theology is anti-Semitic. But every time any doctrine sets itself in contradiction with the explicit promises of God, which He carefully outlined in prophecy and set in the Bible for the Jewish people, the potential dangers cannot be inflated. Replacement Theology is also one of the direct causes preventing Jews from knowing Christ. This is because of their long history of persecution by Christians throughout the centuries. This persecution was because of what these ideas or lies promoted.

WHAT ABOUT ISRAEL?

Israel is God's chosen people. They will play a vital role in the End Times and are necessary for critical Biblical prophecies to make sense. Foremost, Israel must make a treaty with the Antichrist. This begins the Tribulation, as foretold by Daniel.

The Romans destroyed Israel in AD 70. At that time, most of Israel's people were dispersed worldwide. However, they came back together as a nation in 1948. This return of the Jews to the Promised Land was foretold in prophecy. Prophecy also states that Israel must make a peace covenant between themselves and the future antichrist before the Tribulation will begin. Again, Daniel foretold that this pack's signing would signal the Tribulation's beginning. Most prophecy scholars believe this event will not occur until after the Rapture.

When John wrote Revelation, Israel had already been destroyed by Rome. John knew it, he saw it, and he lived through it. However, John knew that in God's plan, the Jews would be back as a nation on the Promised Land. Israel must be a viable political entity in the end times. This makes the year 1948 very significant from a prophetic understanding. Also, the Jewish Temple, which was destroyed in AD 70, will be rebuilt and will exist during the Tribulation period.

Israel had previously been in bondage to single nations, such as the Egyptians, the Assyrians, the Babylonians, and the Persians. In each case, God delivered them. However, never in biblical history had the Israelites been delivered from all over the world and then brought back together after so many centuries.

63 And as the LORD took delight in doing you good and multiplying you, so the LORD will take delight in bringing ruin upon you and destroying you. And you shall be plucked off the land that you are entering to take possession of it. 64 And the LORD will scatter you among all peoples, from one end of the earth to the other, and there you shall serve other gods of wood and stone, which neither you nor your fathers have known. 65 And among these nations you shall find no respite, and there shall be no resting place for the sole of your foot, but the LORD will give you there a trembling heart and failing eyes and a languishing soul. 66 Your life shall hang in doubt before you. Night and day you shall be in dread and have no assurance of your life. 67 In the morning you shall say, 'If only it were evening!' and at evening you shall say, 'If only it were morning!' because of the dread that your heart shall feel, and the sights that your eyes shall see. ⁶⁸ And the LORD will bring you back in ships to Egypt, a journey that I promised that you should never make again; and there you shall offer yourselves for sale to your enemies as male and female slaves, but there will be no buyer." (Deuteronomy 28:63-68)

¹ And when all these things come upon you, the blessing and the curse, which I have set before you, and you call them to mind among all the nations where the LORD your God has driven you, ²and return to the LORD your God, you and your children, and obey his voice in all that I command you today, with all your heart and with all your soul, ³ then the LORD your God will restore your fortunes and have compassion on you, and he will gather you again from all the peoples where the LORD your God has scattered you. ⁴ If your outcasts are in the uttermost parts of heaven, from there the LORD your God will gather you, and from there he will take you. ⁵ And the LORD your God will bring you into the land that your fathers possessed, that you may possess it. And he will make you more prosperous and numerous than your fathers. ⁶And the LORD your God will circumcise your heart and the heart of your offspring, so that you will love the LORD your God with all your heart and with all your soul, that you may live. ⁷ And the LORD your God will put all these curses on your foes and enemies who persecuted you." (Deuteronomy 30:1-7)

"And I will multiply people on you, the whole house of Israel, all of it. The cities shall be inhabited and the waste places rebuilt." (Ezekiel 36:10).

This event did not find fulfillment until 1948. Ezekiel was written in 700 BC, and God knew that in AD 70, Israel would be destroyed and the people dispersed, then in 1948, become a nation again. Ezekiel speaks of a future redemption, a restored Jerusalem, and a worldwide recognition of God and His Messiah. Due to God's faithfulness to His Word, He will revive His people once more through His covenants. He will again shepherd them compassionately and rebuild them as a perfect expression of His Kingdom. Under the hand of *"David,"* He will overwhelm all the forces and powers arrayed against them. His glory shall shine to all the nations of the world by His magnificent presence.

[1] The hand of the LORD was upon me, and he brought me out in the Spirit of the LORD and set me down in the middle of the valley; it was full of bones. [2] And he led me around among them, and behold, there were very many on the surface of the valley, and behold, they were very dry. [3] And he said to me, Son of man, can these bones live? And I answered, O Lord GOD, you know. [4] Then he said to me, Prophesy over these bones, and say to them, O dry bones, hear the word of the LORD. [5] Thus says the Lord GOD to these bones: Behold, I will cause breath to enter you, and you shall live. [6] And I will lay sinews upon you, and will cause flesh to come upon you, and cover you with skin, and put breath in you, and you shall live, and you shall know that I am the LORD. "[7] So I prophesied as I was commanded. And as I prophesied, there was a sound, and behold, a rattling, and the bones came together, bone to its bone. [8] And I looked, and behold, there were sinews on them, and flesh had come upon them, and skin had covered them. But there was no breath in them. (Ezekiel 37:1-8)

This is the first portion of Ezekiel's prophecy about Israel's physical restoration as a nation. This happened in 1948 without a spiritual restoration, which will come later.

[9] Then he said to me, Prophesy to the breath; prophesy, son of man, and say to the breath, Thus says the Lord GOD: Come from the four winds, O breath, and breathe on these slain, that they may live. [10] So I prophesied as he commanded me, and the breath

came into them, and they lived and stood on their feet, an exceedingly great army. (Ezekiel 37:9-10)

This predicts Israel's spiritual restoration, the second portion of Ezekiel's prophecy. This occurs after Israel is restored as a nation and they are physically on the land God gave them.

¹¹ Then he said to me, "Son of man, these bones are the whole house of Israel. Behold, they say, 'Our bones are dried up, and our hope is lost; we are indeed cut off. (Ezekiel 37:11)

What *"they say"* used in this verse is comparable to what the Replacement Theology practitioners teach. They say or teach that the Nation of Israel is finished and has no future as a distinct people or nation. However, God identifies the bones as representing *"the whole house of Israel."* This prophecy is factually predicting the restoration and spiritual rebirth of the whole nation of Israel. Do not believe those who say Israel is dead. It was restored by God in 1948.

¹² 'Therefore prophesy, and say to them, Thus says the Lord GOD: Behold, I will open your graves and raise you from your graves, O my people. And I will bring you into the land of Israel. ¹³ And you shall know that I am the LORD, when I open your graves, and raise you from your graves, O my people. ¹⁴ And I will put my Spirit within you, and you shall live, and I will place you in your own land. Then you shall know that I am the LORD; I have spoken, and I will do it, declares the LORD."I Will Be Their God, They Shall Be My People. ¹⁵ The word of the LORD came to me: ¹⁶ Son of man, take a stick and write on it, For Judah, and the people of Israel associated with him; then take another stick and write on it, For Joseph (the stick of Ephraim) and all the house of Israel associated with him. ¹⁷ And join them one to another into one stick, that they may become one in your hand. ¹⁸ And when your people say to *you, Will you not tell us what you mean by these? ¹⁹ say to them, Thus says the Lord GOD: Behold, I am about to take the stick of Joseph (that is in the hand of Ephraim) and the tribes of Israel associated with him. And I will join with it the stick of Judah, and make them one stick, that they may be one in my hand. ²⁰ When the sticks on which you write are in your hand before their eyes, ²¹ then say to them, Thus says the Lord GOD: Behold, I will take the people of Israel from the nations among which they have gone, and will gather them from all around, and bring them to their own land.²² And I will make them one nation in the land, on the mountains of Israel. And one king shall be king over them all, and they shall be no longer two nations, and no longer divided into two kingdoms. ²³ They shall not defile themselves anymore with their idols and their detestable things, or with any of their transgressions. But I will save them from all the backslidings in which they have sinned, and will cleanse them; and they shall be my people, and I will be their God. ²⁴ My servant David shall be king over them, and they shall all have one shepherd. They shall walk by my rules and be careful to obey my statutes. ²⁵ They shall dwell in the land that I gave to my servant Jacob, where your fathers lived. They and their children and their children's children shall dwell there forever, and David my servant shall be their prince forever. ²⁶ I will make a covenant of peace with them. It shall be an everlasting covenant with them. And I will set them in their land and multiply them, and will set my sanctuary in their midst forevermore. ²⁷ My dwelling place shall be with them, and I will be their God, and they shall be my people. ²⁸ Then the nations will know that I am the LORD who sanctifies Israel, when my sanctuary is in their midst forevermore."* (Ezekiel 37:12-28)

Ezekiel Chapter 37 prophesies are key prophecies about the end times. The scattered dry bones represent the whole House of Israel, all the Jews. They were scattered around the world for two millennia. It seemed impossible for Israel ever to be a nation again.

How can life come to disjointed bones? However, in 1948, by God's power, Israel became a nation again.

The graves, in this context, symbolize the nations where the Jews were scattered. Each grave or nation was akin to a tomb for the Jews, as they were not in the promised land, Israel. The coming together of the bones and the flesh that came upon them symbolizes the miraculous restoration of the Jews as a nation in the Promised Land, Israel. The absence of breath is symbolic of the lack of spiritual life, with the breath representing the Holy Spirit. The act of breathing life into them symbolizes a spiritual rebirth.

God's covenant with Israel is the cornerstone of this prophecy. It is a divine assurance that Israel is His people, and He will restore Them. This prophecy, in itself, is a refutation of Replacement Theology. The dry bones receiving skin and flesh, and the wind being told to blow upon them, is a testament to the power of God in restoring life. The wind, in this context, is a sign of the Spirit of God. This prophecy was a source of encouragement for Israel, foretelling their restoration from the long-continued scattering over the centuries. It also alludes to the Messiah's resurrection of the dead. We are urged to look to Him (the Messiah), who will ultimately open graves, bringing people to judgment. The Messiah will deliver us from sin. God will put His Spirit within us, and through faith, we will have salvation through His Messiah.

This sign shows the people (Israel) that the Lord will unite Judah and Israel. Christ is the true David, Israel's most famous King. Events yet to come will further explain His prophecies. As prophesized by Ezekiel, God's program of restoring Israel has been in progress since 1881, setting the stage for the future Tribulation. Here are a few key points in Israel's history since 1881:

- ❖ **1881-1900**: About 30,000 Jews who had been persecuted in Russia moved to Palestine.
- ❖ **1897**: The goal of establishing a home in Palestine for Jewish people received great energy when the first Zionist Congress convened in Basel, Switzerland, and adopted Zionism as a program.
- ❖ **1904-1914**: 32,000 more Jews who had been persecuted in Russia moved to Palestine.
- ❖ **1924-1932**: 78,000 Polish Jews move to Palestine.
- ❖ **1933-1939**: 230,000 Jews who had been persecuted in Germany and central Europe moved to Palestine.
- ❖ **1948**: Israel becomes a nation after being destroyed in AD 70.
- ❖ **1967**: Israel captured Jerusalem and the West Bank during the Six-Day War after an Arab invasion of the new state of Israel.
- ❖ **2017**: The US officially recognized Jerusalem as Israel's capital by President Donald Trump and opened the US Embassy there.
- ❖ **2020**: The Abraham Accords, brokered by President Donald Trump, are bilateral agreements on Arab–Israeli normalization. As part of the agreements, both the UAE and Bahrain recognized Israel's sovereignty, enabling the establishment of full diplomatic relations.
- ❖ **? Yet To Come**: the 144,000 evangelical Jews, 12,000 from each Tribe of Israel after the Rapture of the Church, who will fill a spiritual void or emptiness left on earth due to the removal of all true believers. These 144,000 new Jewish believers will proclaim that salvation is through Jesus. (More in Revelation 7:4-8)

[17] Do not think that I have come to abolish the Law or the Prophets; I have not come to abolish them but to fulfill them.

[18] For truly, I say to you, until heaven and earth pass away, not an iota, not a dot, will pass from the Law until all is accomplished. (Matthew 5:17-18)

[1] I ask, then, has God rejected his people? By no means! For I myself am an Israelite, a descendant of Abraham, a member of the tribe of Benjamin. [2] God has not rejected his people whom he foreknew. Do you not know what the Scripture says of Elijah, and how he appeals to God against Israel? (Romans 11:1,2)

"For the gifts and the calling of God (promises and covenants) *are irrevocable."* (Romans 11:29)

REVELATION CHAPTER 1

[1] The revelation of Jesus Christ, which God gave him to show his servants the things that must soon take place. He made it known by sending his angel to his servant John, [2] who bore witness to the word of God and the testimony of Jesus Christ, even to all that he saw. [3] Blessed is the one who reads aloud the words of this prophecy, and blessed are those who hear, and who keep what is written in it, for the time is near. Greetings to the Seven Churches." (Revelation 1:1-3)

Revelation 1:1–3 gives us:

- ❖ **The Title**, *"The Revelation of Jesus Christ."*
- ❖ **The Transmission**(How it was given): *"He made it known by sending his angel to his servant John."*
- ❖ The **Genre** and a Promise of a blessing. *"Blessed is the one who reads aloud the <u>words of this prophecy</u>, and <u>blessed are those who hear</u> and who keep what is written in it, for the time is near."*

The opening paragraph identifies this book's genre as a revelation, a prophecy, or a disclosure of unseen realities, its divine author (***Jesus Christ***), and the process by which he conveys them through the human author (***his servant John***) to believers (***his servants***).

The theme of the Book: *"The Revelation of Jesus Christ, a Prophecy."*

Source and Purpose: *"The word of God and to the testimony of Jesus Christ, even to all that he saw."* Sent by His angel: The intermediary, *"to his servant John"* recipient and recorder. The chain of progression is from the Father to the Son (Jesus), to the messenger (the angel), to John, and to (the reader). John stresses that he saw and heard everything he wrote; everything is a literal vision or record from God of things that are GOING TO HAPPEN. Revelation then pronounces the first of seven benedictions to seven specific churches. *"Greeting to the Seven Churches".*

Many call this the revelation of John. However, it should be titled the *Revelation of Jesus Christ*. This is the title given in the first line of the book itself. Revelation 1:1: *"**The revelation of Jesus Christ**."* God transmits the revealed truth to Jesus, and His angel conveys it to John.

This prophecy **WILL TAKE PLACE** because it is a sovereign act by God. In conclusion, John is not told to seal his prophecy, unlike Daniel. John's visions are essential to all readers from that time to today. He was speaking to generations of believers. Giving a factual observation of the *End Times*, recording God's judgment on unbelievers (*The Tribulation*), the second coming of Christ, and God's final judgment. It also tells of Jesus' earthly Millennial Kingdom, the New Jerusalem, and New Earth.

Recall that Daniel was also given visions of the *End Times*, but God instructed him to shut up the words, seal them in a book because its contents were not entirely understandable, and keep them safe for that time.

"But you, Daniel, shut up the words and seal the book, until the time of the end." (Daniel 12:4)

Dr. C.I. Scofield (a great Bible scholar) wrote about Revelation in 1903: *"The book is so written that as the actual time of the events approach, the current events will unlock the meaning of the book."* He pointed out that the book of Revelation didn't have meaning for many centuries, so very few people studied it. Revelation is written so that the meaning will unfold as the events get closer. Since the 1950's, the most significant interest in prophecy has grown. Look at all the recent books written and movies made about the *End Times*.

4 John to the seven churches that are in Asia: Grace to you and peace from him who is and who was and who is to come, and from the seven spirits who are before his throne, 5 and from Jesus Christ the faithful witness, the firstborn of the dead, and the ruler of kings on earth. To him who loves us and has freed us from our sins by his blood 6 and made us a kingdom, priests to his God and Father, to him be glory and dominion forever and ever. Amen. (Revelation 1:4-6)

John's greeting of *"grace"* and *"peace"* were usual greetings of the times. At that time, the oppression of Christians was high; therefore, John's greeting was a meaningful greeting to these seven besieged churches. John then reiterates explicitly the trustworthy source of Revelation by describing its givers. In the line *"and from the seven spirits who are before his throne,"* many theologians reason these seven spirits represent the Holy Spirit. The number seven stands for completeness or perfection in Biblical symbolism. Since the line refers to God the Father and God the Son, the seven Spirits are thought to refer to the third member of the Godhead, the Holy Spirit.

⁵ and from Jesus Christ the faithful witness, the firstborn of the dead, and the ruler of kings on earth. To him who loves us and has freed us from our sins by his blood ⁶ and made us a kingdom, priests. (Revelation 1:5-6).

Christ is the faithful witness, acting as a true prophet. He revealed God to men, not only through His words but His actions. Jesus has always been, from the beginning of time. He is a perfect revelation and witness of all that God is. Regarding the phrase "Firstborn of the Dead," the point is that Christ is the first in a long line of people who will be resurrected with glorified bodies. Look at the clarification of this in Colossians, which says:

¹⁵ He is the image of the invisible God, the firstborn of all creation. ¹⁶ For by him all things were created, in heaven and on earth, visible and invisible, whether thrones or dominions or rulers or authorities—all things were created through him and for him. ¹⁷ And he is before all things, and in him, all things hold together. ¹⁸ And he is the head of the body, the church. He is the beginning, the firstborn from the dead, that in everything he might be preeminent. ¹⁹ For in him all the fullness of God was pleased to dwell, ²⁰and through him to reconcile to himself all things, whether on earth or in heaven, making peace by the blood of his cross." (Colossians 1:15–20)

"To him who loves us and has freed us from our sins by his blood" (Revelation 1:5). Meaning we are cleaned (forgiven) of our sins in the blood of Christ by God's grace. Notice the past tense **"has freed us**." We have been cleaned from our sins and eternal judgment, freed by His blood. The fullness of God's love is a reality. His forgiveness of our sins is a past fact through His sacrifice. We don't have to work to be forgiven, it was fully accomplished when Christ shed His blood for us on the cross. All we must do is accept and believe in His grace and love by faith.

Revelation: A Line by Line Breakdown

¹ And you were dead in the trespasses and sins ² in which you once walked, following the course of this world, following the prince of the power of the air, the spirit that is now at work in the sons of disobedience- ³ among whom we all once lived in the passions of our flesh, carrying out the desires of the body and the mind, and were by nature children of wrath, like the rest of mankind. ⁴ But God, being rich in mercy, because of the great love with which he loved us, ⁵ even when we were dead in our trespasses, made us alive together with Christ-by grace you have been saved- ⁶ and raised us up with him and seated us with him in the heavenly places in Christ Jesus, ⁷ so that in the coming ages he might show the immeasurable riches of his grace in kindness toward us in Christ Jesus. ⁸ For by grace you have been saved through faith. And this is not your own doing; it is the gift of God, ⁹ not a result of works, so that no one may boast. (Ephesians 2:1–9)

All believers have been ordained as priests of God by Jesus Himself. A priest's job is simply that of representing God before men and men before God. Every believer has this privilege of priesthood. *"...and made us a kingdom, priests to his God and Father."* (Revelation 1:6)

⁷ Behold, he is coming with the clouds, and every eye will see him, even those who pierced him, and all tribes of the earth will wail on account of him. Even so. Amen. ⁸"I am the Alpha and the Omega," says the Lord God, who is and who was and who is to come, the Almighty. (Revelation 1:7-8)

This is a direct prediction of the *Second Coming of Christ*. Many believe His coming in clouds is not about the weather, but His believers or witnesses are with Him. All those who died, who believed and trusted in His grace, and all those believers Raptured (more later) before the Tribulation, a time of God's judgments on an unbelieving world.

"Therefore, since we are surrounded by so great a cloud of witnesses, let us also lay aside every weight, and sin which clings so closely, and let us run with endurance the race that is set before us." (Hebrews 12:1)

"I am the Alpha and the Omega," says the Lord God, "who is and who was and who is to come." (Revelation 1:8).

This verse proclaims Jesus Christ is the beginning to the end, A to Z. Jesus is at the first line of the Bible to the last line.

⁹ I, John, your brother and partner in the tribulation and the kingdom and the patient endurance that are in Jesus, was on the island called Patmos on account of the word of God and the testimony of Jesus. ¹⁰ I was in the Spirit on the Lord's Day, and I heard behind me a loud voice like a trumpet ¹¹ saying, "Write what you see in a book and send it to the seven churches, to Ephesus and to Smyrna and to Pergamum and to Thyatira and to Sardis and to Philadelphia and to Laodicea." (Revelation 1:9-11)

John was an old man when he was exiled to Patmos. He was sent there because the Romans feared making him a martyr, so exile was the solution. The Romans never comprehended the impact that John's letters would have. John states he was *"in the Spirit on the Lord's Day,"* meaning the Holy Spirit controlled him. John was unfailing in recording what he saw as a literal prophecy from God. He heard *"a loud voice like a trumpet,"* trumpets in the Bible signify essential messages from God.

There were several hundred churches at the time John wrote Revelation. Nonetheless, the angel told John to write to only seven and specified them. Why? First, these churches had problems typical of all churches then and continue to today. Second, these seven church situations were analogous to the changing circumstances of the church then and throughout the church age up to the rapture.

¹² Then I turned to see the voice that was speaking to me, and on turning, I saw seven golden lampstands, ¹³ and in the midst of the lampstands one like a son of man, clothed with a long robe and with a golden sash around his chest. ¹⁴ The hairs of his head were white, like white wool, like snow. His eyes were like a flame of fire, ¹⁵ his feet were like burnished bronze, refined in a furnace, and his voice was like the roar of many waters. ¹⁶ In his right hand, he held seven stars, from his mouth came a sharp two-edged sword, and this face was like the sun shining in full strength. ¹⁷ When I saw him, I fell at his feet as though dead. But he laid his right hand on me, saying, "Fear not, I am the first and the last, ¹⁸ and the living one. I died, and behold I am alive forevermore, and I have the keys of Death and Hades. (Revelation 1:12-18)

    The most important thing John saw was a vision of Christ Himself. This shows that Jesus is alive in his resurrected body. Christ is the dominant figure in the Book of Revelation. John saw Jesus standing in the middle of seven lampstands, symbolizing the seven churches. These lampstands would be comparable to those that stood in the ancient Jewish Tabernacle, which provided all the light in the Tabernacle. Their purpose was to light up all the articles of worship, giving them clarity. This representation shows that Jesus is the Messiah, the light of the world, illuminating all of mankind to the true meaning of God.

Again Jesus spoke to them, saying, "I am the light of the world. Whoever follows me will not walk in darkness, but will have the light of life." (John 8:12)

¹ "In the beginning was the Word, and the Word was with God, and the Word was God. ² He was at the beginning with God. ³ All things were made through him, and without him was not anything made that was made. [4] In him was life, and life was the light of men. [5] The light shines in the darkness, and the darkness has not overcome it." (John 1:1-5)

Why were these "*lampstands*" selected to symbolize the church? The Church is the body of Christ on earth. Its purpose is to spread the light of the gospel to everyone, everywhere. Jesus called his followers "*the light of the world."* John describes Jesus as wearing the clothing of a priest and a judge, a long robe with a golden sash. He is the priest for all His people and the judge of everyone and everything. His white hair symbolizes pure wisdom, while His flaming eyes seem to burn a hole through the unrighteous. His feet are like burnished bronze glowing in a furnace. In the Bible, bronze is always a symbol of judgment, showing He is the Judge of the living and the dead.

[19] Write therefore the things that you have seen, those that are, and those that are to take place after this. [20] As for the mystery of the seven stars that you saw in my right hand, and the seven golden lampstands, the seven stars are the angels of the seven churches, and the seven lampstands are the seven churches. (Revelation 1:19-20)

Verse 19 gives God a simple outline of the entire *Book of Revelation*. It refers to the visions John will have. A look at the whole church age up to Christ's return, plus the events that occur afterward. First, he must record "***the things that you have seen.***" The vision of the resurrected Christ, who appeared to him and conversed with him. Then he was to write about "***those that are,***" referring to the early church. Then, the things which "***are to take place after this,***" referring to the end of the Church Age, the Tribulation, Final Judgment, and Christ's Kingdom on the New Earth. This is everything from Revelation 4 to the end of the book.

John was given candid insight about things to come. In verse 20 God tells us what the seven stars and seven lampstands mean.

"As for the mystery of the seven stars that you saw in my right hand, and the seven golden lampstands, the seven stars are the angels of the seven churches, and the seven lampstands are the seven churches." (Revelation 1:20)

Review Of The Central Facts of Revelation

- ❖ Theme: *"The revelation of Jesus Christ; a prophecy."*
- ❖ John emphasizes that he saw and heard everything he wrote.
- ❖ Christ is the faithful witness. He revealed God to men.
- ❖ Christ's Firstborn of the dead means that Christ is the first in a long line who will be resurrected with glorified bodies. The promise of resurrection.
- ❖ We have been ordained as a priest of God by Jesus Himself.
- ❖ A direct prophecy of the Second Coming of Christ
- ❖ Jesus Christ is everything from the beginning to the end, A to Z. Jesus is at the first line of the Bible to the last line. Called the Alpha and the Omega.
- ❖ God speaks to the church through situations that parallel the changing conditions of the church as a whole through the entire church age.
- ❖ Jesus is both a priest and a judge of everything.

REVELATION CHAPTER 2

Revelation 2 starts with the *Letters to the Seven Churches*. Each of the seven letters is addressed to a literal church. A representative received the letter at each church and read it to the congregation. Each of the seven letters follows the same standard format:

1. **The Destination:** The city where the church is.
2. **Description of Christ:** In each letter, Jesus describes Himself designed to meet the church's needs.
3. **Commendation:** Jesus seeks to praise each church, but unfortunately, nothing can be found praiseworthy about Thyatira or Laodicea.
4. **Rebuke:** There are only two churches Jesus doesn't rebuke for sinful activities: Smyrna and Philadelphia.
5. **Exhortation:** Jesus encourages and counsels each church. To add what would help and remove what hinders.
6. **Promise:** Jesus promises a blessing to *"who has an ear"* and heeds His advice.
7. **Prophetic Application:** The historical role each church is to have in the church.

TO THE CHURCH IN EPHESUS

¹"To the angel of the church in Ephesus write: 'The words of him who holds the seven stars in his right hand, who walks among the seven golden lampstands. ²"'I know your works, your toil, and your patient endurance, and how you cannot bear with those who are evil but have tested those who call themselves apostles and are not, and found them to be false. ³ I know you are enduring patiently and bearing up for my name's sake, and you have not grown weary. ⁴ But I have this against you, that you have abandoned the love you had at first. ⁵ Remember therefore from where you have fallen; repent, and do the works you did at first. If not, I will come to you and remove your lampstand from its place, unless you repent. ⁶ Yet this you have: you hate the works of the Nicolaitans, which I also hate. ⁷ He who has an ear, let him hear what the Spirit says to the churches. To the one who conquers I will grant to eat of the tree of life, which is in the paradise of God.' (Revelation 2:1-7)

The Destination: Ephesus is located near the modern town of Selçuk in present-day Turkey. At the time of John, it was a large harbor city known as the *Marketplace of Asia*. It was also a banking center because it had a great vault in the Temple of Artemis (Diana was her Roman name). It was considered the safest place in Asia Minor. The Temple of Diana was also considered one of the seven wonders of the ancient world. The city had a widespread practice of occult and black magic. Paul faced these occultists, leading many to Christ. (See Acts Chapter 19). The Church at Ephesus was exceptionally well taught by past pastors Paul, Apollos, Timothy, and John. *The Book of Ephesians* was written by Paul and sent to Ephesus.

Description of Christ: Jesus describes himself as the one **"who holds the seven stars in his right hand, who walks among the seven golden lampstands,"** showing that Christ is with them. He walks among them. He knows their thoughts and attitudes. He sees everything that happens to them and by them. Jesus knows their affections and motives.

Commendation: The church believers were passionate about doing good works and serving the Lord. Twice, the letter speaks of how they labored for Christ. They stood against false teaching and false deacons and labeled immorality precisely as it was. From outward appearance, they looked like a model church. In verse 6, Jesus says, **"Yet this you have: you hate the works of the Nicolaitans, which I also hate."** The *Nicolaitans* were false teachers who claimed that the actions of your body did not affect your spirit, so go out and sin. The teaching of the Nicolaitans was thought to have originated with Nicholaus, one of the seven original deacons of the church of Ephesus; the *Book of Acts* tells of this.

⁴ But we will devote ourselves to prayer and the ministry of the word." ⁵ And what they said pleased the whole gathering, and they chose Stephen, a man full of faith and the Holy Spirit, and

Philip, and Prochorus, and Nicanor, and Timon, and Parmenas, and Nicolaus, a proselyte of Antioch. ⁶ These they set before the apostles, and they prayed and laid their hands on them.
(Acts 6:4-6).

Nicholaus idolized Greek philosophy and acknowledged its view that man is fundamentally sound and naturally evil. He believed a man's indulgence in his body didn't defile the spirit. This gave religious sanction to sexual deviations. He taught that going to both pagan and Christian meetings was acceptable, seeking to merge Christianity with pagan doctrine. The world was his teacher, not God.

Rebuke: Despite all their pros, the Lord discerned a deadly danger creeping in. They had abandoned their first love – Jesus Christ. Though outwardly warm, they were inwardly cold. They went through the proper routines, said the right words, and dished out the correct clichés but withered inside.

Exhortation: Jesus tells them: ***"Remember therefore from where you have fallen; repent, and do the works you did at first. If not, I will come to you and remove your lampstand from its place, unless you repent."*** Remembering and repenting are two significant words because many Christians forget their origins and fall back on old ways. Remember why you follow Jesus.

Promise: Jesus tells them, ***"To the one who conquers I will grant to eat of the tree of life, which is in the paradise of God."*** The one who conquers is the one who believes Jesus is the Son of God and receives Him as Savor and Lord.

Prophetic Application: The Ephesian church is a prophetic picture of the Apostolic Church. The dominant historical characteristics of the era were correct doctrine, prudent conduct, and zealous labor for God. As their love for Jesus began to wane, they served out of a sense of duty. Their acceptance by God depended on their performance, not by grace or through faith. This format led to legalism and rituals.

Revelation: A Line by Line Breakdown

TO THE CHURCH IN SMYRNA

⁸ And to the angel of the church in Smyrna, write The words of the first and the last, who died and came to life. ⁹ I know your tribulation and your poverty (but you are rich) and the slander of those who say that they are Jews and are not but are a synagogue of Satan. ¹⁰ Do not fear what you are about to suffer. Behold, the devil is about to throw some of you into prison, that you may be tested, and for ten days you will have tribulation. Be faithful unto death, and I will give you the crown of life. ¹¹ He who has an ear, let him hear what the Spirit says to the churches. The one who conquers will not be hurt by the second death. (Revelation 2:8-11)

The Destination: Smyrna was about 40 miles north of Ephesus and considered the safest seaport of its time. It was a thriving city on the main trade route from Rome to India and Persia. The original town was laid out by Alexander the Great. It was known as the *Ornament of Asia* due to its splendor and beauty. The main street was known as *The Street of Gold*. On one end was the Temple of Zeus and the Temple of Cybele on the other. Many Jews lived there, yet the city was primarily pagan.

Description of Christ: The Christians at Smyrna were experiencing severe surfing, even martyrdom; Jesus says that these are *"words of the first and the last, who died and came to life."* Christ refers to Himself as the One who suffered, died, and is now alive again. Because He has conquered death, they will too. He has already died for them so they may have everlasting life through His sacrifice.

Commendation: Jesus assures the Smyrna believers that He knows about their faithful service, and *"I know your tribulation and your poverty."* They are rich in his sight. Even though they lose everything in this life for His sake, they earn everlasting rewards in Heaven. The Christians in Smyrna were victims of people who reported them to the Romans so they could get ten percent of their belongings. This devastated many; many more were sent to prison or martyred. Likewise, many of the Jews turned in the Christians, **"the slander of those who say that they are Jews and are not, but are a synagogue of Satan."** Jesus stated that these were not Jews, for they did not believe in the Lord God; if they had, Satan would not have inspired them to hate the Christians.

Rebuke: There is not one word of rebuke to the Smyrna Church. A church of individual suffering and persecution usually inspires the devoted, more than an untested believer.

Exhortation: Jesus encourages the church about the coming trials and holds to their belief in God and Heaven; they will be rewarded with the Crown of Life. **"Do not fear what you are about to suffer. Behold, the devil is about to throw some of you into prison, that you may be tested, and for ten days you will have tribulation. Be faithful unto death, and I will give you the crown of life."**

Promise: Jesus promises no second death to those who heed his words. **"He who has an ear, let him hear what the Spirit says to the churches. The one who conquers will not be hurt by the second death."** The Second Death is noted in Revelation 20:14,15, **"Then Death and Hades were thrown into the lake of fire. This is the second death, the lake of fire. And if anyone's name was not found written in the book of life, he was thrown into the lake of fire."**

Prophetic Application: Jesus tells of the upcoming persecution: **Behold, the devil is about to throw some of you into prison, that you may be tested, and for ten days you will have tribulation. Be faithful unto death."** Many Bible scholars say that these *"ten days"* was a prophetic warning of the years of coming persecution under ten Caesars: Nero (AD 64-68); Domitian (AD 90-95); Aurelius (AD 161-180; Maximus (AD 235-237); Decius (AD 250-253); Valerian (AD 257-260); Aurelian (AD 270-275); and Diocletian (AD 303-312). During this period, millions of Christians met a cruel martyrs' death rather than renouncing Christ to save their earthly death. This long period was a time when the examples of these early believers purified the church. This period of tremendous witnesses and heroic faith finally astonished the Roman Empire by demonstrating the Christian faith.

TO THE CHURCH IN PERGAMUM

¹²"And to the angel of the church in Pergamum write: 'The words of him who has the sharp two-edged sword. ¹³"'I know where you dwell, where Satan's throne is. Yet you hold fast my name, and you did not deny my faith even in the days of Antipas my faithful witness, who was killed among you, where Satan dwells. ¹⁴ But I have a few things against you: you have some there who hold the teaching of Balaam, who taught Balak to put a stumbling block before the sons of Israel so that they might eat food sacrificed to idols and practice sexual immorality. ¹⁵ So also you have some who hold the teaching of the Nicolaitans. ¹⁶ Therefore repent. If not, I will come to you soon and war against them with the sword of my mouth. ¹⁷ He who has an ear, let him hear what the Spirit says to the churches. To the one who conquers, I will give some of the hidden manna, and I will give him a white stone, with a new name written on the stone that no one knows except the one who receives it.'(Revelation 2:12-17)

The Destination: The City of Pergamum (Pergamos) was a political power, a center for academics, and filled with pagan worshipers. It was the capital of Asia Minor and was filled with royal officials, beautiful palaces, and idols. There was an altar to Zeus, a wonder of the ancient world. The patron god of the city was Aesculapius, the god of healing. The rod of Asclepius, a snake-entwined staff, remains a symbol of medicine today. Also, one of the great universities of the era was located there, with a library of over 200,000 books, second only to Alexandria, before it burned.

Description of Christ: Jesus describes Himself as having a sharp sword with two edges. This symbol refers to the Word of God's keen discernment of men's thoughts and motives. Jesus acknowledged that although their outward behavior was not all it could be, their motives towards Him were right.

Commendation: Jesus assures them that He knows they're dwelling where Satan's throne is, that is, that the city's heart was under Satan's control. He, therefore, understands the persecutions and temptations they're experiencing from the rampant Satanic religions. Jesus praises these saints for continuing to boldly proclaim Him as the only Lord in the face of great danger and opposition. He also commends them for sticking steadfastly to the truth rather than watering it down or perverting it with the aberrations of the pagan religions.

Rebuke: Jesus deals with our sins according to our maturity and the circumstances of our failure. This church tolerated severe evil in the teachings and practices of Balaam and the Nicolaitans. Yet Jesus's rebuke shows an understanding of the pressures Satan brings. Balaam drew God's people away by using voluptuous women as enticement through sexual persuasion. The *Nicolaitans* were false teachers who claimed that the actions of your body didn't affect your spirit, so go out and sin.

Exhortation: Jesus hated these teachings because they lured believers away from fellowship with Him and compelled Him to discipline them. No sin can be committed in the body or mind that doesn't affect the believer's communion with Christ until it is judged and forsaken. Jesus warns the church to expel all who teach and practice such errors until they repent. Otherwise, He will fight them with the sword of His Word.

Promise: The people of that time were enamored with the *"mysteries"* of the pagan rites. Jesus promises greater *"mysteries"* for his followers to enjoy forever. **"To the one who conquers, I will give some of the hidden manna."** Just as Israel received manna from heaven while in the wilderness so that Christ's believers will be sustained by the Bread of Life, Jesus Christ. He adds, *"I will give him a white stone, with a new name written on the stone that no one knows except the one who receives it."*

In John's Day, the Roman court gave a white stone to a defendant when he was acquitted and a black stone when he was found guilty. Giving a white stone with a new name suggests the believer's complete acceptance and favor with God.

Prophetic Application: Pergamum symbolizes the church merged with the state. Emperor Constantine made Christianity the official religion of the Roman Empire, and massive persecution ended. However, this blessing became a curse. The church compromised its position to gain favor and power with the emperor. A church hierarchy began to develop, with the Bishop of Rome claiming to be head of the church due to their proximity to the Emperor. This led to the claim of apostolic succession, alleging that this office in Rome was linked directly to Peter, known as the *Big Fisherman*. This was a compromise with paganism and immorality, just like the Church of Pergamum.

TO THE CHURCH IN THYATIRA

[18]"And to the angel of the church in Thyatira, write: 'The words of the Son of God, who has eyes like a flame of fire, and whose feet are like burnished bronze. [19]"'I know your works, love, faith, service, and patient endurance, and that your latter works exceed the first. [20] But I have this against you, that you tolerate that woman Jezebel, who calls herself a prophetess and is teaching and seducing my servants to practice sexual immorality and to eat food sacrificed to idols. [21] I gave her time to repent, but she refuses to repent of her sexual immorality. [22] Behold, I will throw her onto a sickbed, and those who commit adultery with her I will throw into great tribulation unless they repent of her works, [23] and I will strike her children dead. And all the churches will know that I am he who searches mind and heart, and I will give to each of you

according to your works. ²⁴ But to the rest of you in Thyatira, who do not hold this teaching, who have not learned what some call the deep things of Satan, to you I say, I do not lay on you any other burden. ²⁵ Only hold fast what you have until I come. ²⁶ The one who conquers and who keeps my works until the end, to him I will give authority over the nations, ²⁷ and he will rule them with a rod of iron, as when earthen pots are broken in pieces, even as I myself have received authority from my Father. ²⁸ And I will give him the morning star. ²⁹ He who has an ear, let him hear what the Spirit says to the churches.' (Revelation 2:18-29)

The Destination: The City of Thyatira was the least important of the seven cities addressed. It was famous for dyeing red and purple cloth. The town had many trade guilds, and it was almost impossible to do business unless one belonged to a guild. That became a problem for Christians because guilds were widespread with paganism and immorality.

Description of Christ: Jesus describes Himself as having eyes like a flame of fire. This depicts His appraisal of their hearts, a search that exposed impure motivations in their worship. Jesus's feet of bronze symbolized the judgment that was going to fall on this church if it didn't shape up.

Commendation: The Lord praises Thyatira for their love, faith, service, patience, and work. He even mentions work twice, due to a growing church, their service for Christ in recent years has been great.

Rebuke: Some of the church leaders and certain other believers had allowed an occultist prophetess to trap some of the immature believers in the church. Her name was Sambathe, but here she is given the very descriptive name "***Jezebel***." In the Old Testament, Jezebel led many of the Israelites into idolatrous religious rites and debased sexuality; now, in Thyatira, this prophetess had induced the people to mix idolatry and sexual impurity with their Christianity. Even today, some church leaders and "Christian" institutes, who ought to know better, are doing the same thing as happened in Thyatira.

Exhortation: At Thyatira, instead of destroying or removing the prophetess, Christ cast her *"into a bed"* so that those who lack genuine love for God will confirm their infidelity by consorting with this spiritual harlot. Those who commit adultery with her will be brought into *"great tribulation"* unless they repent of her works. Also, Christ states, **"and I will strike her children dead."** Those who mix occultism with the teachings of the Bible and Christianity will perish. Christ declares that all churches will realize through His treatment of the harlot and her followers that He examines the motives behind religious practices. Many people don't desire a personal relationship with God, which has too many demands on them, they only want religion to boost their ego from time to time.

Promise: To those who do not fall to the false teachings and are sincere seekers of Christ, He assures them that no other burden will be added. They are told to hold fast to what they have until Christ returns. This indicates that this kind of church will continue until the Second Coming. They are also promised:

[26]*"The one who conquers and who keeps my works until the end, to him I will give authority over the nations,* [27] *and he will rule them with a rod of iron, as when earthen pots are broken in pieces, even as I myself have received authority from my Father.* [28] *And I will give him the morning star."* (Revelation 2:26-28)

Prophetic Application: Thyatira's significant characteristics fit the church era of the Middle Ages when the church became a fabricated system that bound the people to image worship, superstition, and priestcraft. However, the believing remnant of this prostituted form of the church will endure to the time of the Second Coming.

²⁵ Only hold fast what you have until I come. ²⁶ The one who conquers and who keeps my works until the end, to him, I will give authority over the nations. (Revelation 2:25-26)

REVELATION CHAPTER 3

TO THE CHURCH IN SARDIS

¹ And to the angel of the church in Sardis write: 'The words of him who has the seven spirits of God and the seven stars. "'I know your works. You have the reputation of being alive, but you are dead. ² Wake up, and strengthen what remains and is about to die, for I have not found your works complete in the sight of my God. ³ Remember, then, what you received and heard. Keep it, and repent. If you will not wake up, I will come like a thief, and you will not know at what hour I will come against you. ⁴ Yet you have still a few names in Sardis, people who have not soiled their garments, and they will walk with me in white, for they are worthy. ⁵ The one who conquers will be clothed thus in white garments, and I will never blot his name out of the book of life. I will confess his name before my Father and before his angels. ⁶ He who has an ear, let him hear what the Spirit says to the churches.' (Revelation 3:1-6)

The Destination: Sardis was one of the world's wealthiest and most influential cities. It was ethically content, morally degenerate, and was conquered by Cyrus of Persia, then Alexander the Great. In AD 17, the city was destroyed by an earthquake, but the Romans rebuilt it because it was an important city. However, it never came back to its former glory. The people tended to live in the past, and the church in Sardis was guilty of the same backward-looking attitude. The city was also noted for its idolatrous worship of the goddess Cybele.

Description of Christ: Jesus says he " ***has the seven spirits of God and the seven stars.***" This refers to God's omnipresent and omniscient nature, the Holy Spirit; unfortunately, He saw no evidence that they (the Church of Sardis) had the Spirit. The ministry of the Holy Spirit is to empower, teach, guide, and equip believers for living in Christ. In Sardis, this was tragically missing. The Spirit wasn't absent, but saying they were dead, showing the need for the filling ministry of the Holy Spirit. Christ speaks of holding the seven spirits of God and the seven stars or the messengers responsible for delivering Christ's message to the church. These words are intended to remind all messengers or ministers of their responsibility to proclaim the valid message of Christ. God holds the minister accountable to Him, demonstrating the absolute necessity of walking in the Spirit.

"Not many of you should become teachers, my brothers, for you know that we who teach will be judged with greater strictness." (James 3:1).

Commendation: There is very little praise for this church because ***"still a few names in Sardis, people who have not soiled their garments, and they will walk with me in white, for they are worthy."*** This refers to those walking in the ways of the world and following its mold, not God's, so have soiled garments. This happens when we fail to appreciate the great gift God has given us through the cross.

Rebuke: The church in Sardis had once been spiritually vibrant but now existed in the flesh, or what Christ called dead. ***"You have the reputation of being alive, but you are dead."*** They now have only a handful of genuine followers.

[4]"Yet you have still a few names in Sardis, people who have not soiled their garments, and they will walk with me in white, for they are worthy. [5] The one who conquers will be clothed thus in

white garments, and I will never blot his name out of the book of life." (Revelation 3:4,5)

Exhortation: Jesus tells the church of Sardis to *"Wake up, and strengthen what remains and is about to die, for I have not found your works complete in the sight of my God. Remember, then, what you received and heard. Keep it, and repent. If you will not wake up, I will come like a thief, and you will not know at what hour I will come against you."*

He is telling them to revitalize the good things they have. No believer can live on past spiritual victories. A lack of forward vision leads to stagnation or deterioration. A church or believer who has lost his vision of moving forward soon falls behind the ever-changing world. This is what is meant by being told to wake up.

Promise: Jesus promises those who wake up and repent *"will be clothed thus in white garments, and I will never blot his name out of the book of life. I will confess his name before my Father and before his angels."* The promise is your name will remain in the Book of Life, meaning you are one with Christ, and he will acknowledge you to his Father and all the angels. However, if a person does not receive Jesus as his personal Savior by the time he dies, his name will not be found in the Book of Life, and Jesus will say he does not know you, and that person will not enter Heaven.

"And I tell you, everyone who acknowledges me before men, the Son of Man also will acknowledge before the angels of God, but the one who denies me before men will be denied before the angels of God." (Luke 12:8)

Prophetic Application: The Church of Sardis symbolized the Reformation Era of church history, from 1417 to 1648, when the church was reformed but not revived. Some essential doctrines were reclaimed, such as the idea that people can be justified by

God only by faith. However, the Reformation Era did not shake loose the elaborate rituals and manmade traditions of the medieval church or the legalism that had set in.

TO THE CHURCH IN PHILADELPHIA

⁷"And to the angel of the church in Philadelphia write: 'The words of the holy one, the true one, who has the key of David, who opens and no one will shut, who shuts and no one opens. ⁸"'I know your works. Behold, I have set before you an open door, which no one can shut. I know that you have but little power, and yet you have kept my word and have not denied my name. ⁹ Behold, I will make those of the synagogue of Satan who says that they are Jews and are not, but lie—behold, I will make them come and bow down before your feet, and they will learn that I have loved you. ¹⁰ Because you have kept my word about patient endurance, I will keep you from the hour of trial that is coming on the whole world, to try those who dwell on the earth. ¹¹ I am coming soon. Hold fast what you have, so that no one may seize your crown. ¹² The one who conquers, I will make him a pillar in the temple of my God. Never shall he go out of it, and I will write on him the name of my God, and the name of the city of my God, the new Jerusalem, which comes down from my God out of heaven, and my own new name. ¹³ He who has an ear, let him hear what the Spirit says to the churches.' (Revelation 3:7-13)

The Destination: Philadelphia is about 30 miles southeast of Sardis and was destroyed by the same earthquake. The Romans also rebuilt it. Philadelphia was known for its excellent vineyards and thriving wine industry. Bacchus, the god of wine, was its patron god, so there was the chronic social problem of drunkenness. There was also a substantial Jewish population that was responsible for some of the persecution of the Christians.

Description of Christ: To this missionary church, Jesus says He is the One who opens doors for evangelistic opportunity. No man can open a door of witness or shut one except by the will of God. When Jesus says He has the key of David, it reminds the Jews in Philadelphia of God's covenant to David, promising that through David will come the Messiah, which was fulfilled by Jesus himself. Then, He states that the Jews will come and worship at the feet of the Christians and acknowledge Jesus as the true Messiah, the true God of everything.

Commendation: Jesus praises the church in Philadelphia for its evangelism work. He gives them an open door for witnesses that no one can shut. They relied only on Christ to open the way and had to trust in Him, for they knew that human maneuvering to do God's work does not produce fruit.

Rebuke: There is no rebuke to this church.

Exhortation: Jesus tells the church to hold fast to their actions.

Promise: This letter is comprised of many promises. The most significant promise to the church of Philadelphia is that their believers will not go through the time of tribulation. Revelation 3:10 says: *"Because you have kept my word about patient endurance, I will keep you from the hour of trial that is coming on the whole world, to try those who dwell on the earth."* This is a reference that all true believers will not be around for the tribulation, showing a clear reference to the Rapture before the tribulation. Jesus promises to open the door to an unbelieving world.

Prophetic Application: This speaks of a significant missionary era when believers awakened millions around the world. Unfortunately, missionary evangelistic zeal began to wane after World War One. Due to the Philadelphia-type churches, there are still evangelistic churches, which are still present until the Rapture.

TO THE CHURCH IN LAODICEA

¹⁴"And to the angel of the church in Laodicea write: 'The words of the Amen, the faithful and true witness, the beginning of God's creation. ¹⁵"'I know your work: you are neither cold nor hot. Would that you were either cold or hot! ¹⁶ So, because you are lukewarm and neither hot nor cold, I will spit you out of my mouth. ¹ For you say, I am rich, I have prospered, and I need nothing, not realizing that you are wretched, pitiable, poor, blind, and naked. ¹⁸ I counsel you to buy from me gold refined by fire, so that you may be rich, and white garments so that you may clothe yourself and the shame of your nakedness may not be seen, and salve to anoint your eyes, so that you may see. ¹⁹ Those whom I love, I reprove and discipline, so be zealous and repent. ²⁰ Behold, I stand at the door and knock. If anyone hears my voice and opens the door, I will come into him and eat with him, and he with me. ²¹ The one who conquers, I will grant him to sit with me on my throne, as I also conquered and sat down with my Father on his throne. ²² He who has an ear, let him hear what the Spirit says to the churches. (Revelation 3:14-22)

The Destination: Laodicea was an extremely wealthy banking center about 40 miles east of Ephesus. It had a famous medical school noted for treating eyes. The city was inclined to pleasure, with three theaters and a large race track.

Description of Christ: Jesus first reveals himself as *"Amen,"* which means *"I believe."* Amen is usually spoken in response to some truth or promise from God. This affirmation was sadly lacking in the church. This was meant to convict and rebuke the people into sounding their *"Amen"* to God. Jesus wanted these indifferent church members to look at him in a different light. They held Christ in low esteem, giving casual consideration to his teaching. Jesus describes here as the *"Beginning of God's Creation,"* which appears nowhere else in the Bible. This church was so satiated and smug with all its worldly goods that it had forgotten its reason for existence, which was to proclaim Christ.

Commendation: There is no commendation for this unbelieving church.

Rebuke: This church was neutral, neither apathetic nor fervent for God by their adoption of world views. Next, Jesus rebukes their focus on amassing material wealth. *"For you say, I am rich, I have prospered, and I need nothing, not realizing that you are wretched, pitiable, poor, blind, and naked."*

Exhortation: Christ's exhortation is toward individuals instead of the church, which was almost past reforming. There is little hope for a church when the leadership lacks spiritual life or concern for teaching and leading those to Christ.

Promise: He speaks of the one who conquers, granting him to sit with Him on His throne, *"as I also conquered and sat down with my Father on his throne."*

Prophetic Application: Thousands of churches call themselves Christian, yet Christ is not found in them. *"Behold, I stand at the door and knock. If anyone hears my voice and opens the door, I will come into him and eat with him, and he with me."*

SUMMARY OF THE LETTERS TO THE SEVEN CHURCHES

The Seven Letters to the Churches start in Chapter Two and go through Chapter Three. Each message was to a church that existed at the time of the writing of Revelation. Many other churches existed at that time, but these churches were representative of the spiritual conditions Christ wanted to point out. Also, according to history, the Church has passed through eras similar to that described in each of the seven churches.

These extraordinary messages were written to specific churches, but all the same strengths and weaknesses can be found in today's Church. Their messages can also be applied to each of us independently. Study the message to each church, then ask yourself how you measure up personally to that message. In Chapter 1, John was told to write what he saw in a book and then send that book to the seven churches. And a blessing was pronounced upon all who would read, hear, and keep the words contained in this prophecy.

"Write what you see in a book and send it to the seven churches, to Ephesus and to Smyrna and to Pergamum and to Thyatira and to Sardis and to Philadelphia and to Laodicea."
(Revelation 1:10-11)

As a whole, Christ's messages to the seven churches are a warning to the churches of today to hear what the Spirit is saying. ***"He who has an ear, let him hear what the Spirit says to the churches."***
The church in Ephesus represents the danger of losing love and devotion to Christ. The church at Smyrna represents the danger of the fear of suffering. To this day, this has once again become very real. The church at Pergamum (Pergamos) illustrates the constant threat of doctrinal compromise and the danger of not following the fundamentals of the Bible.

The church of Thyatira shows the danger of moral compromise of Biblical standards. The church of Sardis is a warning not to become dead in the Spirit, only giving an outward appearance of living for Christ. The church in Philadelphia is encouraged to keep enduring with patience and waiting for the return of the Lord. The church at Laodicea is warned of being only warm in their works for Christ.

Christ sent these letters out of love. Christ sent these communications to the seven churches to empower all disciples to overcome sin. Jesus wanted true believers to know He saw their good works, faithfulness, and patience. He also saw the bad, including their compromise, apostasy, indifference, and lukewarmness. He wanted them to know that despite persecution from without and corruption from within. Jesus stood in their midst as a mighty conqueror, and through Him, they could overcome. His purpose was to raise His people in victory, to make them strong.

Christ is always walking among His people, preparing His Bride, the Church, for His coming. He calls us to repentance, bringing us to a new, more vital position of dedication and commitment and releasing a fresh anointing of His Spirit upon us.

THE RAPTURE

The first part of Revelation is about the Church as the central theme, and then, beginning in Chapter 4, the Tribulation begins, and the Church is no longer the focus. It is not seen again until returning with Christ in Revelation Chapter 19. Before moving on to Revelation Chapter 4, let's examine what happens to the Church before the Tribulation. This is where we will first look at the Rapture. According to the Webster's dictionary, "Rapture" is defined as (1) an expression or manifestation of ecstasy or passion; (2) an experience of being carried away by overwhelming emotion; (3) a mystical experience in which the spirit is exalted to a knowledge of divine things; Rapture comes from the Latin *rapare*, meaning to take away or snatch up. This comes from the Greek word *harpazo*, meaning *"to carry away"* or *"seize."* The word *harpazo* occurs fourteen times in the New Testament.

The Rapture is the glorious occurrence in which the departed in Christ will be resurrected alongside all living believers in Christ. They will be instantaneously converted into their resurrection bodies, and both groups, the living and the dead, will be gathered up to meet Jesus in the sky. Then, both groups are taken to heaven. This means there will be one generation of Christians who will never face death. They will be alive on earth at the time of the Rapture when, in an instant, they will be with Jesus in immortal bodies. This will occur before the Tribulation period, so the Church will not go through God's judgments prophesied in

Revelation Chapters 4 through 17. This view is the most consistent with a literal interpretation of Scripture.

The Old Testament does not teach about the Rapture but alludes to it and teaches of the Messiah's Second Coming. It does not teach about it because it is part of the mystery. The Apostle Paul called it a "mystery," a word that, when used in the Bible, usually refers to a secret no one can know until God chooses to reveal it. The Church itself was a mystery until after Jesus' resurrection, ushering in the birth of the Church.

51 Behold! I tell you a mystery. We shall not all sleep, but we shall all be changed, 52 in a moment, in the twinkling of an eye, at the last trumpet. For the trumpet will sound, and the dead will be raised imperishable, and we shall be changed. 53 For this perishable body must put on the imperishable, and this mortal body must put on immortality. 54 When the perishable puts on the imperishable, and the mortal puts on immortality, then shall come to pass the saying that is written: "Death is swallowed up in victory." (1 Corinthians 15:51-54).

15 For this we declare to you by a word from the Lord, that we who are alive, who are left until the coming of the Lord, will not precede those who have fallen asleep. 16 For the Lord himself will descend from heaven with a cry of command, with the voice of an archangel, and with the sound of the trumpet of God. And the dead in Christ will rise first. 17 Then we who are alive, who are left, will be caught up together with them in the clouds to meet the Lord in the air, and so we will always be with the Lord. 18 Therefore encourage one another with these words.
(1 Thessalonians 4:15-18)

The mystery revealed here is the promise that a group of people would not die before going to be with God. They will be changed from mortals to immortals without physical death first.

"We shall not all sleep." It is evident from these verses, and others, that there will be a time when Jesus raises the bodies of the departed believers to be immortals with him while at the same time, all living true believers will rise to be with Him without first dying, by His grace.

The Rapture begins with Jesus Christ's second coming from heaven. Jesus comes Himself to Rapture His church as He promised. He does not send an angel. It is not the return of Elijah.

Why does Jesus promise that a group of believers would be taken from the earth without dying first? The simple answer is twofold. First is that the followers of Christ, who are alive just before the Tribulation, will be raised to Christ before death because God's judgments will be so terrible that He isn't going to let His Church go through it. The Tribulation is for those who reject Christ.

The promise from Jesus is that His believers will not go through the Tribulation. Revelation 3:10 states: ***"Because you have kept my word about patient endurance, I will keep you from the hour of trial that is coming on the whole world, to try those who dwell on the earth."*** This is a reference that all believers will not be on earth at the time of tribulation, showing a clear reference that the Rapture will happen before the "***hour of trial that is coming on the whole world, to try those who dwell on the earth."***

The second reason is that all the believers in Christ are filled with the Holy Spirit, so they must be removed from the earth to allow Satan to have his way without the influence of Christians. This also means that the Holy Spirit will be out of the way, and His influence will be significantly reduced right after the Rapture. His work after the Rapture will not be identical to that during the Church Age.

The Church Age is a time when Christians are filled with the Holy Spirit by believing in Christ through being Born Again. When this group is supernaturally removed from the earth, ending the age, what is removed also is the Holy Spirit's power from working

Revelation: A Line by Line Breakdown

through the Church. Until this happens, Satan cannot bring about his plan.

After the Rapture, the Holy Spirit will continue bringing people to salvation during the Tribulation. During this time, evangelism through the Holy Spirit will be more effective than at any other time. As Satanic activity increases, so will the Holy Spirit's activity.

However, some Bible scholars believe the Church will have to endure the Tribulation with the unbelieving world. This creates confusion and anxiety throughout the body of Christ worldwide. Many do not consider God's grace towards His followers or a literal interpretation of the Scriptures. It comes from an uncertainty about whether the Church, composed of all true believers in Jesus, regardless of denomination, will endure the Tribulation or go through part of it called *the Mid- or Post-Tribulation Rapture. After the Tribulation,* there is no need for the Rapture.

Through the study of the Bible, we know God is not an unforgiving God to His believers. Accordingly, by His love and grace, the followers of Christ who are alive just before the Tribulation will be raised or Raptured to be with Jesus before their earthly death. This is called the *Pre-Tribulation Rapture*.

Confusion might arise from a failure to distinguish that Jesus' second coming has distinct stages. Scripture speaks of Christ coming in secret. Then scripture also tells of Christ coming in power, glory, and majesty, with every eye seeing him. Both of these can only be true if there are separate appearances of Christ, one before the Tribulation, the other at the end of it. The first part is the Rapture, which is part of the mystery and ends the Church Age. The second part is when Jesus comes in His full glory.

Now, concerning the coming of our Lord Jesus Christ and our being gathered together to him, (2 Thessalonians 2:1)

Paul is specifically referring to the Rapture of the Church because there will be no *"gathering together"* at Jesus' Second Coming to earth. At the Rapture of the Church, Jesus does not come to earth, He appears in the sky for His followers.

"Then we who are alive, who are left, will be caught up together with them in the clouds to meet the Lord in the air, and so we will always be with the Lord." (1 Thessalonians 4:17)

As we move forward in Revelation, it should be noted the Church is mentioned nineteen times in the first 3 chapters and is not mentioned at all from Chapters 4 through 19, the chapters of the Tribulation. Another sign that the church was removed before the Tribulation is that in Chapters 2 and 3, we read, **"He who has an ear, let him hear what the Spirit says to the churches."** Then, in Chapter 13, we read: **"He who has an ear, let him hear what the Spirit says."** The same warning but without mention of the Church. Why did God omit the Church in Chapter 13? It must be because the Church was removed from the earth before God's judgments. The best authority on Jesus' return is Jesus himself. Jesus uses the illustration of Noah and Lot because first, God removes His believers, and then comes the judgment.

[38]"For as in those days before the flood they were eating and drinking, marrying and giving in marriage, until the day when Noah entered the ark, [39] and they were unaware until the flood came and swept them all away, so will be the coming of the Son of Man. [40] Then, two men will be in the field; one will be taken and one left. [41] Two women will be grinding at the mill; one will be taken and one left. [42] Therefore, stay awake, for you do not know on what day your Lord is coming. [43] But know this, that if the master of the house had known in what part of the night the thief was coming, he would have stayed awake and would not have let

his house be broken into. ⁴⁴ Therefore you also must be ready, for the Son of Man is coming at an hour you do not expect".
(Matthew 24:38-44)

Jesus also uses Lot as an example: *²⁸"Likewise, just as it was in the days of Lot - they were eating and drinking, buying and selling, planting and building, ²⁹ but on the day when Lot went out from Sodom, fire, and sulfur rained from heaven and destroyed them all ³⁰ so will it be on the day when the Son of Man is revealed. ³¹ On that day, let the one who is on the housetop, with his goods in the house, not come down to take them away, and likewise let the one who is in the field not turn back. ³² Remember Lot's wife. ³³ Whoever seeks to preserve his life will lose it, but whoever loses his life will keep it. ³⁴ I tell you, in that night there will be two in one bed. One will be taken and the other left. ³⁵ There will be two women grinding together. One will be taken and the other left."*
(Luke 17:28-35)

Paul also wrote in 1 Thessalonians 1:10, *"and to wait for his Son from heaven, whom he raised from the dead, Jesus who delivers us from the wrath to come."* The term, *wait*, is only used here in the New Testament. Also, the Greek dictionary (*Grimm-Thayer*) suggests that to wait is looking to the future for someone expected and trusted. This emphasizes that the believer is to expect Christ's return constantly. The second part of the verse states, *"Jesus who delivers us from the wrath to come."* This means that Christ will remove his Church before the Tribulation. This is the pattern God always uses: He first gives a prophetic warning, and then God removes his people from harm, and the judgment falls on the unbelievers. This was also seen at the Passover. So how will we know when Jesus' return is?

³²"From the fig tree, learn its lesson: as soon as its branch becomes tender and puts out its leaves, you know that summer is near. ³³

So also, when you see all these things, you know that he is near, at the very gates. ³⁴ Truly, I say to you, this generation will not pass away until all these things take place. ³⁵ Heaven and earth will pass away, but my words will not pass away."
(Matthew 24:32-35)

This parable involves a fig tree sprouting, indicating summer is near. So, there will be signs that will signal Jesus' arrival. Only the Father knows the exact time, day, or hour, but the generation that sees these signs will see the coming of Christ. Jesus called these signs birth pains. Like birth pains, as they get closer together and more robust, it means the baby is due, so it is with the signs of His coming. They will start small and build. Revelation will go into more detail as we advance in our study, but the most obvious is the increase in earthquakes, storms, and volcanos. Also, there will be a departure of many Christian churches from the true word of God as pagan and occult practices increase. These are some of the birth pains or the new leaves on the fig tree.

¹ But understand this that in the last days there will come times of difficulty. ² For people will be lovers of self, lovers of money, proud, arrogant, abusive, disobedient to their parents, ungrateful, unholy, ³ heartless, unappeasable, slanderous, without self-control, brutal, not loving good, ⁴ treacherous, reckless, swollen with conceit, lovers of pleasure rather than lovers of God, ⁵ having the appearance of godliness, but denying its power. Avoid such people. ⁶ For among them are those who creep into households and capture weak women, burdened with sins and led astray by various passions, ⁷ always learning and never able to arrive at a knowledge of the truth. ⁸ Just as Jannes and Jambres opposed Moses, so these men also oppose the truth, men corrupted in mind and disqualified regarding the faith.
(2 Timothy 3:1-8)

Note that the Rapture agrees with God's dogma of action. Deliverance of His believers from the tribulation before it starts concurs with all of God's dealings with His believers in the past. Like with Noah and Lot, and as in the time of Moses, we can see examples of God's directly stated principle of God's action toward His believers. They do not go through the judgments of God. God always protects his people.

God has a reason to deliver all who are believers in Him from the Tribulation, where all His people would be targets of persecution, even death. God does not change. We see from the past how God will act in the future, as He always has. To transport believers from a period of universal trial and physical destruction, such as tribulation, necessitates the removal of the Church from the earth by the Rapture, which is also a promise from Jesus.

"Because you have kept my word about patient endurance, I will keep you from the hour of trial that is coming on the whole world, to try those who dwell on the earth." (Revelation 3:10)

Summary of What The Scriptures Teach About The Rapture:

- ❖ The Rapture was unknown until it was revealed to the church, primarily by Paul.
- ❖ ALL believers living when the Rapture occurs will not experience death.
- ❖ Jesus Himself will descend from His Father's house, where He is preparing a place for us to gather all His believers (John 14:1-3; 1 Thessalonians 4:16).
- ❖ *[1] "Let not your hearts be troubled. Believe in God; believe also in me. [2] In my Father's house are many rooms. If it were not so, would I have told you that I go to prepare a place for you? [3] And if I go and prepare a place for you, I*

will come again and will take you to myself, that where I am you may be also. (John 14:1-3)
- *¹⁶ For the Lord himself will descend from heaven with a cry of command, with the voice of an archangel, and with the sound of the trumpet of God. And the dead in Christ will rise first. ¹⁷ Then we who are alive, who are left, will be caught up together with them in the clouds to meet the Lord in the air, and so we will always be with the Lord. ¹⁸ Therefore encourage one another with these words.* 1 Thessalonians 4:16-18)
- All who believe in Christ will hear the archangel's voice and hear God's trumpet call. *For the Lord himself will descend from heaven with a cry of command, with the voice of an archangel, and with the sound of the trumpet of God. And the dead in Christ will rise first.* (1 Thessalonians 4:16).
- The Rapture will occur suddenly, without warning, and will be instantaneous.
- In the Rapture, every believer in Christ will be instantly transformed from mortal to immortal, with glorified bodies.
- Those Raptured will be caught up in the air to meet Jesus, along with the resurrected Church Age believers who have died.
- At the time of the Rapture, all true believers in Christ will be taken into God the Father's presence to the dwelling place Jesus has prepared.
- Then, after the church is Raptured, the world will suffer the unprecedented outpouring of God's wrath, the Tribulation. (Matthew 24:21)

How Long Will The Tribulation Last?

"For then there will be great tribulation, such as has not been from the beginning of the world until now, no, and never will be. And if those days had not been cut short, no human being would

be saved. But for the sake of the elect those days will be cut short." (Matthew 24:21-22)

Revelation Chapters 4 through 19 record God's judgment on the earth. This time is known as the Tribulation, which starts after the Rapture and ends when Jesus physically returns to earth. The sign starting the Tribulation will be the signing of a treaty between Israel and the Arab nations orchestrated by the Antichrist. This starts the final countdown to Jesus' return, ending the age.

Many wonder how long this treaty will be after the Rapture. No one knows how long this gap will be: a few days, weeks, months, or even years. However long this gap is, it will be a time of trying to explain the Rapture and the rise of the Antichrist as a great peacemaker and statesman. He will be the one behind world peace, but beware.

² For you yourselves are fully aware that the day of the Lord will come like a thief in the night. ³ While people are saying, "There is peace and security," then sudden destruction will come upon them as labor pains come upon a pregnant woman, and they will not escape. (1 Thessalonians 5:2-3)

Many ask how long the Tribulation will last. Here, we'll look at God's timeline for the Tribulation or his judgments. It will be the worst time the world has ever known, as God has an outpouring of his wrath on those who rejected His Son.

¹⁶"For God so loved the world, that he gave his only Son, that whoever believes in him should not perish but have eternal life. ¹⁷ For God did not send his Son into the world to condemn the world, but so that the world might be saved through him. ¹⁸ Whoever believes in him is not condemned, but whoever does not believe is condemned already, because he has not believed in the name of the only Son of God. ¹⁹ And this is the judgment: the light has come into the world, and people loved the darkness rather than the light because their works were evil." (John 3:16-19)

The Tribulation will be seven years of appalling torment and disasters, which will bring great suffering to the world. When Jesus told of the end times before His second coming, He said there would be a "great tribulation." During this time, approximately 70% of the world's population died (as assumed from the judgments in Revelation).

"For then there will be great tribulation, such as has not been from the beginning of the world until now, no, and never will be. And if those days had not been cut short, no human being would be saved. But for the sake of the elect those days will be cut short." (Matthew 24: 21-22)

The Tribulation is a significant event mentioned several times in Scripture. In the Old Testament, the prophets mention it at least forty-nine times, and at least fifteen times in the New Testament. But how do we know it will last seven years? The Tribulation will start after the Rapture, permitting the antichrist to make a covenant or treaty with Israel. This relates directly to Daniel's prophecy. The length of the Tribulation is foretold in the Book of Daniel, chapter 9.

God provides a prophetic timetable for the nation of Israel. Daniel records a prophecy known as the prophecy of 70 weeks, or 490 years. From it, we learn the Tribulation will last one "week." In Hebrew terminology, this refers to seven years, known as a week of years or seven years. The first 69 weeks of years started with King Artaxerxes' decree to rebuild Jerusalem and ended with the rejection of Jesus, a period of exactly 483 years. The last week, the 70th week, or the last seven years complete the 490 years prophesied by Daniel. This 70th week has not taken place yet. We're now in a gap called the *"Church Age."* The Tribulation is the last seven years.

²⁴ "Seventy weeks are decreed about your people and your holy city, to finish the transgression, to put an end to sin, and to atone for iniquity, to bring in everlasting righteousness, to seal both vision and prophet and to anoint the holiest place. ²⁵ Know, therefore and understand that from the going out of the word to restore and build Jerusalem to the coming of an anointed one, a prince, there shall be seven weeks. Then for sixty-two weeks it shall be built again with squares and moat, but in a troubled time. ²⁶ And after the sixty-two weeks, an anointed one shall be cut off and shall have nothing. And the people of the prince who is to come shall destroy the city and the sanctuary. Its end shall come with a flood, and to the end there shall be war. Desolations are decreed. ²⁷ And he shall make a strong covenant with many for one week, and for half of the week he shall put an end to sacrifice and offering. And on the wing of abominations shall come one who makes desolate, until the decreed end is poured out on the desolator." (Daniel 9:24-27)

The New Testament also tells us about the length of the Tribulation. It will be divided into two periods of 1260 days or three-and-a-half years. The first half is called just the "Tribulation," and the second half is called "The Great Tribulation." The period that is known as the Tribulation starts when the anti-Christ stops a war between Israel and its Arab enemies. This will then permit Israel to rebuild their Temple. Also, during this time, there will be a global rejection of God in favor of a rise in idols, the occult, and all types of sexual perversion or the return to life as it was in ancient Babylon. This will last for the first half of the Tribulation, and then the Anti-Christ declares himself god, making all the world worship him. Thus begins the Great Tribulation, lasting 1260 days or three-and-a-half years.

"But do not measure the court outside the temple; leave that out, for it is given to the nations, and they will trample the holy city for forty-two months. And I will grant authority to my two witnesses, and they will prophesy for 1,260 days, clothed in sackcloth." (Revelation 11:2-3)

"And the woman fled into the wilderness, where she has a place prepared by God, in which she is to be nourished for 1,260 days." (Revelation 12:6)

"And the beast was given a mouth uttering haughty and blasphemous words, and it was allowed to exercise authority for forty-two months." (Revelation 13:5)

REVELATION CHAPTER 4

[1]After this I looked, and behold, a door standing open in heaven! And the first voice, which I had heard speaking to me like a trumpet, said, "Come up here, and I will show you what must take place after this." [2]At once I was in the Spirit, and behold, a throne stood in heaven, with one seated on the throne. [3]And he who sat there had the appearance of jasper and carnelian, and around the throne was a rainbow that had the appearance of an emerald. (Revelation 4:1-3)

John was commanded to enter heaven, and his first sight was the glorious throne of God and the indescribable person sitting upon it. John is entitled to observe what will transpire in the End Times, after the Rapture of the Church. God grants him a vision of what occurs at that time in heaven and on earth, plus records it. The throne becomes the key location throughout the rest of Revelation. Around it, everything else revolves. From it, God pours forth his judgments towards all the unrepentant on the earth.

In verse 3, John describes the one upon the throne as "the appearance of jasper and carnelian, and around the throne was a rainbow that had the appearance of an emerald." Jasper is a precious stone whose name means spotted or speckled stone, and it was known to have been a favorite gem in the ancient world. Carnelian is a reddish-red brown mineral commonly used as a semi-precious gemstone.

Jasper depicts the glowing radiance of God's holiness and flawless perfection, while the deep red of Carnelian symbolizes the shed blood of Christ's grace. By His grace, we were saved.

Additionally, verse 3 speaks of a rainbow: **"And around the throne was a rainbow that had the appearance of an emerald."** The rainbow's purpose around God's throne is a gracious reminder that He will remember His post-flood promise of mercy, even during the Tribulation. The promise is given in Genesis 9:

[11] I establish my covenant with you, that never again shall all flesh be cut off by the waters of the flood, and never again shall there be a flood to destroy the earth." [12] And God said, "This is the sign of the covenant that I make between me and you and every living creature that is with you, for all future generations: [13] I have set my bow in the cloud, and it shall be a sign of the covenant between me and the earth. [14] When I bring clouds over the earth and the bow is seen in the clouds, [15] I will remember my covenant that is between me and you and every living creature of all flesh. And the waters shall never again become a flood to destroy all flesh. 16 When the bow is in the clouds, I will see it and remember the everlasting covenant between God and every living creature of all flesh that is on the earth." [17] God said to Noah, "This is the sign of the covenant that I have established between me and all flesh that is on the earth." (Genesis 9:11-17)

Finally, it has the **"appearance of an emerald"** as the rainbow circles the throne. In the Bible, green symbolizes life, and a circle represents eternity. Therefore, the circular, emerald-colored rainbow shows God's gift of eternal life to those who follow God and have their name in the Book of Life.

⁴ Around the throne were twenty-four thrones, and seated on the thrones were twenty-four elders, clothed in white garments, with golden crowns on their heads. (Revelation 4:4).

The identity of these twenty-four Elders is unknown. Many Bible scholars think they are a special group of angels. Another thought is that these Elders represent the Church. Why? Because twenty-four is the number associated with priestly service and is symbolic of the Church acting as a priest. Also, these Elders are clothed in white and wearing gold crowns; both are associated with born-again humans, but not angels.

White robes symbolize the righteous attire given to believers the moment they trust in Christ, and the golden crowns are the victors' laurel. The crown represents victory over death and hell, which angels have never faced. Goods are only promised to believers as rewards for various kinds of faithfulness.

⁵ From the throne came flashes of lightning, and rumblings and peals of thunder, and before the throne were burning seven torches of fire, which are the seven spirits of God, ⁶ and before the throne there was as it were a sea of glass, like crystal. And around the throne, on each side of the throne, are four living creatures, full of eyes in front and behind: ⁷ the first living creature like a lion, the second living creature like an ox, the third living creature with the face of a man, and the fourth living creature like an eagle in flight. ⁸ And the four living creatures, each of them with six wings, are full of eyes all around and within, and day and night they never cease to say, "Holy, holy, holy, is the Lord God Almighty, who was and is and is to come!" (Revelation 4:5-8)

The throne of God is the center of heaven, and everyone is fixed upon it and the objects around it. The first of these objects is the seven lamps on the throne. These are the same seven lamps on earth in Chapter One, representing the Church as Jesus walks among them.

"I saw seven golden lampstands, and in the midst of the lampstands one like a son of man" (Revelation 1:12-13)

Now we see the seven lamps are in heaven, further evidence that God will remove (Rapture) His Church from the earth before the outpouring of His judgments. The seven Spirits of God symbolize the sevenfold characteristics of the Holy Spirit. They were introduced in Revelation Chapter 1:4, ***"and from the seven spirits who are before his throne."*** Isaiah describes these seven spirits as:

"And the Spirit of the LORD shall rest upon him, the Spirit of wisdom and understanding, the Spirit of counsel and might, the Spirit of knowledge and the fear of the LORD." (Isaiah 11:2)

"And before the throne, there was as it were a sea of glass, like crystal" (Revelation 4:6).

The word *'sea'* in Biblical symbolism often describes mankind. Here, the sea is like glass or calm. This is assumed to represent the believers in heaven who are tranquil in the presence of God.

Revelation 4:6 continues, **"And around the throne, on each side of the throne, are four living creatures, full of eyes in front and behind."** It is thought that these *"creatures"* are angels who represent Christ's four portraits found in the four Gospels – Matthew, Mark, Luke, and John.

"The first living creature is like a lion." The lion is the king of the beast, representing Jesus as the King of the Jews, which is emphasized in the gospel of Matthew. The lion symbolizes Christ as the King of everything, conquering the ruler of all. Jesus is the promised son of David, established by the authority to sit enthroned at the right hand of God. Before him, all crowns must be thrown down. He is the King of kings and Lord of lords.

"The second living creature like an ox." The ox is hardworking, just as Jesus works hard to get about his Father's business and obey His will. This is the picture of Christ in the Book of Mark. Also, a young ox is a calf, symbolizing Christ's sacrifice for our sins. He can wash away our sins in his blood.

"The third living creature with the face of a man" represents Jesus as the ideal and perfect man, as portrayed in the Gospel of Luke. Jesus Christ is the Son of Man, born of woman, God made flesh, and he precedes us as the firstborn from the dead, yet remains close to us, knocking at our door, seeking to sup and abide with us.

"The fourth living creature like an eagle in flight," suggests Jesus' heavenly origin, His complete oneness with God in heaven. This is the message of the Gospel of John. Jesus was truly God from eternity, divine, and having risen from the dead and ascended into heaven, living forever.

"And the four living creatures, each of them with six wings, are full of eyes all around." The creatures are described as *"living"* to signify that Jesus, whom each creature portrays, *"was dead"* but now is *"alive forevermore."* The six wings symbolize all the fullness of Christ and his universal authority. The many eyes represent Christ's eternal wisdom and knowledge, whose judgments are true and righteous.

⁹ And whenever the living creatures give glory and honor and thanks to him who is seated on the throne, who lives forever and ever, ¹⁰ the twenty-four elders fall before him who is seated on the throne and worship him who lives forever and ever. They cast their crowns before the throne, saying, [11]"Worthy are you, our Lord and God, to receive glory and honor and power, for you created all things, and by your will they existed and were created." (Revelation 4:9-11)

Whenever the four living beings praise God, the twenty-four elders fall before the throne worshiping God, casting their crowns at his feet. This shows that God is to be worshipped and given praise, glory, and honor. The crowns represent eternal life. A crown, like a throne, is a symbol of authority. However, these elders are giving glory to God. They fall before Him, casting their authority to God so that God might be recognized as the only source of all authority, power, and dominion.

REVELATION CHAPTER 5

[1] Then I saw in the right hand of him who was seated on the throne a scroll written within and on the back, sealed with seven seals. [2] And I saw a strong angel proclaiming with a loud voice, "Who is worthy to open the scroll and break its seals?" [3] And no one in heaven or on earth or under the earth was able to open the scroll or to look into it, [4] and I began to weep loudly because no one was found worthy to open the scroll or to look into it.
(Revelation 5:1-4)

John tells us that one of the first events after the Rapture of the Church will be unsealing a scroll. This scroll is thought to be from Daniel, of whom God revealed many predictions, and of Christ. Daniel was told to seal them up until the end of the age.

"But you, Daniel, shut up the words and seal the book, until the time of the end." (Daniel 12:4).

John describes a search for someone worthy to open the scroll.

"Who is worthy to open the scroll and break its seals?" (Revelation 5:2).

Sealing a scroll was a common practice, and the more important the document, the more seals upon it; the most important had seven seals. For a seven-seal scroll, a scribe would take a long roll of parchment and then begin writing. After a period of writing, he would roll it up to hide what was written, then place a seal on it. Afterward, he would begin writing again. This process would continue until what was being written was finished, at which time the scroll would have seven seals. The scroll was meant to be read one seal at a time as it was opened.

This was done to prevent what was written from being read or tampered with by anyone unauthorized. Only a worthy person with proper authority and legal rights could access the message.

"And I began to weep loudly because no one was found worthy to open the scroll or to look into it." (Revelation 5:4)

John knew that the scroll characterized the coming New Heaven and New Earth, that one worthy would be one untainted with Adam's sin. When God created Adam and Eve, he gave them dominion over the earth and everything in it. However, when Adam submitted to Satan, he turned his back on God and officially forfeited to Satan his authority to rule the world. Earth rightly belongs to man, but due to Adam's actions, none of mankind is worthy. No man or angel has the right to open the scroll.

[5] And one of the elders said to me, "Weep no more; behold, the Lion of the tribe of Judah, the Root of David, has conquered so that he can open the scroll and its seven seals." [6] And between the

throne and the four living creatures and among the elders I saw a Lamb standing, as though it had been slain, with seven horns and with seven eyes, which are the seven spirits of God sent out into all the earth. ⁷ And he went and took the scroll from the right hand of him who was seated on the throne. ⁸ And when he had taken the scroll, the four living creatures and the twenty-four elders fell down before the Lamb, each holding a harp, and golden bowls full of incense, which are the prayers of the saints. (Revelation 5:5-8)

As John is weeping, one of the Elders assures him a person worthy to open the scroll has been found. He is the Lion of the tribe of Judah, the Root of David, the Deliverer of Israel, and the Redeemer of man, Christ. Judah was one of the twelve sons of Jacob.

"The scepter shall not depart from Judah, nor the ruler's staff from between his feet, until tribute comes to him; and to him shall be the obedience of the peoples." (Genesis 49:10)

This verse speaks of the fact that the ruler's ship shall not depart from the tribe of Judah, from which King David came, until the Messiah.

John sees the lamb appearing "as though it had been slain." This means that John saw the wounds that were there, and on several occasions, Jesus showed His wounds to those who both believed in Him and rejected Him. We need to stop and remember that Jesus could have had a perfect resurrected body, yet he chose to have his scars on his new immortal body. This is a reminder of his sacrifice for all of mankind so all who look upon him will see.

John sees this lamb: **"with seven horns and with seven eyes, which are the seven spirits of God sent out into all the earth"** (Revelation 5:6). This symbolizes a composite image of Christ. The number seven denotes perfection and completeness. Horns represent power, and multiple eyes imply knowledge and intelligence. It is also thought to speak of the Holy Spirit, which ***"God sent out into all the earth."***

Jesus has described two ways in Revelation 5:5 as a Lion and a Lamb – ***"behold, the Lion of the tribe of Judah, the Root of David,"*** then in Revelation 5:6: ***"I saw a Lamb standing, as though it had been slain."*** This appears contradictory: a lion and a lamb. However, when Jesus first came to earth, it was in humility that he offered himself as a sacrificial lamb to die for all the sins of all mankind. But when Jesus returns, it will be in power and glory, in the supremacy and strength of a lion.

Finally, Christ, as the lamb, takes the seven-seal scroll. The elders fall in worship because they realize that the events of redemption that started at creation are coming to a close.

[8] And when he had taken the scroll, the four living creatures and the twenty-four elders fell down before the Lamb, each holding a harp, and golden bowls full of incense, which are the prayers of the saints. [9] And they sang a new song, saying, "Worthy are you to take the scroll and to open its seals, for you were slain, and by your blood, you ransomed people for God from every tribe and language and people and nation, [10] and you have made them a kingdom and priests to our God, and they shall reign on the earth." [11] Then I looked, and I heard around the throne and the living creatures and the elders the voice of many angels, numbering myriads of myriads and thousands of thousands, [12] saying with a loud voice, "Worthy is the Lamb who was slain, to receive power and wealth and wisdom and might and honor and glory and blessing!" [13] And I heard every creature in heaven and on earth and under the earth and in the sea, and all that is in them, saying, "To him who sits on the throne and to the Lamb be blessing and honor and glory and might forever and ever!" [14] And the four living creatures said, "Amen!" and the elders fell down and worshiped. (Revelation 5:8-14)

Heaven hears a new song about Jesus never heard before. *"And they sang a new song."* Music – a song is a form of Praise, and the new song is a form of praise to God. We sing when happy or sad, at weddings, funerals, or in the shower. Heaven will have music and songs.

REVELATION CHAPTER 6

¹ Now I watched when the Lamb opened one of the seven seals, and I heard one of the four living creatures say with a voice like thunder, "Come!" ² And I looked, and behold, a white horse! And its rider had a bow, and a crown was given to him, and he came out conquering, and to destroy. (Revelation 6:1-2)

This first part of Revelation 6 introduces and unleashes the "Four Horsemen of the Apocalypse."

"Behold the White Horse." As the first seal is opened, a warrior rider on a white horse is sent out to conquer. This is the Antichrist being given his release to take over the earth by war. *"The White Horse"* is the symbol of conquest. When a victorious general or king made his triumph in a newly conquered city, he always entered on a white horse.

"And its rider had a bow, and a crown was given to him," the Antichrist carries a bow, symbolizing his control over the weapons of war. On his head is a crown, showing his claim as the sovereign king of all he conquers, wanting all the world's countries. This is the Antichrist, who is thought will rule from a revised Rome. The vital thing to note about this charismatic leader is that he is the first of the judgments God places on the world. The world will initially see him as the savior of everything, but he's the world's greatest curse. This is just his first appearance, and there is much more in Revelation to follow.

³ When he opened the second seal, I heard the second living creature say, "Come!" ⁴ And out came another horse, bright red. Its rider was permitted to take peace from the earth so that people should slay one another, and he was given a great sword. (Revelation 6:3-4)

"Behold the Red Horse". Red is the color of war. During the first half of the Tribulation, the Antichrist brings peace. People will hail him as the greatest leader in world history. However, after three and a half years, the second seal is opened at the mid-point of the Tribulation, and the red horse takes away the peace. This loss of peace is described in Ezekiel 38 and Daniel 11.

⁵ When he opened the third seal, I heard the third living creature say, "Come!" And I looked, and behold, a black horse! And its rider had a pair of scales in his hand. ⁶ And I heard what seemed to be a voice in the midst of the four living creatures, saying, "A quart of wheat for a denarius, and three quarts of barley for a denarius, and do not harm the oil and wine!" (Revelation 6:5-6)

"Behold The Black Horse" represents financial catastrophe. As war expands around the globe, food, fuel, medicine, and all other commodities become increasingly scarce. Trade will come to a crawl or even stop. *"And its rider had a pair of scales in his hand."* The scales indicate a scarcity of food. Food will be measured out as if it were gold. There are numerous passages in the Bible associated with the weighing of food. *"A quart of wheat for a denarius, and three quarts of barley for a denarius"* means that food will cost a day's pay. A denarius was a day's pay. During the Tribulation, one will have to pay all that he makes to eat. Most likely, the Antichrist won't have a food stamp program. No work, no food. *"And do not harm the oil and wine!"* When John wrote Revelation, Olive oil and wine were luxury food items in Roman times. The black horseman

was told not to harm these items. All foods will be available to temp people, but only the rich can buy them.

⁷ When he opened the fourth seal, I heard the voice of the fourth living creature say, "Come!" ⁸ And I looked, and behold, a pale horse! And its rider's name was Death, and Hades followed him. And they were given authority over a fourth of the earth, to kill with sword and with famine and with pestilence and by wild beasts of the earth. (Revelation 6:7-8)

"Behold the Pale Horse," which represents Death. With war and famine comes plagues, and then death soon follows. The rider of the pale horse was given the authority to kill over a fourth of the world's population. Based on current world population estimates, that means 1,750,000,000 will die in a very short time. *"And with pestilence."* Many used to think the pestilence would be related to war and famine, which always followed them, but we have seen how pestilence destroyed the world's economy in a few weeks. It brought the United States and the whole world to a collapse in a few weeks. A pestilence called coronavirus. Of course, there is also biological warfare.

⁹ When he opened the fifth seal, I saw under the altar the souls of those who had been slain for the word of God and for the witness they had borne. ¹⁰ They cried out with a loud voice, "O Sovereign Lord, holy and true, how long before you will judge and avenge our blood on those who dwell on the earth?" ¹¹ Then they were each given a white robe and told to rest a little longer until the number of their fellow servants and their brothers should be complete, who were to be killed as they themselves had been. (Revelation 6:9-11)

During the Great Tribulation, countless brothers and sisters in Christ will be persecuted and martyred. We all can be saved now without much worry of persecution or death; those who wait until the signs of the times to convince them, such as after the Rapture, will only be saved from the lake of fire, not the Tribulation. This means that during a time like the early Christians', your life was on the line.

The Antichrist will require that all the people of the earth worship him. All who refuse and do not take his mark (The Mark of The Beast) will be prohibited from buying and selling (discussed later in our study). All these tribulation saints will be given a white robe and told to wait. Many believe the wait is for Jesus's return. The white cloud Jesus returns with is thought to be the white-robed tribulation saints.

12 When he opened the sixth seal, I looked, and behold, there was a great earthquake, and the sun became black as sackcloth, the full moon became like blood, 13 and the stars of the sky fell to the earth as the fig tree sheds its winter fruit when shaken by a gale. 14 The sky vanished like a scroll that is being rolled up, and every mountain and island was removed from its place.
(Revelation 6:12-14)

As the sixth seal is opened there is a great earthquake. An earthquake is always a scary experience, and anyone in one remembers it quite well. As we move into the twentieth century, earthquakes have increased in number and severity. In the early twenty-first century, areas that never had earthquakes are having earthquakes. Many believe these are the birth pains leading to the Tribulation, the End Times—a warning. When the tribulation comes, there will be tremendous earthquakes like the world has never seen before.

"And the sun became black as sackcloth, the full moon became like blood, and the stars of the sky fell to the earth." The word star can also mean a meteor. Meteors that John, a first-century man, refers to maybe missiles. Missiles streaking through

the air resemble meteors. Now place a warhead on these missiles, conventional or nuclear, and we have massive amounts of dust and debris blowing into the sky, blackening the sun. The moon will appear red from the atmospheric dust.

"The sky vanished like a scroll that is being rolled up, and every mountain and island was removed from its place." A great description of a nuclear blast. In the area of a nuclear blast, the atmosphere rolls back on itself. A vacuum is created at ground zero as the blast spreads out, and the air comes rushing back in. This is what creates much of the destruction. It looks like the earth is being moved. Watch a nuclear blast film on YouTube filmed in the mountains, at sea, and on islands. You will see the sky roll up, and the land seems to be removed from its place.

[15] Then the kings of the earth and the great ones and the generals and the rich and the powerful, and everyone, slave and free, his in the caves and among the rocks of the mountains, [16] calling to the mountains and rocks, "Fall on us and hide us from the face of him who is seated on the throne, and from the wrath of the Lamb, [17] for the great day of their wrath has come, and who can stand?" (Revelation 6:15-17)

Everyone on the earth tries to hide. They go to the caves and mountains to get away from the destruction. There is a saying I learned in the Army: bombs and bullets don't care who you are. Everyone tries to hide from kings to slaves, rich and poor, even the generals. They pray for the mountains and rocks to hide them. Another Army saying is that there are no atheists in a foxhole. Yet, the people didn't pray to God, even though they knew this was the wrath of the Lamb.

Summary of The Four Horsemen of the Apocalypse

1. **The White Horse** represents conquest, the Antichrist
2. **The Red Horse** represents violence and warfare
3. **The Black Horse** represents financial catastrophe and famine.
4. **The Pale Horse** represents widespread death.

REVELATION CHAPTER 7

[1] After this I saw four angels standing at the four corners of the earth, holding back the four winds of the earth, that no wind might blow on earth or sea or against any tree. [2] Then I saw another angel ascending from the rising of the sun, with the seal of the living God, and he called with a loud voice to the four angels who had been given power to harm earth and sea, [3] saying, "Do not harm the earth or the sea or the trees, until we have sealed the servants of our God on their foreheads." (Revelation 7:1-3)

Angels play an essential role in the workings of God and heaven. They are not mythological creatures, as many want us to believe. They are real and spoken of as a matter of fact in the Bible. They have a vital role to play in the end times. For future reference, the Bible speaks of essentially three categories of angles:

- **First** are the Angels of God. These angels remained faithful to God when Lucifer led a rebellion against Him.
- **Second** are the angels who followed Lucifer and are called demons. They are unbound, still free to work against God's plans.
- **Third** are the bound and imprisoned fallen angels. God casts These particularly vicious groups into *"The Abyss."* They are there to await the final judgment.

Because angels have supernatural power and superior intelligence, the four here are given authority over the weather. They were also given the power to harm the earth and sea, but not immediately.

"another angel ascending from the rising of the sun, with the seal of the living God, and he called with a loud voice to the four angels... "Do not harm the earth or the sea or the trees, until we have sealed the servants of our God on their foreheads." (Revelation 7:2-3)

This angel has the seal of the living God, being sent by God to mark the foreheads of those God has chosen as His evangelists. These are the 144,000 witnesses. God never allowed Himself to be without witnesses to proclaim His way to receive forgiveness. After the Rapture, there will be a spiritual void or emptiness left on earth due to the removal of all true believers-the church. These 144,000 new believers will fill the void and proclaim the way to salvation through Jesus.

The Angel had **"the seal of the living God,"** a seal at that time in history meant to make an imprint, usually with a signet ring. This was done to show that the one who bears the seal is given the authority of the one whose seal it is. It is a visible sign of ownership and a guarantee of protection by the one whose seal it is. Revelation 7:3 states the servants of God shall wear a mark upon their foreheads, no one will be able to mistake them, **"...we have sealed the servants of our God on their foreheads."** The seal guarantees protection for the person wearing it because those marked will be under constant attack by the Antichrist and demonic forces.

As we shall see, all true believers will suffer from hunger, exposure, ridicule, torture, imprisonment, and, at times, even death. Still, the 144,000 evangelists will survive to the end of the Tribulation. God will supernaturally protect them from death and protect all other believers from the coming plagues of the Tribulation. We know the 144,000 will survive the Tribulation due to Revelation Chapter 14 notes that the 144,000 witnesses are standing on Mount Zion with Jesus.

"Then I looked, and behold, on Mount Zion stood the Lamb, and with him, 144,000 who had his name and his Father's name written on their foreheads." (Revelation 14:1)

Who will these 144,000 be? Revelation 7:4-8 tells us exactly.

⁴ And I heard the number of the sealed, 144,000, sealed from every tribe of the sons of Israel: ⁵ 12,000 from the tribe of Judah were sealed, 12,000 from the tribe of Reuben, 12,000 from the tribe of Gad, ⁶ 12,000 from the tribe of Asher, 12,000 from the tribe of Naphtali, 12,000 from the tribe of Manasseh, ⁷ 12,000 from the tribe of Simeon, 12,000 from the tribe of Levi, 12,000 from the tribe of Issachar, ⁸ 12,000 from the tribe of Zebulun, 12,000 from the tribe of Joseph, 12,000 from the tribe of Benjamin were sealed. (Revelation 7:4-8)

Many say this has to be a symbol; it can't mean what it says, and nonetheless, it does. God spells it all out who these 144,000 will be. Don't fall into Preterism Theology, which means everything in Revelation has already happened and is only symbolic. God's word is always true. God redeems 144,000 literal Jews and ordains them as His evangelists. Twelve thousand from each tribe of Israel make up the 144,000. This is the word of God.

"And I heard the number of the sealed, 144,000, sealed from every tribe of the sons of Israel" (Revelation 7:4)

To properly understand why, during the Tribulation, God chose only Jews to be His witnesses, it is because the Jews were to be God's representatives to the Gentiles about the Messiah. Biblical history reveals that they failed this task because they did not recognize Jesus as the Messiah.

As we look at the list of the twelve tribes, note that two original tribes, Dan and Ephraim, are missing. The tribes of Levi and Joseph are substituted for them. Why is this? Many believe it is due to the tribes of Dan and Ephraim having led Israel into idolatry. As noted in the Ten Commandments, the first is *"You shall have no other gods before me"* (Exodus 20:3).

Additionally, many also believe that Dan is missing because the Jewish False Prophet is thought to come from the tribe of Dan, due to Jacob stating that in the last days:

"Dan shall be a serpent in the way, a viper by the path, that bites the horse's heels so that his rider falls backward." (Genesis 49:17).

The Tribe of Ephraim may also be left out because it caused the civil war that divided Israel. Individual members of the tribes of Dan and Ephraim will not be given the honor of being evangelists during the Tribulation.

⁹ After this I looked, and behold, a great multitude that no one could number, from every nation, from all tribes and peoples and languages, standing before the throne and before the Lamb, clothed in white robes, with palm branches in their hands, ¹⁰ and crying out with a loud voice, "Salvation belongs to our God who sits on the throne, and to the Lamb!" ¹¹ And all the angels were standing around the throne and the elders and the four living creatures, and they fell on their faces before the throne and worshiped God, ¹² saying, "Amen! Blessing and glory and wisdom and thanksgiving and honor and power and might be to our God forever and ever! Amen." (Revelation 7:7-12)

This great multitude is from every corner of the earth. As evidenced by their white robes, they are all believers in Jesus. The effectiveness of evangelism during the Tribulation will be overwhelming. It will be like nothing that has ever been seen before. These Saints are standing before the throne with palm branches declaring, **"Salvation belongs to our God who sits on the throne and to the Lamb!"** As they say this, every being at the throne falls on their faces, worshiping God.

[13] Then one of the elders addressed me, saying, "Who are these, clothed in white robes, and from where have they come?" [14] I said to him, "Sir, you know." And he said to me, "These are the ones coming out of the great tribulation. They have washed their robes and made them white in the blood of the Lamb. [15] "Therefore they are before the throne of God, and serve him day and night in his temple, and he who sits on the throne will shelter them with his presence. [16] They shall hunger no more, neither thirst anymore; the sun shall not strike them, nor any scorching heat. [17] For the Lamb in the midst of the throne will be their shepherd, and he will guide them to springs of living water, and God will wipe away every tear from their eyes." (Revelation 7:13-17)

John is asked if he knows who those clothed in white are. In verse 7:14, he is told, **"These are the ones coming out of the great tribulation. They have washed their robes and made them white in the blood of the Lamb."**

Due to Jesus, we are no longer unclean; because of the blood of the Lamb, we are clean. Christ took on all our sins and died for us. We are all no longer soiled but washed clean. There shall be no hunger or thirst, and the heat shall no longer bother us. The Lamb will guide us to living water, and God will wipe away our tears.

Even while God is justly punishing the world for its rejection of Christ, He offers both Jews and Gentiles the opportunity to receive Jesus as Savor. Even in the Tribulation, there can be salvation, and millions will come to Christ.

REVELATION CHAPTER 8

¹ When the Lamb opened the seventh seal, there was silence in heaven for about half an hour. ² Then I saw the seven angels who stand before God, and seven trumpets were given to them. ³ And another angel came and stood at the altar with a golden censer, and he was given much incense to offer with the prayers of all the saints on the golden altar before the throne, ⁴ and the smoke of the incense, with the prayers of the saints, rose before God from the hand of the angel. ⁵ Then the angel took the censer and filled it with fire from the altar and threw it on the earth, and there were peals of thunder, rumblings, flashes of lightning, and an earthquake. ⁶ Now the seven angels who had the seven trumpets prepared to blow them. (Revelation 8:1-6)

Chapter 8 starts with the opening of the seventh seal; this brings on silence in heaven for about half an hour. This silence is overwhelming in meaning, starkly contrasting the joyous sounds heard in heaven prior. This half-hour of silence is the lull before the storm since the seventh seal brings the most incredible judgment yet.

The seven angels, who stand in God's presence, will announce the ensuing seven judgments with a trumpet blast. The Bible designates distinct ranks of angels, and the highest are these seven angels, known as archangels.

Then, before they sound the first trumpet, *"another angel"* appears holding a golden censer and is given *"much incense"* to offer with the prayers of all the saints on the golden altar before the throne. Many believe this is not an angel but Jesus acting as High Priest.

The high priest only used the golden censer in the Holy of Holies. In the Old Testament, incense was used to represent the coming of the Messiah. He has the prayers of all the saints, which means all who have died with Christ, all who were Raptured before the Tribulation, and all who have been martyred since the Tribulation started.

After all the prayers are offered, the censer is filled with fire from the altar and throws it onto the earth. This results in thunder, rumblings, flashes of lightning, and an earthquake. Now, the seven angels with the trumpets are prepared to sound them.

The first angel blew his trumpet, and there followed hail and fire, mixed with blood, and these were thrown upon the earth. And a third of the earth was burned up, and a third of the trees were burned up, and all green grass was burned up. (Revelation 8:7)

The first trumpet sounds start the seven judgments, which are known as the *"Judgments of Thirds."* At the first trumpet blast, ***"a third of the earth was burned up, and a third of the trees were burned up, and all green grass was burned up."*** This devastation seems related to a nuclear exchange on the earth, more significant than the one described in Chapter Six.

John did not know modern warfare, so hail and fire thrown upon the earth is an excellent description of a missile attack. The size of the destruction appears to be from nuclear missiles. The massive loss of vegetation will cause worldwide famine. Farm grains such as wheat, rice, and oats were all known as *grass*.

⁸ The second angel blew his trumpet, and something like a great mountain, burning with fire, was thrown into the sea, and a third of the sea became blood. ⁹ A third of the living creatures in the sea died, and a third of the ships were destroyed. (Revelation 8:8-9)

Verse 8 sounds the second trumpet and states: ***"Something like a great mountain, burning with fire, was thrown into the sea."*** What could this be that brings an end to a third of everything living in the oceans? It might be a meteor that hits the earth, or it might be nuclear missiles attacking naval or merchant vessels in the seas. Whichever it is, it destroys a third of all ships and everything living in the sea. Look at the pictures of a nuclear warhead test in the oceans. The explosion looks like a mountain burning with fire. With the loss of a third of the marine life added to the loss of a third of the grass (farmland), there will be even more famine and all the complications that follow that much destruction.

10 The third angel blew his trumpet, and a great star fell from heaven, blazing like a torch, and it fell on a third of the rivers and on the springs of water. 11 The name of the star is Wormwood. A third of the water became wormwood, and many people died from the water because it had been made bitter.
(Revelation 8:10-11)

The third trumpet sounds and a third of the freshwater is destroyed. First, a third of the salt water – the oceans, now ***"a third of the rivers and on the springs...became wormwood."*** This is brought about by a great star falling from the sky named *Wormwood*. Again, this could be related to nuclear missiles leaving fallout on the waters. Wormwood is a bitter herb, implying that a third of the freshwater will be so tainted that no one can drink it.

The fourth angel blew his trumpet, and a third of the sun was struck, and a third of the moon, and a third of the stars, so that a third of their light might be darkened, and a third of the day might be kept from shining, and likewise a third of the night.
(Revelation 8:12)

The fourth trumpet sounds, and a third of the light from the sky, day and night, is weakened. This may be due to volcanos and/or nuclear explosions causing the soot and smoke in the air to decrease the ambient light by one-third.

Then I looked, and I heard an eagle crying with a loud voice as it flew directly overhead, "Woe, woe, woe to those who dwell on the earth, at the blasts of the other trumpets that the three angels are about to blow!" (Revelation 8:13)

God pauses after four judgments before the next three befall the earth. It is important to note that this pause allows those on earth to repent. Note that a third of all vegetation has been destroyed, a third of all marine life has been destroyed, and a third of all freshwater has become tainted. This is followed by all ambient light being reduced by one-third. Think of the significance of this harm to man and the earth. Hopefully, this will motivate men to turn to Christ for forgiveness. However, most will have a hardened heart and do not heed the *"eagle crying with a loud voice. Woe, woe, woe to those who dwell on the earth."*

REVELATION CHAPTER 9

¹ And the fifth angel blew his trumpet, and I saw a star fallen from heaven to earth, and he was given the key to the shaft of the bottomless pit. ² He opened the shaft of the bottomless pit, and from the shaft rose smoke like the smoke of a great furnace, and the sun and the air were darkened with the smoke from the shaft. ³ Then, from the smoke came locusts on the earth, and they were given power like the power of scorpions of the earth. ⁴ They were told not to harm the grass of the earth or any green plant or any tree, but only those people who do not have the seal of God on their foreheads. ⁵ They were allowed to torment them for five months, but not to kill them, and their torment was like the

Revelation: A Line by Line Breakdown

torment of a scorpion when it stings someone. ⁶ And in those days people will seek death and will not find it. They will long to die, but death will flee from them. ⁷ In appearance the locusts were like horses prepared for battle: on their heads were what looked like crowns of gold; their faces were like human faces, ⁸ their hair like women's hair, and their teeth like lions' teeth; ⁹ they had breastplates like breastplates of iron, and the noise of their wings was like the noise of many chariots with horses rushing into battle. ¹⁰ They have tails and stings like scorpions, and their power to hurt people for five months is in their tails. ¹¹ They have as king over them the angel of the bottomless pit. His name in Hebrew is Abaddon, and in Greek he is called Apollyon. (Revelation 9:1-11)

The *"star"* is a person rather than a literal star since *"he"* is given a key that opens the bottomless pit. The fallen star is Lucifer, known as the *"Star of the Morning"* or Satan. He receives the key from Christ since Jesus possesses the key of hell.

"...Fear not, I am the first and the last, and the living one. I died, and behold I am alive forevermore, and I have the keys of Death and Hades." (Revelation 1:17-18)

The opening of the bottomless pit unleashes a judgment of severe torment, the *"locusts."* The bottomless pit holds the worst demons of hell. These fallen angels are so ferocious that God has kept them bound. Their leader is a demon almost equal in power and authority to Satan.

"They have as king over them the angel of the bottomless pit. His name in Hebrew is Abaddon, and in Greek he is called Apollyon." (Revelation: 9:11).

God permits the release of these demons because men have failed to heed the judgments and have not asked for mercy.

The locusts in this chapter are unlike any found on earth today. These demons of the pit possess them. They have a king named Abaddon – The Destroyer. They will have a scorpion-like stinger in their tail to torment men for five months, but not believers in Christ, those who have God's seal.

They were told not to harm the grass of the earth or any green plant or any tree, but only those people who do not have the seal of God on their foreheads. (Revelation 9:4)

It is thought that those who believe in Jesus as the Messiah will receive the seal of God on their foreheads. Just like the 144,000 evangelists at the beginning of the Tribulation, in Revelation Chapter 7:3, they will also be protected from many of the judgments during the Tribulation. Nonetheless, they will suffer from hunger, exposure, ridicule, torture, and imprisonment, sometimes even death, for Christ.

These loci that are released will have a sting, which will be so painful that their victims will wish they could die but won't. The demon-possessed locusts are not permitted to kill anyone. As with Job in the Old Testament, God allows Satan to torment but not kill. Also, they cannot touch those protected by God, having the Seal of God on their foreheads. Just as God has always protected his people, read about Noah, Lot, and the Jews in the time of Moses, to name a few examples. This stands for the faithfulness of God for his people.

[12] The first woe has passed; behold, two woes are still to come. [13] Then the sixth angel blew his trumpet, and I heard a voice from the four horns of the golden altar before God, [14] saying to the sixth angel who had the trumpet, "Release the four angels who are bound at the great river Euphrates." [15] So the four angels, who had been prepared for the hour, the day, the month, and the year, were released to kill a third of mankind. [16] The number of mounted

troops was twice ten thousand times ten thousand; I heard their number. ¹⁷And this is how I saw the horses in my vision and those who rode them: they wore breastplates the color of fire and of sapphire and of sulfur, and the heads of the horses were like lions' heads, and fire and smoke and sulfur came out of their mouths. ¹⁸By these three plagues a third of mankind was killed, by the fire and smoke and sulfur coming out of their mouths. ¹⁹ For the power of the horses is in their mouths and in their tails, for their tails are like serpents with heads, and by means of them they wound. (Revelation 9:12-19)

    Verse 13 begins with the second woe (the sixth trumpet) as the four most wicked and powerful of all the fallen angels are released to kill a third of mankind! This after one-fourth of the world's population has already been slain from the judgment in Revelation Chapter 6:8:

"And I looked, and behold, a pale horse! And its rider's name was Death, and Hades followed him. And they were given authority over a fourth of the earth, to kill with sword and with famine and with pestilence and by wild beasts of the earth." (Revelation 6:8)

    Then add in all the people killed by poisoning of fresh water, and now another 33% of the population will die.
    These four angels are restrained at the river Euphrates. God bound them because they were tremendously powerful representatives of Satan. The location is significant because it's the area of the Garden of Eden, where the first human sin was committed. It is an area where many significant events in history took place. It is the recognized boundary line between East and West, back to the Babylonians, Greeks, and Romans. It is here Kipling wrote: *"East is East, and West is West, and never the twain shall meet."* These four angels will mobilize an army of 200 million east of the Euphrates.

"The number of mounted troops was twice ten thousand times ten thousand; I heard their number." (Revelation 9:1-16)

Red China has more than this in its army right now. It is believed that when these four evil angels are unbound, they will mobilize the giant war machine of the East led by Red China. Remember that when John wrote this, there was no number even close to this in the entire world population.

[20] The rest of mankind, who were not killed by these plagues, did not repent of the works of their hands nor give up worshiping demons and idols of gold and silver and bronze and stone and wood, which cannot see or hear or walk, [21] nor did they repent of their murders or their sorceries or their sexual immorality or their thefts. (Revelation 9:20-21)

Two of the most incredible verses in the Bible are that no matter what God has allowed to happen to mankind, man is still not willing to repent and turn to Christ. They also reveal another remarkable prediction that man will once again turn his back on God to worship demons and idols.

REVELATION CHAPTER 10

[1] Then I saw another mighty angel coming down from heaven, wrapped in a cloud, with a rainbow over his head, and his face was like the sun, and his legs like pillars of fire. [2] He had a little scroll open in his hand. And he set his right foot on the sea, and his left foot on the land, [3] and called out with a loud voice, like a lion roaring. When he called out, the seven thunders sounded. [4] And when the seven thunders had sounded, I was about to write, but I heard a voice from heaven saying, "Seal up what the seven thunders have said, and do not write it down." [5] And the angel whom I saw standing on the sea and on the land raised his right

hand to heaven ⁶ and swore by him who lives forever and ever, who created heaven and what is in it, the earth and what is in it, and the sea and what is in it, that there would be no more delay, ⁷ but that in the days of the trumpet call to be sounded by the seventh angel, the mystery of God would be fulfilled, just as he announced to his servants the prophets. (Revelation 10:1-7)

There is an interlude of peace between the sixth and seventh trumpets near the end of the tribulation. Up to this point, twelve specific judgments have overwhelmed the earth. God again gives man a chance to turn to Him for mercy and forgiveness. This mighty angel is of the same rank, power, and authority as the strong angel of Revelation *5:2*.

"And I saw a strong angel proclaiming with a loud voice, 'Who is worthy to open the scroll and break its seals?'" (Revelation 5:2)

We know this because the Greek word used here for "*another*" means "*another of the same kind*." The Bible sets forth many levels of rank, power, and authority in the angelic realm. Angels designated as "*strong*" are the supreme angels that stand continually in the presence of God on the throne known as Archangels. The two most people have heard of are Michael and Gabriel.

"But when the archangel Michael, contending with the devil..." (Jude 1:9)

"The angel said to him, "I am Gabriel. I stand in the presence of God, and I have been sent to speak to you and to tell you this good news." (Luke 1:19)

His appearance reveals the supreme authority of this mighty being:

"wrapped in a cloud, with a rainbow over his head, and his face was like the sun, and his legs like pillars of fire." (Revelation 10:1).

This dramatic event takes place in the spiritual realm, being witnessed by the angelic host of heaven, Satan, and his legions of demons. This angel claims possession of the earth for Jesus. The fact that Satan does nothing to prevent this angel from accomplishing his mission bears witness to the angel's great power and authority. The angel came down from heaven wrapped in a cloud, symbolizing a heavenly visit. God gave him this honor.

He lays the beams of his chambers on the waters; he makes the clouds his chariot; he rides on the wings of the wind; (Psalm 104:3)

"…Behold, the LORD is riding on a swift cloud and comes to Egypt;" (Isaiah 19:1)

"He was still speaking when behold, a bright cloud overshadowed them, and a voice from the cloud said, 'This is my beloved Son, with whom I am well pleased; listen to him.'" (Matthew 17:5)

This angel is crowned with a rainbow, God's sign of remembrance, showing that God keeps his covenants and promises. He will keep His covenant to show mercy and grace to all who believe in His Son. It also indicates that He will keep His judgment, as in the time of Noah, Lot, and Moses.

"For God so loved the world, that he gave his only Son, that whoever believes in him should not perish but have eternal life." (John 3:16)

"For by grace, you have been saved through faith. And this is not your own doing; it is the gift of God, not a result of works, so that no one may boast." (Ephesians 2:8-9)

The angel is noted, **"his face was like the sun,"** to remind us of the glory of whose presence he had just come from. When Moses descended Mount Sinai after being in the presence of God, his face glowed.

"When Moses came down from Mount Sinai, with the two tablets of the testimony in his hand as he came down from the mountain, Moses did not know that the skin of his face shone because he had been talking with God." (Exodus 34:29)

The angel carries a small scroll, considered the deed to the earth. The angel also has **"legs like pillars of fire,"** symbolizing judgment. The angel places **"his right foot on the sea, and his left foot on the land"** to show the taking possession of the planet Earth, all land, and seas. He takes possession by divine judgment. Thus, he carries the deed redeemed by Christ. The angel **"called out with a loud voice, like a lion roaring."** After which, he is answered. **"When he called out, the seven thunders sounded."** These seven thunders that sounded give a message that John begins to take down but is told to stop.

⁴ And when the seven thunders had sounded, I was about to write, but I heard a voice from heaven saying, "Seal up what the seven thunders have said and do not write it down." (Revelation 10:4)

Nowhere else in the rest of John's vision (Revelation) is he ever permitted to reveal what he heard. Over the centuries, much speculation about what this message was has been. All we can conclude is it must be very potent. Something the world can't handle. Verse 6 says, **"That there would be no more delay."** This tells us Christ will no longer delay His coming. The big question comes from Revelation 10:7.

"but that in the days of the trumpet call to be sounded by the seventh angel, the mystery of God would be fulfilled, just as he announced to his servants the prophets." (Revelation 10:7)

What is the mystery proclaimed to the prophets? The age-old paradox is considered: Why has God allowed evil to continue? Why has God not put down His enemies and established His kingdom of the earth? Second, Peter 3:9-10 clears up this mystery.

"The Lord is not slow to fulfill his promise as some count slowness but is patient toward you, not wishing that any should perish, but that all should reach repentance. But the day of the Lord will come like a thief, and then the heavens will pass away with a roar, and the heavenly bodies will be burned up and dissolved, and the earth and the works that are done on it will be exposed."
(2 Peter 3:9-10)

God wants to give time for as many people as possible to repent. This time, through all these centuries, has allowed many people to repent and receive Jesus as their Savior.

⁸ Then the voice that I had heard from heaven spoke to me again, saying, "Go, take the scroll that is open in the hand of the angel who is standing on the sea and on the land." ⁹ So I went to the angel and told him to give me the little scroll. And he said to me, "Take and eat it; it will make your stomach bitter, but in your mouth it will be sweet as honey." ¹⁰ And I took the little scroll from the hand of the angel and ate it. It was sweet as honey in my mouth, but when I had eaten it my stomach was made bitter. ¹¹ And I was told, "You must again prophesy about many peoples and nations and languages and kings.". (Revelation 10:8-11)

John is told to take the scroll from the angel. *"Take and eat it; it will make your stomach bitter, but in your mouth it will be*

sweet as honey." Tasting and eating are often used in the Bible to portray hearing and believing. Some Old Testament prophets were commanded to "*eat*" a scroll containing scripture.

But how can it be both bitter and sweet? It's sweet to learn of God's love for man and his plan for eternal salvation. It's bitter when we discover that all who reject Christ will suffer God's judgment. This was John; he rejoiced in the coming of Jesus but was greatly saddened by those who would not repent.

REVELATION CHAPTER 11

Chapter 11 of Revelation focuses on Jerusalem and the significant events that transpire there. Throughout world history, no city has been more important than Jerusalem. Consider these facts about that city:

- ❖ It was where Melchizedek blessed Abraham over 4,000 years ago. Melchizedek was the King of ancient Salem and "*priest of the Most High God."* Ancient Salem is understood to have been the nucleus of the later city of Jerusalem, and its name was incorporated in that of Jerusalem, which is sometimes referred to as "Salem."
- ❖ **"And Melchizedek, king of Salem, brought out bread and wine. (He was a priest of God Most High.) And he blessed him and said, "Blessed be Abram by God Most High, Possessor of heaven and earth"** (Genesis 14:18, 19)
- ❖ Captured by King David and exalted as the national capital of Israel 3000 years ago.
- ❖ It was the site of the Temple of Israel, the first built by Solomon and a wonder of the ancient world.
- ❖ It was established as the spiritual center of life, where God dwelt.

- ❖ It is the ONLY city God ever called "My city." The Bible has nearly 800 references to Jerusalem, called *"the City of our God."*
- ❖ It was the site of numerous invasions each time the Israelis forsook their faith in God.
- ❖ It was where Jesus was crucified and ascended into heaven.
- ❖ It is considered holy by Judaism, Christianity, and Islam.
- ❖ It was reaffirmed as the capital of Israel by President Donald Trump. The US formally recognized Jerusalem as Israel's capital in 2017 and opened the US embassy there in May 2018.

[1] Then I was given a measuring rod like a staff, and I was told, "Rise and measure the temple of God and the altar and those who worship there, [2] but do not measure the court outside the temple; leave that out, for it is given over to the nations, and they will trample the holy city for forty-two months. (Revelation 11:1-2)

John wrote the Book of Revelation about AD 95, which means the Temple that stood in Jerusalem in Christ's day, known as the "Second Temple," was non-existent. The Romans destroyed it twenty-five years earlier under Titus when he leveled the Temple and the Holly City in AD 70. So, what Temple is John referring to? There can be only one answer, a not-yet-built one.

In Revelation 11:1-2 John was told to measure this future Temple, including the altar. An extensive study of the Temple Mount shows that the location of the Temple is not where the Dome of the Rock sits, as many believe. After a sixteen-year study, renowned archaeologist Dr. Asher Kaufman, a professor at Hebrew University, found evidence that the Golden Dome of the Rock is at least 150 meters south of the Eastern gate.

Dr. Kaufman has laid out the exact Temple foundation. It fits precisely as ancient descriptions of the Temple describe it. God knew of the Moslem Mosque and prophetically in Revelation 11:1

stated to measure this area for a future Temple. This means that the Temple could be rebuilt at any time without the destruction of the third-holiest shrine of the Muslim faith - the Dome of the Rock. Also, in Revelation 11:1-2, John was told to measure the Temple and its worshippers. When God takes measurements of his worshippers, it's to evaluate the spiritual condition of His people.

³ And I will grant authority to my two witnesses, and they will prophesy for 1,260 days, clothed in sackcloth." ⁴ These are the two olive trees and the two lampstands that stand before the Lord of the earth. ⁵ And if anyone would harm them, fire pours from their mouth and consumes their foes. If anyone would harm them, this is how he is doomed to be killed. ⁶ They have the power to shut the sky, that no rain may fall during the days of their prophesying, and they have power over the waters to turn them into blood and to strike the earth with every kind of plague, as often as they desire. (Revelation 11:3-6)

The two witnesses that God will raise at this time will preach so effectively that no one can plead ignorance about the realities of salvation. They will make it a point to prove that Jesus has already fulfilled everything about the Messiah.

Before God allows the murder of these two witnesses, they will be allowed to preach for 1,260 days and destroy anyone who comes against them. Using the Biblical year 360 days, this comes out to three and a half years or the first half of the seven-year Tribulation. Now, who are the two witnesses? Many Biblical scholars believe they will be Moses and Elijah. There are many reasons why. One is in Malachi 4; God predicted the coming of Elijah.

"Behold, I will send you Elijah the prophet before the great and awesome day of the LORD comes. And he will turn the hearts of fathers to their children and the hearts of children to their fathers,

lest I come and strike the land with a decree of utter destruction." (Malachi 4:5-6)

"The great and awesome day of the LORD." Refers specifically to the last half of the Tribulation period. Notice in Revelation 11:6 that the two witnesses have the power to cause drought by withholding the rain (Elijah's most famous Old Testament miracle) and can turn the earth's waters into blood (one of Moses' most famous miracles). Among all the prophets of the Old Testament, Moses and Elijah were removed from the earth before their ministries were finished.

Moses was removed prematurely and not allowed to enter the Promised Land because he relied on himself, not God. He put his faith in man, a replication of mankind's sin since Adam and Eve—relying on ourselves rather than on God. Moses sinned because he moved away from his obedience to God. He was allowed to see the *Promised Land* but not enter. No one knows where his body is.

So Moses the servant of the LORD died there in the land of Moab, according to the word of the LORD, And he buried him in the valley in the land of Moab opposite Beth-Peor; but no one knows the place of his burial to this day. (Deuteronomy 34:5-6)

But when the archangel Michael, contending with the devil, was disputing about the body of Moses, he did not presume to pronounce a blasphemous judgment, but said, "The Lord rebuke you." (Jude 1:9)

Elijah asked God to kill him because he was being persecuted. So, God told him to appoint a new prophet in his place.

And Jehu the son of Nimshi you shall anoint to be king over Israel, and Elisha the son of Shaphat of Abel-meholah you shall anoint to be prophet in your place (1 Kings 19:16).

God took Elijah to heaven in a whirlwind and chariot of fire. *And as they still went on and talked, behold, chariots of fire and horses of fire separated the two of them. And Elijah went up by a whirlwind into heaven.* (2 Kings 2:11)

⁷ And when they have finished their testimony, the beast that rises from the bottomless pit will make war on them and conquer them and kill them, ⁸ and their dead bodies will lie in the street of the great city that symbolically is called Sodom and Egypt, where their Lord was crucified. ⁹ For three and a half days some from the peoples and tribes and languages and nations will gaze at their dead bodies and refuse to let them be placed in a tomb, ¹⁰ and those who dwell on the earth will rejoice over them and make merry and exchange presents, because these two prophets had been a torment to those who dwell on the earth. ¹¹ But after the three and a half days a breath of life from God entered them, and they stood up on their feet, and great fear fell on those who saw them. ¹² Then they heard a loud voice from heaven saying to them, "Come up here!" And they went up to heaven in a cloud, and their enemies watched them. ¹³ And at that hour there was a great earthquake, and a tenth of the city fell. Seven thousand people were killed in the earthquake, and the rest were terrified and gave glory to the God of heaven. ¹⁴ The second woe has passed; behold, the third woe is soon to come. (Revelation 11:7-14)

"The beast that rises from the bottomless pit" refers to the coming Antichrist. He hears the two witnesses and becomes so angry at their straightforward gospel that he makes war against them and kills them.

"Their dead bodies will lie in the street of the great city that symbolically is called Sodom and Egypt, where their Lord was crucified." (Revelation 11:8)

This is an insulting reference to Jerusalem. *"Sodom"* refers to its immorality and *"Egypt"* to its worldliness, while the remainder of its crucifixion of Jesus emphasizes its consistent rejection.

And those who dwell on the earth will rejoice over them and make merry and exchange presents, because these two prophets had been a torment to those who dwell on the earth.
(Revelation 11:10).

The people will celebrate their death like Christmas. After three and one-half days, the joy is over as the bodies come to life again. The two rise to heaven in a cloud before speechless witnesses. At that moment, an earthquake strikes the city of Jerusalem, killing seven thousand people. Those left alive are petrified, giving glory to God. At last, many Jews receive the Gospel.

[15] Then the seventh angel blew his trumpet, and there were loud voices in heaven, saying, "The kingdom of the world has become the kingdom of our Lord and his Christ, and he shall reign forever and ever." [16] And the twenty-four elders who sit on their thrones before God fell on their faces and worshiped God, [17] saying, "We give thanks to you, Lord God Almighty, who is and who was, for you have taken your great power and begun to reign. [18] The nations raged, but your wrath came, and the time for the dead to be judged, and for rewarding your servants, the prophets and saints, and those who fear your name, both small and great, and for destroying the destroyers of the earth." (Revelation 11:15-18)

The seventh angel sounds his trumpet, signaling the last swift and terrible judgments to commence. The people of God surrounding His throne, see the long-awaited Kingdom of God is about to be established, so they burst into praise. This desire for a Kingdom of peace and prosperity on earth had been the dearest desire of all the Old Testament believers. It was the primary hope of Judaism. The Jews always hoped for a new earthly kingdom and a new David. Just before Jesus's ascension, the apostles inquired about this from Jesus.

So, when they had come together, they asked him, "Lord, will you at this time restore the kingdom to Israel?" He said to them, "It is not for you to know times or seasons that the Father has fixed by his own authority. (Acts 1:6-7).

The apostles didn't realize that the Kingdom promised to Israel had been temporarily deferred until the Gentiles were given a chance to accept His Messiah. God wants all the people of the earth to be entitled to the blessings promised to Israel.

[19] Then God's temple in heaven was opened, and the ark of his covenant was seen within his temple. There were flashes of lightning, rumblings, peals of thunder, an earthquake, and heavy hail. (Revelation 11:19)

There is a complete temple in heaven, and the earthly one is only a replica. We see this heavenly Temple open, revealing the Ark of God's covenant. This opening of heaven's Temple shows the Jews and everyone that God is unconditionally faithful about His covenant of salvation through forgiveness. This chapter closes with flashes of lightning and thunder, earthquakes, and hail – a warning that God's final climactic judgments are on the way to those who reject the Messiah.

REVELATION CHAPTER 12

¹ And a great sign appeared in heaven: a woman clothed with the sun, with the moon under her feet, and on her head a crown of twelve stars. ² She was pregnant and was crying out in birth pains and the agony of giving birth. ³ And another sign appeared in heaven: behold, a great red dragon, with seven heads and ten horns, and on his heads seven diadems. ⁴ His tail swept down a third of the stars of heaven and cast them to the earth. And the dragon stood before the woman who was about to give birth, so that when she bore her child, he might devour it. ⁵ She gave birth to a male child, one who is to rule all the nations with a rod of iron, but her child was caught up to God and to his throne, ⁶ and the woman fled into the wilderness, where she has a place prepared by God, in which she is to be nourished for 1,260 days. (Revelation 12:1-6)

The significant point in this chapter is "And a great sign appeared in heaven," a woman in celestial clothing. She is introduced as pregnant and crying out in birth pains. The identity of this woman can be partly established by the symbols that make up her unusual clothing. In his prophetic dream, the Hebrew patriarch Joseph saw the sun, moon, and eleven stars bowing to him.

"Then he dreamed another dream and told it to his brothers and said, "Behold, I have dreamed another dream. Behold, the sun, the moon, and eleven stars were bowing down to me. But when he told it to his father and his brothers, his father rebuked him and said to him, "What is this dream that you have dreamed? Shall I and your mother and your brothers indeed come to bow ourselves to the ground before you?" (Genesis 37:9-10)

Jacob, Joseph's father, indignantly pointed out that the dream meant that there would come a time when Joseph's family would bow down to Joseph. In the dream the sun symbolizes Jacob, the moon stands for his mother, Rachel, and the eleven stars represent his brothers. Joseph's dream did come true, confirming the symbols represented his family. Accordingly, we can reason that the symbols in Revelation 12:1 identify the woman as Israel and the stars as the tribes of Israel.

The woman is further identified by the fact she gives birth to a male child who is to rule all nations with a rod of iron. It's clear that the male child is the Messiah, and the woman who gives birth to this child must symbolically refer to Israel.

"I will tell of the decree: The LORD said to me, "You are my Son; today I have begotten you. Ask of me, and I will make the nations your heritage, and the ends of the earth your possession. You shall break them with a rod of iron and dash them in pieces like a potter's vessel." (Psalm 2:7-9)

Chapter 12:3 talks of a *"great red dragon"*. Usually, a dragon represents the villain in most stories. The same is true here; this dragon represents Satan. It is thought that this dragon is red because he's covered with the blood of all the people slaughtered and all the wars he instigated. The dragon has seven heads and ten horns, which many authorities think represents the seven continents of the world, and the ten horns are the ten-nation confederation, believed to be the rebirth of Rome led by the Antichrist.

"His tail swept down a third of the stars of heaven and cast them to the earth. And the dragon stood before the woman who was about to give birth, so that when she bore her child, he might devour it." (Revelation 12:4)

Satan, the red dragon, and his followers, all the angels that stand with him called demons, are the stars swept down by his tail as they are cast out of heaven. The dragon, or Satan, is ready to kill the child, the Messiah, as he is born.

⁷ Now war arose in heaven, Michael and his angels fighting against the dragon. And the dragon and his angels fought back, ⁸ but he was defeated, and there was no longer any place for them in heaven. ⁹ And the great dragon was thrown down, that ancient serpent, who is called the devil and Satan, the deceiver of the whole world--he was thrown down to the earth, and his angels were thrown down with him. ¹⁰ And I heard a loud voice in heaven, saying, "Now the salvation and the power and the kingdom of our God and the authority of his Christ have come, for the accuser of our brothers has been thrown down, who accuses them day and night before our God. (Revelation 12:7-10)

Satan makes one last attempt to take over, but God's champion is the archangel, Michael. Satan and his angels are kicked out of heaven, thrown down to the earth, and never allowed to come before God again with accusations against God's people for any reason.

¹¹ And they have conquered him by the blood of the Lamb and by the word of their testimony, for they loved not their lives even unto death. ¹² Therefore, rejoice, O heavens and you who dwell in them! But woe to you, O earth and sea, for the devil has come down to you in great wrath, because he knows that his time is short!" (Revelation 12:11-12)

In verse 11, we see the secret of defeating the Devil through the blood of the Lamb and the word of testimony. We must remind Satan about the blood of Jesus, the cross, and Christ's triumph over death and hell. We are more than conquerors over the Devil because Christ loves us and gave His life for us. Now, do we recognize this and live like it?

"No, in all these things, we are more than conquerors through him who loved us. For I am sure that neither death nor life, nor angels nor rulers, nor things present nor things to come, nor powers, nor height nor depth, nor anything else in all creation, will be able to separate us from the love of God in Christ Jesus our Lord." (Romans 8:37-39)

The second weapon believers have for the Devil's attacks is **"by the word of their testimony"**. Satan uses every clever device he has to keep us from sharing with others the word of God, telling what He has done in our lives. Many seekers have a great impression when hearing others and hearing the stories of how lives have changed due to Christ. The reason this is a menace to Satan is that God gave His children the privilege of bringing others into His kingdom.

¹³ And when the dragon saw that he had been thrown down to the earth, he pursued the woman who had given birth to the male child. ¹⁴ But the woman was given the two wings of the great eagle so that she might fly from the serpent into the wilderness, to the place where she is to be nourished for a time, and times, and half a time. ¹⁵ The serpent poured water like a river out of his mouth after the woman, to sweep her away with a flood. ¹⁶ But the earth came to the help of the woman, and the earth opened its mouth and swallowed the river that the dragon had poured from his mouth. ¹⁷ Then the dragon became furious with the woman and went off to make war on the rest of her offspring, on those who keep the commandments of God and hold to the testimony of Jesus. And he stood on the sand of the sea. (Revelation 12:13-17)

The dragon, or Satan, gets thrown out of heaven. He attacks *"the woman"* or the Jews (Israel). There will be a tremendous Satanic fury against them.

"So when you see the abomination of desolation spoken of by the prophet Daniel, standing in the holy place (let the reader understand), then let those who are in Judea flee to the mountains. Let the one who is on the housetop not go down to take what is in his house, and let the one who is in the field not turn back to take his cloak." (Matthew 24:15-18)

During the Tribulation, Satan will control a man who will rule the entire world, known as the Antichrist. He'll pretend to be a great friend of Israel for the first three and one-half years of the Tribulation. In the second half of the Tribulation, known as the Great Tribulation, he will turn on Israel when Satan is cast out of heaven. When this happens, there will be many Jews who will have their eyes opened and see the Antichrist is the evil one, not the Messiah. They will then see that God's Messiah is Jesus. This group of Jewish believers will be led to a protective place in the wilderness.

"But the woman was given the two wings of the great eagle so that she might fly from the serpent into the wilderness, to the place where she is to be nourished for a time, and times, and half a time." (Revelation 12:14)

Bible scholars believe this to be Petra, *"the City of Rock"* in the Jordanian wilderness, south of the Dead Sea. It appears there will be some airlift that will rapidly transport these fleeing Jews across the rugged terrain to their place of protection. The Antichrist, or Satan, won't stand for these Jewish believers getting away from him, so will send a *"flood"* of pursuers after them.

This *flood* will be a great army to trap and kill them, just like when the Jews fled Pharaoh in the time of Moses, who sent his army after them. However, God will cause the earth to open to swallow them up, just like the Red Sea swallowed up Pharaoh's. This will motivate the Antichrist to attempt to kill everyone who believes in Christ.

REVELATION CHAPTER 13

¹ And I saw a beast rising out of the sea, with ten horns and seven heads, with ten diadems on its horns and blasphemous names on its heads. ² And the beast that I saw was like a leopard; its feet were like a bear's, and its mouth was like a lion's mouth. And to it the dragon gave his power and his throne and great authority. ³ One of its heads seemed to have a mortal wound, but its mortal wound was healed, and the whole earth marveled as they followed the beast. ⁴ And they worshiped the dragon, for he had given his authority to the beast, and they worshiped the beast, saying, "Who is like the beast, and who can fight against it?" ⁵ And the beast was given a mouth uttering haughty and blasphemous words, and it was allowed to exercise authority for forty-two months. ⁶ It opened its mouth to utter blasphemies against God, blaspheming his name and his dwelling, that is, those who dwell in heaven. ⁷ Also it was allowed to make war on the saints and to conquer them. And authority was given it over every tribe and people and language and nation, ⁸ and all who dwell on earth will worship it, everyone whose name has not been written before the foundation of the world in the Book of Life of the Lamb who was slain. ⁹ If anyone has an ear, let him hear: ¹⁰ If anyone is to be taken captive, to captivity he goes; if anyone is to be slain with the sword, with the sword must he be slain. Here is a call for the endurance and faith of the saints.
(Revelation 13:1-10)

Revelation 13 introduces the Antichrist, also known as the *"Beast,"* because that is what he is in God's sight. More than 100 prophecies clearly predict the rise of the Antichrist in the end times. The Scripture clearly describes the Antichrist's origin, nationality, career, and how he rules the world.

So why does the Antichrist emerge from the sea? The sea represents the restless strivings of all the nations of the world. John explains in Revelation 17:15: **"And the angel said to me, The waters that you saw, where the prostitute is seated, are peoples and multitudes and nations and languages."** Isaiah stated that the Antichrist would rise from the sea because of the chaos of the nations.

"But the wicked are like the tossing sea; for it cannot be quiet, and its waters toss up mire and dirt." (Isaiah 57:20).

What do the ten horns and crowns represent? In Bible symbolism, horns almost always represent political power. The Beast's ten horns represent the ten nations that form a confederacy, and the Beast will rule. The seven heads are thought to be the seven continents of the earth, showing the Antichrist will rule the world. This is first covered in Daniel chapter 8.

"His power shall be great-but not by his own power; and he shall cause fearful destruction and shall succeed in what he does, and destroy mighty men and the people who are the saints. By his cunning he shall make deceit prosper under his hand, and in his own mind he shall become great. Without warning he shall destroy many. And he shall even rise up against the Prince of princes, and he shall be broken-but by no human hand."
(Daniel 8:24-25)

Daniel is very symbolic, and his prophecies are rather elaborate. However, he talks of four successive world empires that will rise and fall (Babylon, Persia, Greece, and Rome). When God is about to peak world history, ten nations will emerge from the fourth empire, Rome, and form a confederation that will be a political entity.

At that point, a brilliant personality will rise to world prominence and lead this nation, but with the help of Satan. Daniel also states this confederacy would be the most significant Gentile power ever to rule the world. Revelation 13:2 says the beast is compared with a leopard, a bear, and a lion. These images represent that the Beast will have similarities to all three empires from the past.

The ancient Greeks, under Alexander the Great, were like a leopard. The Persian Empire was like a bear. The Babylonian Empire was thought of as a lion, the king of the beast.

The Beast-Antichrist will combine all these features into himself. As the leopard, he will be like Alexander, striking with brilliant attacks of swiftness, giving no quarter. He will be like a bear (Persia), very powerful and unstoppable. He will rule the world. And like the lion (Babylon), he will have regal splendor and regal tricks due to being empowered by Satan.

The Bible has several other titles for the beast or antichrist Each one gives a unique glimpse into his sinister nature.

He will be known as a man of lawlessness and destruction.
³ *Let no one deceive you in any way. For that day will not come, unless the rebellion comes first, and the <u>man of lawlessness</u> is revealed, <u>the son of destruction</u>,* (2 Thessalonians 2:3)

He will be known as the little horn. ***"I considered the horns, and behold, there came up among them <u>another horn, a little one</u>, before which three of the first horns were plucked up by the roots. And behold, in this horn were eyes like the eyes of a man, and a mouth speaking great things."*** (Daniel 7:8)

He shall be a *king*. ***"And at the latter end of their kingdom, when the transgressors have reached their limit, <u>a king of bold face</u>, one who understands riddles, shall arise."*** (Daniel 8:23)

The prince who is to come. ***"And after the sixty-two weeks, an anointed one shall be cut off and shall have nothing. And the people of <u>the prince who is to come</u> shall destroy the city and the sanctuary. Its end shall come with a flood, and to the end there shall be war. Desolations are decreed."*** (Daniel 9:26)

The worthless shepherd. ***"Woe to my <u>worthless shepherd</u>, who deserts the flock! May the sword strike his arm and his right eye! Let his arm be wholly withered, his right eye utterly blinded!"*** (Zechariah 11:17)

The Abomination. ***"So when you see the <u>abomination</u> of desolation spoken of by the prophet Daniel, standing in the holy place (let the reader understand)"*** (Matthew 24:15)

He is the son of destruction. ***"Let no one deceive you in any way. For that day will not come, unless the rebellion comes first, and the man of lawlessness is revealed, <u>the son of destruction</u>,"*** (2 Thessalonians 2:3)

The lawless one. ***"The coming of <u>the lawless one</u> is by the activity of Satan with all power and false signs and wonders"*** (2 Thessalonians 2:9)

The Antichrist. ***"Children, it is the last hour, and as you have heard that <u>antichrist</u> is coming, so now many antichrists have come. Therefore we know that it is the last hour."*** (1 John 2:18)

He is called the beast. ***"And I saw a <u>beast</u> rising out of the sea, with ten horns and seven heads, with ten diadems on its horns and blasphemous names on its heads."*** (Revelation 13:1)

The Bible does not clearly identify the Antichrist as a Jew or Gentile. Most Biblical scholars believe he will be a Gentile, most likely from Europe or one of the countries that made up the Roman Empire. Scripture tells us that in the Book of Daniel, he will come from a kingdom of ten kingdoms. Many hold that these ten kingdoms are the European Union. These nations making up the European Union were all part of the Roman Empire. Daniel also states he will make a covenant with Israel promising them Gentile protection. Luke tells us that the Antichrist will come during the times of the Gentiles.

The Antichrist will be the most unbelievable political leader the world has ever known. He will be like Caesar, Napolean, Thomas Jefferson, and John Adams all in one man. With the world's emphasis today on a one-world global government that can bring peace and coexistence between all nations, we can see how a person like this could take world power.

Scripture describes the characteristics of the Antichrist as:
- An intellectual Genius
- Commercial Genius
- Administrative Genius
- Political Genius
- Oratorical Genius
- Military Genius
- Religious Genius

"One of its heads seemed to have a mortal wound, but its mortal wound was healed, and the whole earth marveled as they followed the beast." (Revelation 13:3)

His greatest attribute is that he is a master of deception. Amazingly the Antichrist will appear to rise from the dead due to a mortal head wound he receives in the last half of the Tribulation. God will allow Satan to give the Antichrist-Beast tremendous supernatural ability. This trick of Satan makes the whole earth marvel and worship him. Now, as ruler of the earth, his facade of peace and prosperity ends. He directly attacks God's people, Christians, ultimately killing a great many tribulation saints.

In Revelation 13:8, John speaks of a book called "**The Book of Life of the Lamb.**" In the Book of Life are written the names of every person who ever lived on earth. In the Book of Life of the Lamb is everyone who accepted Jesus. If a person rejects Jesus as

Savior, and God knows he will never accept Jesus as Christ, his name is blotted out of the Book of Life. Those who are not found in the Lamb's Book and those who worship the Beast-Antichrist and take his mark will suffer for it at the final judgment.

⁸ and all who dwell on earth will worship it, everyone whose name has not been written before the foundation of the world in the book of life of the Lamb who was slain. (Revelation 13:8)

Revelation speaks of the Book of Life here and in Chapter 20.

"And I saw the dead, great and small, standing before the throne, and books were opened. Then another book was opened, which is the book of life. And the dead were judged by what was written in the books, according to what they had done."
(Revelation 20:12)

God records everyone's thoughts, words, and deeds to be recalled on the Day of Judgement. Jesus determines how we are judged, believers and unbelievers. Both will stand before Him. Believers will be rewarded for their faith in Christ. Their salvation is never in question because Jesus died on the cross for us. However, unbelievers will be judged by Jesus by their deeds according to God's law. They choose not to accept God's free gift of salvation.

²³ for all have sinned and fall short of the glory of God, ²⁴ and are justified by his grace as a gift, through the redemption that is in Christ Jesus, (Romans 3:23,24)

"For by grace, you have been saved through faith. And this is not your own doing; it is the gift of God, not a result of works, so that no one may boast." (Ephesians 2:8-9)

²⁷ And just as it is appointed for man to die once, and after that comes judgment, ²⁸ so Christ, having been offered once to bear the sins of many, will appear a second time, not to deal with sin but to save those who are eagerly waiting for him.
(Hebrews 9:27,28)

The Bible also eludes to two Books of Life. One has been called the Book of Life since the beginning of time, and the other is called Lamb's Book of Life. The difference between the two is the Lamb's Book of Life only has the names of those who received His free gift of salvation. One's name may be removed from the Book of Life but not from the Lamb's. Through Christ, we are saved.

"If anyone is to be taken captive, to captivity he goes; if anyone is to be slain with the sword, with the sword must he be slain. Here is a call for the endurance and faith of the saints."
(Revelation 13:10)

As seen in verse 10, Satan will be so furious with those whose names are still in the Book of Life of the Lamb that the Antichrist will wage war all over the world on believers, who will suffer or die for their faith in Christ.

¹¹ Then I saw another beast rising out of the earth. It had two horns like a lamb and it spoke like a dragon. ¹² It exercises all the authority of the first beast in its presence, and makes the earth and its inhabitants worship the first beast, whose mortal wound was healed. ¹³ It performs great signs, even making fire come down from heaven to earth in front of people, ¹⁴ and by the signs that it is allowed to work in the presence of the beast it deceives those who dwell on earth, telling them to make an image for the beast that was wounded by the sword and yet lived. ¹⁵ And it was allowed to give breath to the image of the beast, so that the image of the beast might even speak and might cause those who

would not worship the image of the beast to be slain. ¹⁶ Also it causes all, both small and great, both rich and poor, both free and slave, to be marked on the right hand or the forehead, ¹⁷ so that no one can buy or sell unless he has the mark, that is, the name of the beast or the number of its name. ¹⁸ This calls for wisdom: let the one who has understanding calculate the number of the beast, for it is the number of a man, and his number is 666.
(Revelation 13:11-18)

Despite the tyranny of the first Beast (the Antichrist), Satan will rise to a second beast. The second beast will be very similar to the first one. The Greek word translated *"another"* in verse 11 specifically means another of the same kind. However, there will be differences. While the first beast comes from the sea, the second emerges from the land. Biblically, earth means land; symbolically, it usually refers to Israel. Many believe this second beast will be a Jew.

This second beast has two horns without crowns. What do these symbolize? Not political power, there are no crowns, this second beast has religious authority, and is called the *"False Prophet."* He'll merge all religious systems into a counterfeit one. Millions will fall for his deception. When this religious merger is complete, Satan will have accomplished one of the most sinister deceptions in world history.

The second beast, or False Prophet, will perform great signs through satanic power. Through these miracles, the False Prophet will convince most people that he is God sent, the awaited Messiah. In verse 15, the second beast gives life to the image of the first beast, the Antichrist, and forces people to worship the image or be put to death. Where will this image be erected? In the reconstructed Temple in Jerusalem. This desecration is noted in Daniel's book when he speaks of the *"abomination of desolation."*

"And he shall make a strong covenant with many for one week, and for half of the week he shall put an end to sacrifice and offering. And on the wing of abominations shall come one who makes desolate, until the decreed end is poured out on the desolator." (Daniel 9:27)

"And from the time that the regular burnt offering is taken away and the abomination that makes desolate is set up, there shall be 1,290 days." (Daniel 12:11)

"If a prophet or a dreamer of dreams arises among you and gives you a sign or a wonder, and the sign or wonder that he tells you comes to pass, and if he says, 'Let us go after other gods,' which you have not known, 'and let us serve them,' you shall not listen to the words of that prophet or that dreamer of dreams. For the LORD your God is testing you, to know whether you love the LORD your God with all your heart and with all your soul. You shall walk after the LORD your God and fear him and keep his commandments and obey his voice, and you shall serve him and hold fast to him." (Deuteronomy 13:1-4)

All will be compelled to receive a distinguishing mark on their forehead or right hand called the *"Mark of the Beast."* Everyone who refuses the mark will be forbidden to buy or sell anything. What will happen to the people who receive the Mark of the Beast? John tells us in the next chapter of Revelation 14.

"And another angel, a third, followed them, saying with a loud voice, "If anyone worships the beast and its image and receives a mark on his forehead or on his hand, he also will drink the wine of God's wrath, poured full strength into the cup of his anger, and he will be tormented with fire and sulfur in the presence of the holy angels and in the presence of the Lamb."(Revelation 14:9-10)

The number 666 will be the number for the beast or Satan.

"This calls for wisdom: let the one who has understanding calculate the number of the beast, for it is the number of a man, and his number is 666" (Revelation 13:18).

Verse 18 states that the number of the beast is 666. Even people who have never read a single verse of the Bible and are not Christians know about this number. So, what does it mean?

No number in history has caused more fear and mystery than 666, the *mark of the beast*. Studies flourish about it. Is this a literal number or some symbol? The number 6 in the Bible stands for humanity, **"for it is the number of a man,"** so many Biblical scholars reason the meaning of 666 is a man trying to imitate the trinity of God. Representing an unholy trinity. Revelation tells us this unholy trinity that is aligned with Satan, will be Satan as the Father, the Antichrist as the Son, and the False Prophet as the Holy Spirit. Anyone who acknowledges the blasphemous trinity by worshipping the beast will be separated forever from the actual Trinity, the true God. In review, the first Beast, or the Antichrist, will proclaim himself God. A violation of the First Commandment:

"I am the LORD your God, who brought you out of the land of Egypt, out of the house of slavery. You shall have no other gods before me." (Exodus 20:2-3).

Some of the Characteristics of the Antichrist:
- He is a charismatic leader;
- He will blaspheme God;
- The number of the antichrist is 666;
- He claims to be God and worshiped;
- He will display miraculous powers;
- He appears to come back to life from a mortal head wound;

- ❖ He rules the earth in full authority and controls the world's economy;
- ❖ He physically defiles God's temple, known as the *"abomination of desolation"*;
- ❖ He tries the destruction of Israel,
- ❖ He has the fight against Christ at Armageddon.

The second beast, known as the False Prophet, will masquerade as the Messiah, and Revelation Chapter 13 lists his influences.

He exercises unlimited authority and forces people to worship the Antichrist. ***"It exercises all the authority of the first beast in its presence, and makes the earth and its inhabitants worship the first beast, whose mortal wound was healed."*** (Revelation 13:12).

He performs great miracles. ***"It performs great signs, even making fire come down from heaven to earth in front of people,"*** (Revelation 13:13).

He deceives the population and forces people to worship the Antichrist's image. ***"and by the signs that it is allowed to work in the presence of the beast it deceives those who dwell on earth, telling them to make an image for the beast that was wounded by the sword and yet lived."*** (Revelation 13:14).

He deceives the world into believing the Antichrist was raised from the dead. ***"And it was allowed to give breath to the image of the beast, so that the image of the beast might even speak and might cause those who would not worship the image of the beast to be slain."*** (Revelation 13:15).

He makes everyone get the mark of the beast. ***"Also it causes all, both small and great, both rich and poor, both free and slave, to be marked on the right hand or the forehead,"*** (Revelation 13:16).

The Antichrist's image made to be worshiped is a violation of the Second Commandment.

"You shall not make for yourself a carved image, or any likeness of anything that is in heaven above, or that is in the earth beneath, or that is in the water under the earth. You shall not bow down to them or serve them, for I the LORD your God am a jealous God, visiting the iniquity of the fathers on the children to the third and the fourth generation of those who hate me, but showing steadfast love to thousands of those who love me and keep my commandments." (Exodus 20:4-6)

The Beast-Antichrist of Revelation 13 differs from the many Antichrist John warns us to beware of. He indicates there will be a future Antichrist but also tells of the coming of lesser Antichrists. These Antichrists will be false teachers who deny Jesus. John tells us to test their teachings to be sure they are from God, not Satan.

[18] Children, it is the last hour, and as you have heard that antichrist is coming, so now many antichrists have come. Therefore we know that it is the last hour. [19] They went out from us, but they were not of us; for if they had been of us, they would have continued with us. But they went out, that it might become plain that they all are not of us. [20] But you have been anointed by the Holy One, and you all have knowledge. [21] I write to you, not because you do not know the truth, but because you know it, and because no lie is of the truth. [22] Who is the liar but he who denies that Jesus is the Christ? This is the antichrist, he who denies the Father and the Son. (1 John 2:18-22)

[1] Beloved, do not believe every spirit, but test the spirits to see whether they are from God, for many false prophets have gone out into the world. [2] By this you know the Spirit of God: every spirit that confesses that Jesus Christ has come in the flesh is from God, [3] and every spirit that does not confess Jesus is not from God. This is the spirit of the antichrist, which you heard was coming and now is in the world already. (1 John 4:1-3)

From these passages, we see that the spirit of the antichrist, or Satan, has been at work since the first century to destroy and reject the truth about Jesus. To stop unbelievers from becoming believers in Christ. From the very day Jesus was born, the very beginning of Christianity, believers in Christ have been convinced that a world ruler possessed by Satan would eventually come.

Studying Scripture, reveals several critical details about the coming Antichrist. These clues can only be applied to one person. Many people have been called the Antichrist, but none have met all the identity markers.

Daniel tells us many things about the coming Antichrist. He will rise to power in the end times, and he will be very intelligent and persuasive. His rule over people will be by deception. He will make a peace treaty with Israel, which will start the Tribulation. Then, he will break that treaty and invade Israel.

The book of Revelation tells us he will rule the world.

[7] *Also it was allowed to make war on the saints and to conquer them. And authority was given it over every tribe and people and language and nation, [8] and all who dwell on earth will worship it, everyone whose name has not been written before the foundation of the world in the book of life of the Lamb who was slain.*
(Revelation 13:7,8)

Many also believe his capital city will be Rome, and his rule will be by international consent.

[12] *And the ten horns that you saw are ten kings who have not yet received royal power, but they are to receive authority as kings for one hour, together with the beast. [13] These are of one mind, and they hand over their power and authority to the beast.*
(Revelation 17:12,13)

Revelation also tells us the beast will control the world's economy by forcing everyone who wants to buy or sell to have his mark.

[16] *Also it causes all, both small and great, both rich and poor, both free and slave, to be marked on the right hand or the forehead, [17] so that no one can buy or sell unless he has the mark, that is, the name of the beast or the number of its name.*
(Revelation 13:16,17)

Finally, he claims to be God from the temple in Jerusalem, what Daniel calls the *abomination of desolation.*

...the man of lawlessness is revealed, the son of destruction, [4] who opposes and exalts himself against every so-called god or object of worship, so that he takes his seat in the temple of God, proclaiming himself to be God. (2 Thessalonians 2:3,4)

Is President Trump The Antichrist?

Many people are saying President Donald Trump is the Antichrist. Many in the mainstream press also have tried to make that assumption. Especially after his near-miss assassination attempt. How does he measure up, or does he meet any of the criteria for being the Antichrist?

The Bible gives us many details about the Antichrist. The general picture of the beast is he is a European. President Trump is from New York. He rises to power as a peacemaker. Scripture does not tell us if he is Jewish or Gentile. Whichever he is, he will control the Gentile world's economy and military. President Trump does not control the world's economy. He will be assisted by the leader of the world's religion, the False Prophet. JD Vance has no resemblance to the False Prophet. Plus, BOTH are devoted Christians subject to the Rapture.

Revelation: A Line by Line Breakdown

Characteristics of the Antichrist vs President Trump

- ❖ He Will Blaspheme God; (President Trump Never has been heard to Blaspheme God. He is a devoted Christian)
- ❖ The number of the antichrist is 666 (President Trump has no known number other than 45)
- ❖ He claims to be God and worshiped; (President Trump has never claimed he is a god.)
- ❖ He Will Display Miraculous Powers (President Trump has never shown any Miraculous Powers)
- ❖ He appears to come back to life from a mortal head wound (President Trump's assassination attempt was a near miss)
- ❖ He rules the earth in full authority (President Trump does not rule most of the known world.)
- ❖ He will control the world's economy (President Trump does not control the world economy);
- ❖ He defiles God's temple in Jerusalem, known as the *"abomination of desolation"* (So far, there is not a rebuilt temple in Jerusalem to defile).
- ❖ So far, President Trump has met NO CRITERIA of the Antichrist.

The False Prophet

The Antichrist will have a partner known as the False Prophet. He will manage a worldwide deception of religion, making the Antichrist their god. This second beast will also murder (Revelation 13:15) and force all people to receive 'the Mark of the Beast' to buy or sell (Revelation 13:16).

[11] Then I saw another beast rising out of the earth. It had two horns like a lamb and it spoke like a dragon. [12] It exercises all the authority of the first beast in its presence, and makes the earth

and its inhabitants worship the first beast, whose mortal wound was healed. (Revelation 13:11,12)

15 And it was allowed to give breath to the image of the beast, so that the image of the beast might even speak and might cause those who would not worship the image of the beast to be slain. 16 Also it causes all, both small and great, both rich and poor, both free and slave, to be marked on the right hand or the forehead, 17 so that no one can buy or sell unless he has the mark, that is, the name of the beast or the number of its name.
(Revelation 13:15-17)

The two beasts will work together. The first, known as the Antichrist, will be the political leader. The second, known as the False Prophet, will rule all religions. Both will oppose Jesus.

Revelation 13 gives us recognizing features of the Fale Prophet:

- ❖ He rises from the earth: *Then I saw another beast rising out of the earth. It had two horns like a lamb and it spoke like a dragon.* (Revelation 13:11)
- ❖ Motivated by Satan: *spoke like a dragon* (Revelation 13:11) the dragon spoke of in Revelation represents Satan
- ❖ Controls religious affairs and promotes the worship of the Antichrist: *It exercises all the authority of the first beast in its presence, and makes the earth and its inhabitants worship the first beast, whose mortal wound was healed.* (Revelation 13:12)
- ❖ Performs signs and miracles: *It performs great signs, even making fire come down from heaven to earth in front of people,* (Revelation 13:13)
- ❖ Deceives the entire world: *and by the signs that it is allowed to work in the presence of the beast it deceives those who dwell on earth, telling them to make an image*

for the beast that was wounded by the sword and yet lived. (Revelation 13:14)

❖ Empowers the image of the Antichrist and kills all who refuse to worship the Antichrist: *And it was allowed to give breath to the image of the beast, so that the image of the beast might even speak and might cause those who would not worship the image of the beast to be slain.* (Revelation 13:15)

❖ Controls all commerce and forces everyone to get the mark of the beast: *[17] so that no one can buy or sell unless he has the mark, that is, the name of the beast or the number of its name. [18] This calls for wisdom: let the one who has understanding calculate the number of the beast, for it is the number of a man, and his number is 666.* (Revelation 13:17,18)

Scripture warns against all types of false prophets.

"Then if anyone says to you, 'Look, here is the Christ!' or 'There he is!' do not believe it. For false christs and false prophets will arise and perform great signs and wonders, so as to lead astray, if possible, even the elect. See, I have told you beforehand. So, if they say to you, 'Look, he is in the wilderness,' do not go out. If they say, 'Look, he is in the inner rooms,' do not believe it. For as the lightning comes from the east and shines as far as the west, so will be the coming of the Son of Man Scripture has several warnings against false prophets and teachers. Jesus himself warned of this." (Matthew 24:23-27)

How Can Believers Recognize a False Prophet?

❖ Prophecies do not come true. *"When a prophet speaks in the name of the LORD, if the word does not come to pass or come true, that is a word that the LORD has not spoken;*

the prophet has spoken it presumptuously. You need not be afraid of him." (Deuteronomy 18:22)
- ❖ Denies the deity of Jesus Christ. **"Therefore, as you received Christ Jesus the Lord, so walk in him, rooted and built up in him and established in the faith, just as you were taught, abounding in thanksgiving. See to it that no one takes you captive by philosophy and empty deceit, according to human tradition, according to the elemental spirits of the world, and not according to Christ. For in him the whole fullness of deity dwells bodily"** (Colossians 2:6-9)
- ❖ Causes people to follow false gods or idols. **"You shall have no other gods before me. You shall not make for yourself a carved image, or any likeness of anything that is in heaven above, or that is in the earth beneath, or that is in the water under the earth. You shall not bow down to them or serve them, for I the LORD your God am a jealous God,"** (Exodus 20:3-5)

REVELATION CHAPTER 14

¹ Then I looked, and behold, on Mount Zion stood the Lamb, and with him 144,000 who had his name and his Father's name written on their foreheads. ² And I heard a voice from heaven like the roar of many waters and like the sound of loud thunder. The voice I heard was like the sound of harpists playing on their harps, ³ and they were singing a new song before the throne and before the four living creatures and before the elders. No one could learn that song except the 144,000 who had been redeemed from the earth. ⁴ It is these who have not defiled themselves with women, for they are virgins. It is these who follow the Lamb wherever he goes. These have been redeemed from mankind as first fruits for God and the Lamb, ⁵ and in their mouth no lie was found, for they are blameless. (Revelation 14:1-5)

This chapter reminds us that many will never give in to the Beast. Among these are the 144,000 converted Jewish evangelists first noted in Revelation 7. Because Christ gives them supernatural insight, they can know the miracles of the Antichrist and False Prophet, are fake from Satan. These 144,000 will be protected by Jesus and preserved throughout the Tribulation. This is a great miracle because, during these seven years, more than half the earth's population will perish. These 144,000 evangelists will be the most wanted people on the planet. They were hunted to be killed by the Antichrist, for they would lead millions to the true Messiah, Jesus.

"and they were singing a new song before the throne and before the four living creatures and before the elders. No one could learn that song except the 144,000 who had been redeemed from the earth." (Revelation 14:3)

No one is allowed to learn the song of the 144,000 because it is a joyous testimony of their miraculous protection by God through the horrors of the Tribulation.

"It is these who have not defiled themselves with women, for they are virgins." (Revelation 14:4).

What does this mean? Since a virgin or celibate has not had any sexual relations or vows not to, it may seem God is against marriage and sexual relations in the end times. However, Biblical scholars have the impression that this verse is not about sexual purity but about separation from sin, called a spiritual virgin, not a physical one. And this is the issue during the Tribulation, steering clear of the Satanically inspired religious system of the Beast-Antichrist.

"You adulterous people! Do you not know that friendship with the world is enmity with God? Therefore, whoever wishes to be a friend of the world makes himself an enemy of God." (James 4:4).

⁶ Then I saw another angel flying directly overhead, with an eternal gospel to proclaim to those who dwell on earth, to every nation and tribe and language and people. ⁷ And he said with a loud voice, "Fear God and give him glory, because the hour of his judgment has come, and worship him who made heaven and earth, the sea and the springs of water." ⁸ Another angel, a second, followed, saying, "Fallen, fallen is Babylon the great, she who made all nations drink the wine of the passion of her sexual immorality." ⁹ And another angel, a third, followed them, saying with a loud voice, "If anyone worships the beast and its image and receives a mark on his forehead or on his hand, ¹⁰ he also will drink the wine of God's wrath, poured full strength into the cup of his anger, and he will be tormented with fire and sulfur in the presence of the holy angels and in the presence of the Lamb. ¹¹ And the smoke of their torment goes up forever and ever, and they have no rest, day or night, these worshipers of the beast and its image, and whoever receives the mark of its name."
(Revelation 14:6-11)

There will be a period in the Tribulation, a phenomenon never seen before in the history of the world. Verse 14:6 states **ANGELS WILL PREACH THE GOSPEL TO THE PEOPLE OF THE WORLD!** God offers one last offer to unbelievers for grace through Jesus before the final judgment. Three angels will fly through the air proclaiming the gospel. He ensures everyone has had the opportunity to hear the Good News, the Gospel. God will announce to everyone on earth *"to every nation and tribe and language and people."*

A second angel speaks of the fallen Babylon the Great, which is not ancient Babylon but a new one. This Babylon is fully discussed in Chapters 17 and 18. A third angel announces that anyone who worships the Beast or receives his mark: *"he also will drink the wine of God's wrath, poured full strength into the cup of his anger, and he will be tormented with fire and sulfur in the presence of the holy angels and in the presence of the Lamb."*(Revelation 14:10). In other words, the choice is between Heaven and Hell. The choice will be either the Messiah (Jesus) or the Beast (Satan). The angels make this clear to everyone on the earth so no one can plead ignorance that Jesus is the Messiah.

¹² Here is a call for the endurance of the saints, those who keep the commandments of God and their faith in Jesus. ¹³ And I heard a voice from heaven saying, "Write this: Blessed are the dead who die in the Lord from now on." "Blessed indeed," says the Spirit, "that they may rest from their labors, for their deeds follow them!" (Revelation 14:12-13)

Blessed are the dead in Christ (martyrs); those who accept Jesus as their savior need not fear death. John speaks of all in the Tribulation who will die for Jesus rather than worship the Beast or receive his mark, called the *Tribulation Saints.*

¹⁴ Then I looked, and behold, a white cloud, and seated on the cloud one like a son of man, with a golden crown on his head, and a sharp sickle in his hand. ¹⁵ And another angel came out of the temple, calling with a loud voice to him who sat on the cloud, "Put in your sickle, and reap, for the hour to reap has come, for the harvest of the earth is fully ripe." ¹⁶ So he who sat on the cloud swung his sickle across the earth, and the earth was reaped. ¹⁷ Then another angel came out of the temple in heaven, and he too had a sharp sickle. ¹⁸ And another angel came out from the altar, the angel who has authority over the fire, and he called with a loud voice to the one who had the sharp sickle, "Put in your sickle and gather the clusters from the vine of the earth, for its grapes are ripe." ⁱ⁹ So the angel swung his sickle across the earth and gathered the grape harvest of the earth and threw it into the great winepress of the wrath of God. ²⁰ And the winepress was trodden outside the city, and blood flowed from the winepress, as high as a horse's bridle, for 1,600 stadia. (Revelation 14:14-20)

The harvest starts here, using terminology similar to Jesus's wheat reaping. Jesus told of this in a parable known as The Parable of the Weeds.

"The kingdom of heaven may be compared to a man who sowed good seed in his field, but while his men were sleeping, his enemy came and sowed weeds among the wheat and went away. So when the plants came up and bore grain, then the weeds appeared also. And the servants of the master of the house came and said to him, 'Master, did you not sow good seed in your field? How then does it have weeds?' He said to them, 'An enemy has done this.' So, the servants said to him, 'Then do you want us to go and gather them?' But he said, 'No, lest in gathering the weeds you root up the wheat along with them. Let both grow together until the harvest, and at harvest time I will tell the reapers, Gather the weeds first and bind them in bundles to be burned, but gather the wheat into my barn." (Matthew 13:24-30)

The Parable of the Weeds Explained: *"Then he left the crowds and went into the house. And his disciples came to him, saying, 'Explain to us the parable of the weeds of the field.' He answered, 'The one who sows the good seed is the Son of Man. The field is the world, and the good seed is the sons of the kingdom. The weeds are the sons of the evil one, and the enemy who sowed them is the devil. The harvest is the close of the age, and the reapers are angels. Just as the weeds are gathered and burned with fire, so will it be at the close of the age. The Son of Man will send his angels, and they will gather out of his kingdom all causes of sin and all law-breakers, and throw them into the fiery furnace. In that place there will be weeping and gnashing of teeth. Then the righteous will shine like the sun in the kingdom of their Father. He who has ears, let him hear'.* (Matthew 13:36-43)

Revelation 14:17 states: **"Then another angel came out of the temple in heaven, and he too had a sharp sickle."** The *"Son of Man"* doesn't oversee this reaping. The angels do this harvest. This angel tells the harvesting angel: **"Put in your sickle and gather the clusters from the vine of the earth, for its grapes are ripe"** (Revelation 14:15). All the clusters of grapes that are gathered in this harvest are cast into **"the great winepress of the wrath of God,"** (Revelation 14:19). This indicates that there's no separation, all are unbelievers intended for destruction.

    The winepress was **"outside the city,"** which could only be Jerusalem. God's judgment is just outside Jerusalem. Armies of all nations will also be gathered outside Jerusalem. The Messiah Jesus will strike first, and blood will flow **"as high as a horse's bridle"** for **"1,600stadia"**(two hundred miles). (Revelation 14:20)

Zechariah foretold of this:

"For I will gather all the nations against Jerusalem to battle, and the city shall be taken and the houses plundered and the women raped. Half of the city shall go out into exile, but the rest of the people shall not be cut off from the city. Then the LORD will go out and fight against those nations as when he fights on a day of battle." (Zechariah 14:2-3)

REVELATION CHAPTER 15

[1] Then I saw another sign in heaven, great and amazing, seven angels with seven plagues, which are the last, for with them the wrath of God is finished. (Revelation 15:1)

Chapters 15 and 16 go together because they describe two aspects of the same events: the seven plagues and the last of God's wrath. John states: **"the wrath of God is finished,"** in the Greek language of the New Testament, it is the same word Jesus shouted from the cross as He died: **"When Jesus had received the sour wine, he said, 'It is finished," and he bowed his head and gave up his spirit.'"** (John 19:30). Jesus meant that the debt of man's sin against God was finished. He died for us so we would not have to. Here, **"God is finished"** refers to God's patience being finished for all those who reject Christ whom He sent on their behalf.

"For God so loved the world, that he gave his only Son, that whoever believes in him should not perish but have eternal life. For God did not send his Son into the world to condemn the world, but in order that the world might be saved through him. Whoever believes in him is not condemned, but whoever does not believe is condemned already, because he has not believed in the name of the only Son of God. And this is the judgment: the light has come into the world, and people loved the darkness rather than the light because their works were evil. (John 3:16-19)

² And I saw what appeared to be a sea of glass mingled with fire- and also those who had conquered the beast and its image and the number of its name, standing beside the sea of glass with harps of God in their hands. ³ And they sing the song of Moses, the servant of God, and the song of the Lamb, saying, "Great and amazing are your deeds, O Lord God the Almighty! Just and true are your ways, O King of the nations! ⁴ Who will not fear, O Lord, and glorify your name? For you alone are holy. All nations will come and worship you, for your righteous acts have been revealed." (Revelation 15:2-4)

John states in verse 2, *"And I saw what appeared to be a sea of glass mingled with fire,"* meaning a great crowd of people.

This same *"**sea of glass**"* was found in Revelation 4:6: *"**and before the throne there was as it were a sea of glass, like crystal**"* and symbolized the mass of believers who were in the Rapture and are now before God's throne. However, now it has all those who died for Christ in the Tribulation, which is the fire. And they sang *"**the song of Moses**,"* which the Jews have sung for thousands of years to praise and thank God for delivering them out of Egypt from Pharaoh. And the *"**song of the Lamb**"* for deliverance from death by the grace of God's Messiah, Jesus.

*⁵ **After this I looked, and the sanctuary of the tent of witness in heaven was opened, ⁶ and out of the sanctuary came the seven angels with the seven plagues, clothed in pure, bright linen, with golden sashes around their chests. ⁷ And one of the four living creatures gave to the seven angels seven golden bowls full of the wrath of God who lives forever and ever, ⁸ and the sanctuary was filled with smoke from the glory of God and from his power, and no one could enter the sanctuary until the seven plagues of the seven angels were finished.*** (Revelation 15:5-8)

John is given a view of the heavenly Tabernacle, of which the earthly Temple was patterned. Out of the sanctuary came the seven angels. Remember that God gave Moses specific instructions (Exodus 25 & 26) on how to build the earthly Tabernacle, and he was told it was to be made the same as the one in heaven.

"And let them make me a sanctuary, that I may dwell in their midst. Exactly as I show you concerning the pattern of the tabernacle, and of all its furniture, so you shall make it."
(Exodus 25:8-9).

The heavenly sanctuary was closed until the seven angels finished their task. The smoke of God's glory and power flowed from the sanctuary, and no one could enter God's presence until the seven plagues had finished.

REVELATION CHAPTER 16

"Then I heard a loud voice from the temple telling the seven angels, "Go and pour out on the earth the seven bowls of the wrath of God." (Revelation 16:1)

God sends forth the seven angels with a loud voice. In His great foresight, He knows unbelievers, still alive on earth, have hardened hearts. The seven angels are dressed as priests in white robes and golden vests.

"and out of the sanctuary came the seven angels with the seven plagues, clothed in pure, bright linen, with golden sashes around their chests." (Revelation15:6)

"So the first angel went and poured out his bowl on the earth, and harmful and painful sores came upon the people who bore the mark of the beast and worshiped its image." (Revelation 16:2)

This begins the *Bowl Judgments*. The first angel's bowl pours on unbelievers and will produce sores; with such intense suffering, death would be preferred. There will be no cure for this judgment. This plague will trouble all unbelievers who have the mark of the beast and worship him. God will supernaturally shield all His believers from these sores, as He did in the days of Moses.

"The second angel poured out his bowl into the sea, and it became like the blood of a corpse, and every living thing died that was in the sea." (Revelation 16:3)

The second bowl judgment follows as this angel pours his bowl into the sea. It becomes like the blood of a dead person. And EVERY living thing in the seas dies EVERYTHING!

⁴ The third angel poured out his bowl into the rivers and the springs of water, and they became blood. ⁵ And I heard the angel in charge of the waters say, "Just are you, O Holy One, who is and who was, for you brought these judgments. ⁶ For they have shed the blood of saints and prophets, and you have given them blood to drink. It is what they deserve!" ⁷ And I heard the altar saying, "Yes, Lord God the Almighty, true and just are your judgments!" (Revelation 16:4-7).

The third angel's bowl turned the rivers and springs into blood. Now, there is no fresh water to drink or any fish to eat. The reason for this judgment is stated in verse 6 which is due to: **"For they have shed the blood of saints and prophets,"** then the verse states, **"It is what they deserve!"** As it was in the time of Moses, when Pharaoh hardened his heart to God, He turned the Nile River to blood. So as man in the end times hardens his heart to God, the freshwater is turned to blood.

"Thus says the LORD, "By this you shall know that I am the LORD: behold, with the staff that is in my hand I will strike the water that is in the Nile, and it shall turn into blood." (Exodus 7:17)

⁸ The fourth angel poured out his bowl on the sun, and it was allowed to scorch people with fire. ⁹ They were scorched by the fierce heat, and they cursed the name of God who had power over these plagues. They did not repent and give him glory. (Revelation 16:8-9)

Many scholars feel the Fourth Bowl will be a full-scale war. Nevertheless, the most astonishing thing is man **"did not repent,"** giving glory to God, even after all the desolation thus far. Unbelievers still remain DEAD SET against God's salvation.

¹⁰ The fifth angel poured out his bowl on the throne of the beast, and its kingdom was plunged into darkness. People gnawed their tongues in anguish ¹¹ and cursed the God of heaven for their pain and sores. They did not repent of their deeds.
(Revelation 16:10-11)

The fifth bowl judgment is upon the Beast and his kingdom. Many believe this kingdom is the revived Roman Empire. The Beast's kingdom will be *"plunged into darkness,"* yet *"they did not repent."*

¹² The sixth angel poured out his bowl on the great river Euphrates, and its water was dried up to prepare the way for the kings from the east.¹³And I saw, coming out of the mouth of the dragon and out of the mouth of the beast and out of the mouth of the false prophet, three unclean spirits like frogs.¹⁴ For they are demonic spirits, performing signs, who go abroad to the kings of the whole world, to assemble them for battle on the great day of God the Almighty.¹⁵ ("Behold, I am coming like a thief! Blessed is the one who stays awake, keeping his garments on, that he may not go about naked and be seen exposed!") ¹⁶ And they assembled them at the place that in Hebrew is called Armageddon.
(Revelation 16:12-16).

Verse 12 states: *"The sixth angel poured out his bowl on the great river Euphrates, and its water was dried up, to prepare the way for the kings from the east."* This is an extension of the sixth trumpet judgment in chapter 9

¹⁵ "So the four angels, who had been prepared for the hour, the day, the month, and the year, were released to kill a third of

mankind. ¹⁶ The number of mounted troops was twice ten thousand times ten thousand; I heard their number".
(Revelation 9:15,16).

These hordes from the east in the sixth bowel judgment are an army staged on the Euphrates. The ancient boundary of east and west. In Revelation 16:12, the waters of the Euphrates dry up, leaving a path for this massive army to move into *"the place that in Hebrew is called Armageddon."* Also, Satan, the Beast, the False Prophet, and the demons perform miraculous signs in front of all world leaders. These signs are for Western leaders since the east is already at the Euphrates. This unholy trinity (666) is trying to fight the East. Revelation Verse 16:16: *"And they assembled them at the place that in Hebrew is called Armageddon."* This place was also named by the Prophet Joel, who foresaw this terrible day:

"Let the nations stir themselves up and come up to the Valley of Jehoshaphat (known as Armageddon), for there I will sit to judge all the surrounding nations. Put in the sickle, for the harvest is ripe. Go in, tread, for the winepress is full. The vats overflow, for their evil is great. Multitudes, multitudes, in the valley of decision! For the day of the LORD is near in the valley of decision."
(Joel 3:12-14)

¹⁷ The seventh angel poured out his bowl into the air, and a loud voice came out of the temple, from the throne, saying, "It is done!" ¹⁸ And there were flashes of lightning, rumblings, peals of thunder, and a great earthquake such as there had never been since man was on the earth, so great was that earthquake. ¹⁹ The great city was split into three parts, and the cities of the nations fell, and God remembered Babylon the great, to make her drain the cup of the wine of the fury of his wrath. ²⁰ And every island fled away, and no mountains were to be found. ²¹ And great hailstones, about one hundred pounds each, fell from heaven on people; and they cursed God for the plague of the hail because the plague was so severe. (Revelation 16:17-21)

While this great battle of Armageddon rages, every city in the world will be leveled. This will be by *"earthquake"*. It was taken from the original text in the Greek word *seimos,* which means a great shaking of the earth. This could mean an actual earthquake, or some have confidence it's foretelling of a full-scale nuclear war.

In this last judgment, no nation will escape, and every city in the world is going to be leveled. In verse 16:20, we are told that the devastation will be so tremendous that all the cities will be destroyed, and the landscape will transform. Every island and mountain will be leveled so that none exist. At the same time, in the next verse (16:21), there is an incredible hailstorm with hailstones of about 100 pounds each, which crush the people, and they curse God for sending them. They still do not repent and accept Jesus.

² For I will gather all the nations against Jerusalem to battle, and the city shall be taken and the houses plundered and the women raped. Half of the city shall go out into exile, but the rest of the people shall not be cut off from the city. ³ Then the LORD will go out and fight against those nations as when he fights on a day of battle. ⁴ On that day his feet shall stand on the Mount of Olives that lies before Jerusalem on the east, and the Mount of Olives shall be split in two from east to west by a very wide valley, so that one half of the Mount shall move northward, and the other half southward. ⁵ And you shall flee to the valley of my mountains, for the valley of the mountains shall reach to Azal. And you shall flee as you fled from the earthquake in the days of Uzziah king of Judah. Then the LORD my God will come, and all the holy ones with him. (Zechariah 14:2-5)

Review of the Tribulation Judgments

The Seal Judgments:

- ❖ Seal 1: The White Horse representing the Antichrist
- ❖ Seal 2: The Red Horse representing Conflicts and War
- ❖ Seal 3: The Black Horse representing Famine and Inflation
- ❖ Seal 4: The Pale Horse representing Death
- ❖ Seal 5: The Martyred Tribulation Saints
- ❖ Seal 6: Great Earthquakes
- ❖ Seal 7: Silence in Heaven a lull before the Trumpet Judgments

The Trumpet Judgments – Called The Judgments of Thirds:

- ❖ Trumpet 1: One-Third of the Earth's Vegetation is Destroyed
- ❖ Trumpet 2: One-Third of the Earth's Seas Are Turned Into Blood
- ❖ Trumpet 3: One-Third of the Earth's Freshwater Are Contaminated
- ❖ Trumpet 4: One-Third of Sky Is Darkened
- ❖ Trumpet 5: The First Woe – Locust Like Creatures Plague the Earth
- ❖ Trumpet 6: The Second Woe – One-Third of All the World's Population Die From War
- ❖ Trumpet 7: The Third Woe – The Seven Bowl Judgments Begin

The Bowl Judgments:

- ❖ Bowl 1: Terrible Sores Appear on those who follow the Antichrist

- Bowl 2: All of the Earth's Seas Are Turned To Blood
- Bowl 3: All of the Earth's Freshwater is Turned To Blood
- Bowl 4: The Earth is Scorched
- Bowl 5: Darkness Covers the Earth
- Bowl 6: The Euphrates River Dries Up, And a Massive Army Moves Toward Armageddon
- Bowl 7: Massive Earthquakes Followed by 100-pound Hailstones Leveled The Earth

REVELATION CHAPTER 17

Revelation Chapters 17 and 18 are not in chronological order, deviating to describe the world system before Satan is given complete control of the earth through the Antichrist and False Prophet. These chapters are about **"Babylon the Great, Mother of Prostitutes,"** which appears entirely in the first half of the Tribulation. The chronological narrative of God's judgments then continues in Chapter 19.

[1] Then one of the seven angels who had the seven bowls came and said to me, "Come, I will show you the judgment of the great prostitute who is seated on many waters, [2] with whom the kings of the earth have committed sexual immorality, and with the wine of whose sexual immorality the dwellers on earth have become drunk." [3] And he carried me away in the Spirit into a wilderness, and I saw a woman sitting on a scarlet beast that was full of blasphemous names, and it had seven heads and ten horns. [4] The woman was arrayed in purple and scarlet, and adorned with gold and jewels and pearls, holding in her hand a golden cup full of abominations and the impurities of her sexual immorality. [5] And on her forehead was written a name of mystery: "Babylon the great, mother of prostitutes and of earth's abominations. [6] And I saw the woman, drunk with the blood of the saints, the blood of the martyrs of Jesus. When I saw her, I marveled greatly. [7] But the

Revelation: A Line by Line Breakdown

angel said to me, "Why do you marvel? I will tell you the mystery of the woman and of the beast with seven heads and ten horns that carries her. ⁸ The beast that you saw was, and is not, and is about to rise from the bottomless pit and go to destruction. And the dwellers on earth whose names have not been written in the book of life from the foundation of the world will marvel to see the beast, because it was and is not and is to come. ⁹ This calls for a mind with wisdom: the seven heads are seven mountains on which the woman is seated; ¹⁰ they are also seven kings, five of whom have fallen, one is, the other has not yet come, and when he does come, he must remain only a little while. ¹¹ As for the beast that was and is not, it is an eighth but it belongs to the seven, and it goes to destruction. ¹² And the ten horns that you saw are ten kings who have not yet received royal power, but they are to receive authority as kings for one hour, together with the beast. ¹³ These are of one mind, and they hand over their power and authority to the beast. ¹⁴ They will make war on the Lamb, and the Lamb will conquer them, for he is Lord of lords and King of kings, and those with him are called and chosen and faithful." ¹⁵ And the angel said to me, "The waters that you saw, where the prostitute is seated, are peoples and multitudes and nations and languages. ¹⁶ And the ten horns that you saw, they and the beast will hate the prostitute. They will make her desolate and naked, and devour her flesh and burn her up with fire, ¹⁷ for God has put it into their hearts to carry out his purpose by being of one mind and handing over their royal power to the beast, until the words of God are fulfilled. ¹⁸ And the woman that you saw is the great city that has dominion over the kings of the earth.
(Revelation 17:1-18)

First, we need to identify the symbols used in Chapter 17. The two central figures are a harlot and a seven-headed, ten-horned beast. The harlot is lavishly dressed in jewels and luxurious purple and scarlet garments, showing royalty and political influence. In her hand is a cup made of gold, full of atrocities.

"The woman was arrayed in purple and scarlet, and adorned with gold and jewels and pearls, holding in her hand a golden cup full of abominations and the impurities of her sexual immorality. And on her forehead was written a name of mystery: Babylon the great, mother of prostitutes and of earth's abominations." (Revelation 17:4-5)

The harlot is sitting on a creature with seven heads, ten horns, and blasphemous names written all over it. The color of this creature is scarlet, the color of blood "...***and I saw a woman sitting on a scarlet beast that was full of blasphemous names, and it had seven heads and ten horns.***" (Revelation 17:3). The most revolting thing about her was she was drunk, not from drink, but on the blood of believers.

"And I saw the woman, drunk with the blood of the saints, the blood of the martyrs of Jesus." (Revelation 17:6)

The angel clarifies this scene for John, stating that all the kings of the earth have committed adultery with her. She ***"sits on many waters,"*** which is another way of saying that she influences vast numbers of people whom she has seduced in one way or another. The seven heads represent influence over the entire earth, while the ten horns represent her influence over the kingdom of the Beast.

The foulest thing anyone can call a woman is a whore. For this woman to be labeled one by the angel has great significance. In biblical terms, the word *"whore", "harlot,"* and *"adultery"* are frequently used to symbolize a spiritual departure from God and His truth by an individual, a city, or a nation.

Revelation: A Line by Line Breakdown

And on her forehead was written a name of mystery: 'Babylon the great, mother of prostitutes and of earth's abominations.' (Revelation 17:5).

When the angel tells John what is written on the woman is a mystery, he is declaring that this harlot is a false mystical system. Its main teachings are the occult and sexual perversions, just as in ancient Babylon. Historically, Babylon established the world's first religious center, practicing sorcery and astrology, under its first dictator Nimrod.

These old Babylon teachings will be the same occult practices renewed in the new Babylon. Her luxurious presence of jewels and royal clothes means she will significantly appeal to men's sensual nature. Her gold cup, which is filled with abominations, represents her corrupt and perverse teachings. Her drunkenness with the saint's blood shows how successful she will be at abolishing all who oppose her.

What is known about the ancient city of Babylon is that it was founded about 600 BC and was controlled by occult influences. Babylon's religion was passed from empire to empire until the days of the Roman Empire (160 BC to 500 AD). The mystery that John was given to expose is that the religion of Babylon will be revived.

This religion is to control the world's political powers in the end times. This religion will be an occult amalgamation of all the world's religions. For the first part of the Tribulation, **"Babylon the great, mother of prostitutes and of earth's abominations."** will relish having great political power and influence over the earth.

In verse 17:18, **"And the woman that you saw is the great city that has dominion over the kings of the earth,"** who is said to be **"Babylon the great, mother of prostitutes and of earth's abominations"** (Revelation 17:5). She does not have a name other than Babylon the great. This is thus the mystery. Many scholars accept that this is not a place but an idea, a religion, a way of life. In the original Greek, the word used is *polis,* from which we get the words politics and metropolitan. According to *Harper's Bible Dictionary,* the meaning of *polis* is *"large areas of high population density."*

The Babylon mentioned here is not a city but an idea or religion that controls large population centers or nations. Verse 17:15 states these *"**are peoples and multitudes and nations and languages.**"* However, many believe this Babylon will be a physical city in the revived Roman Empire or may also be built where the original city of Babylon was in Iraq. There may or may not be a new city of Babylon. A city rebuilt just for the purpose of controlling corruption is a farfetched idea.

"And the angel said to me, 'The waters that you saw, where the prostitute is seated, are peoples and multitudes and nations and languages.'" (Revelation 17:15)

This does not sound like a revised single city or nation. However, many, if not all the nations of the earth. This Babylonian idea represents all the corruption and sexual perverse teaching in the world. With the Rapture being the removal of God's church and the influence of the Holy Spirit, one way to fill this void will be the teachings of Babylon. The woman, Babylon, also sits on seven mountains (17:9). The original Greek word is *oros*. Traditional theology believes these seven mountains are actually hills, so this must mean Rome, called the *"City of Seven Hills."* However, this Babylon does not sit on seven hills but on mountains.

Now take a look at Luke 3:5: ***"Every valley shall be filled, and every mountain and hill shall be made low,"*** and then look at Luke 23:30, ***"Then they will begin to say to the mountains, 'Fall on us,' and to the hills, 'Cover us.'"*** These verses talk of hills and mountains in the same verse. Luke uses the Greek word *buonos,* which means hill, and for mountains, he uses the Greek word *oros,* which means mountains. The same Greek word, *oros,* is used in

Revelation 17:9. Luke differentiates these two types of land masses: mountains and hills. John meant mountains, not hills.

Unmistakably, Rome does not sit on seven mountains but on hills. So, do these seven land masses represent the seven continents, meaning the entire earth? That this perverse Babylon will influence the entire world? This *"mystery"* could mean that this Babylon is not a location but a belief, an idea. Is this to be a perversion of the world to turn people away from God? At the time John wrote Revelation, people did not even know that there were seven continents. However, God knew.

As stated, this Babylonian idea will represent all the corruption and perverse sexual teaching in the world, just as Wall Street in New York City represents the stock market. We all know the stock market is worldwide, not a place. So will be the idea of Babylon. There is a London Stock Exchange, Paris, Tokyo, Hong Kong, Sidney, Los Angeles, Dallas, and Chicago, to name a few going around the world. Again, several places have Stock Exchanges that circle the globe. Destroy Wall Street in New York, and the exchange keeps going. It does not destroy the stock exchange. It would take a correlated worldwide attack on every city with the stock exchange to destroy it. Just as it would take a worldwide attack on the resurrected Babylon.

[10] *they are also seven kings, five of whom have fallen, one is, the other has not yet come, and when he does come, he must remain only a little while. [11] As for the beast that was and is not, it is an eighth but it belongs to the seven, and it goes to destruction."* (Revelation 17:10-11)

This may not seem very clear at first glance. However, we can assemble a coherent and systematic time sequence of the eight providential nations revealed to John. In looking at the providential nations in scripture, we can easily know who six of the eight empires are from verse 17:10. Each empire must be connected directly to Israel. But why is it that every nation throughout history that Scripture refers to always has a direct correlation with Israel? Because in God's eyes, Israel, his chosen people, is the earth's geographical center. God weighs the value of other nations by how they treat Israel.

"I will bless those who bless you, and him who dishonors you I will curse, and in you all the families of the earth shall be blessed." (Genesis 12:3)

The first empire was Egypt, which fulfilled Abraham's prophecy of 400 years of Jewish slavery.

"Then the LORD said to Abram, 'Know for certain that your offspring will be sojourners in a land that is not theirs and will be servants there, and they will be afflicted for four hundred years.'" (Genesis 15:13).

It is important to note that God stated 400 years and Jewish slavery was 400 years. When God gives us a number, that number is literal, absolute.

The second empire was Assyria, which judged Israel for her idolatry and made her a vassal state, fulfilling Isaiah's prophecies.

The third was Babylon. In 587 BC, the ancient Kingdom of Judah was captured by Nebuchadnezzar, ruler of Babylon. He defeated Israel in the Jewish–Babylonian War and destroyed Solomon's Temple in Jerusalem. This event is described in the book of 2 Kings 25:8-9, and its historicity is supported by archaeological and non-biblical evidence.

[8] In the fifth month, on the seventh day of the month--that was the nineteenth year of King Nebuchadnezzar, king of Babylon-Nebuzaradan, the captain of the bodyguard, a servant of the king of Babylon, came to Jerusalem. [9] And he burned the house of the

LORD and the king's house and all the houses of Jerusalem; every great house he burned down. (2 Kings 25:8-9)

    The fourth was the Persian Empire, in 600 BC, which was a major ancient civilization that is Iran today. Daniel was sold to the Persians but rose to become the most trusted advisor to the Persian emperors. The Books of Isaiah, Jeremiah, and Daniel all discuss this and have prophecies about future events.

    The fifth empire was Greece. In 332 BC, Alexander the Great conquered Israel, making the land and people of Israel part of the Hellenistic Empire. Alexander went through Israel on his way to Gaza. Israel and Jerusalem were peacefully absorbed into the Greek Empire. The Greek authorities preserved the rights of the local Jewish population and did not attempt to interfere with Jewish religious practice. The Jews continued flourishing as separate entities, but they were part of the Greek Empire.

    "The one that is" refers to the Roman Empire, which controlled Israel at the time of Jesus. To the Romans, this area was called Judea and Palestine.

    Then there is the other, noted in verse 10: **"The other has not yet come, and when he does come, he must remain only a little while."** (Revelation 17:10). Many believe this to be the United States. America was founded on God's word; our nation's motto is *"In God We Trust."* We accept as true that God has blessed us. America is currently the most wealthy and powerful nation in the world. However, how long will that last? Many presidents made it clear that America was founded on Judeo-Christian principles. They leaned heavily on the Scriptures to form and guide the United States. America has always protected and sided with Israel. President Donald Trump recognized Jerusalem as the one true capital of Israel, establishing the American embassy there.

    By studying American history, one can realize, whether our Founding Fathers knew it or not, that they made a covenant with God when they founded this nation upon biblical principles. They invoked God's protection because of their faith and obedience, as well as America's. Now, America is being strongly influenced by Satan. America's press, schools, and even political America have fallen from Biblical principles. President Biden has rejected Israel in favor of the Arab nations.

A *"covenant"* is an agreement between two parties in which promises are made under oath to perform or refrain from specific actions stipulated. It is implied that each party would receive certain benefits. A covenant with God always invokes the blessings of His provision, guidance, and protection. God has kept all His covenants. Man has not. An example of one of God's convents with a nation is the covenant God made with Israel.

"I will bless those who bless you, and him who dishonors you I will curse, and in you all the families of the earth shall be blessed." (Genesis 12:3)

"And if you faithfully obey the voice of the LORD your God, being careful to do all his commandments that I command you today, the LORD your God will set you high above all the nations of the earth. And all these blessings shall come upon you and overtake you if you obey the voice of the LORD your God. Blessed shall you be in the city, and blessed shall you be in the field. Blessed shall be the fruit of your womb and the fruit of your ground and the fruit of your cattle, the increase of your herds and the young of your flock. Blessed shall be your basket and your kneading bowl. Blessed shall you be when you come in, and blessed shall you be when you go out. (Deuteronomy 28:1-6)

America integrated the same divine principles into her foundation. Read our founding documents, founding laws (the Constitution), and how the original schools were set up with the Bible as their textbook. These declarations invoked divine assistance. Thus, a covenant with God. But as things are rapidly changing today, as America is starting to reject God's values and commandments and even may stop aiding Israel, this may be the beginning of the fall of the United States.

Is America becoming the new Sodom and Gomorrah, whose story is recorded in Genesis chapters 18 and 19? As America rejects God's laws, rejects Israel, and breaks the covenant we enjoyed with God, are we in the fall? Revelation is a warning. Revelation 17:10 says this nation yet to come will remain only a little while. Is America that empire?

"There are also seven kings, five of whom have fallen, one is, the other has not yet come, and when he does come, he must remain only a little while." (Revelation 17:10)

Is this a warning that America's time is up? We have fallen into all types of perversions and are rejecting God's word and His Son, our Savior. Remember what happened to Sodom and Gomorrah when they rejected God in favor of all types of earthly pleasures, even embracing homosexuality? Is America becoming Babylon?

"Then the LORD rained on Sodom and Gomorrah sulfur and fire from the LORD out of heaven. And he overthrew those cities, and all the valley, and all the inhabitants of the cities, and what grew on the ground." (Genesis 19:24-25).

This is America's warning to repent before it's too late. However, on America's behalf, much of the country is Christian and has the largest population of Christians of any country in the world. President Donald Trump made world history serving Israel in making the Abraham Accords. However, at the Rapture, all the Christians are removed, and also the influence of the Holy Spirit. Will the influence of the *"harlot"* take control of America, letting it fall so the Antichrist takes over?

Revelation 17:12 foretells the time that ten kings or nations to come with the beast, or the coming of a New World Order, which is the last empire.

"And the ten horns that you saw are ten kings who have not yet received royal power, but they are to receive authority as kings for one hour, together with the beast." (Revelation 17:12)

Many think this ten-nation confederation will be the remnants of the Roman Empire, of which the European Common Market is already. Before this ten-nation conglomerate of the beast, God will also raise another powerful nation. God refers to this nation as a woman (Revelation 17:3). This woman, or nation, sits upon the waters and also the beast.

The Greek word used in Revelation 17 for sit upon is *kathemia*, which refers to a dignitary sitting in public as a judge. This word *kathemia* is the same word used to describe Jesus when He sits upon His throne as King of Kings and Lord of Lords. In this providential nation of Babylon, the Great rules or presides over the beast before the beast is released upon the world with his religion.

Revelation 17:16 tells that the beast, and the one with ten horns, will hate the one who is called the prostitute – Babylon the Great.

"And the ten horns that you saw, they and the beast will hate the prostitute. They will make her desolate and naked, and devour her flesh and burn her up with fire." (Revelation 17:16)

This is considered the religion of the earth until the one started by the False Profit. When the time comes, this false profit will set up the antichrist, or beast, to be worshiped as a god. Thus, the world will reject the religion of the prostitute Babylon in favor of their new god and religion of the antichrist. Many believe the antichrist will accomplish this hoax by being possessed by Satan. In the final days and will appear to rise from the dead. Also, everyone will be required to get his mark or die.

"One of its heads seemed to have a mortal wound, but its mortal wound was healed, and the whole earth marveled as they followed the beast." (Revelation 13:3).

REVELATION CHAPTER 18

¹ After this I saw another angel coming down from heaven, having great authority, and the earth was made bright with his glory. ²And he called out with a mighty voice, "Fallen, fallen is Babylon the great! She has become a dwelling place for demons, a haunt for every unclean spirit, a haunt for every unclean bird, a haunt for every unclean and detestable beast. ³ For all nations have drunk the wine of the passion of her sexual immorality, and the kings of the earth have committed immorality with her, and the merchants of the earth have grown rich from the power of her luxurious living." ⁴ Then I heard another voice from heaven saying, "Come out of her, my people, lest you take part in her sins, lest you share in her plagues; ⁵ for her sins are heaped high as heaven, and God has remembered her iniquities. ⁶ Pay her back as she herself has paid back others, and repay her double for her deeds; mix a double portion for her in the cup she mixed. ⁷ As she glorified herself and lived in luxury, so give her a like measure of torment and mourning, since in her heart she says, 'I sit as a queen, I am no widow, and mourning I shall never see.' ⁸ For this reason her plagues will come in a single day, death and mourning and famine, and she will be burned up with fire; for mighty is the Lord God who has judged her." ⁹ And the kings of the earth, who committed sexual immorality and lived in luxury with her, will weep and wail over her when they see the smoke of her burning.

¹⁰ They will stand far off, in fear of her torment, and say, "Alas! Alas! You great city, you mighty city, Babylon! For in a single hour your judgment has come." ¹¹ And the merchants of the earth weep and mourn for her, since no one buys their cargo anymore, ¹²cargo of gold, silver, jewels, pearls, fine linen, purple cloth, silk, scarlet cloth, all kinds of scented wood, all kinds of articles of ivory, all kinds of articles of costly wood, bronze, iron, and marble, ¹³ cinnamon, spice, incense, myrrh, frankincense, wine, oil, fine flour, wheat, cattle and sheep, horses and chariots, and slaves, that is, human souls. ¹⁴ "The fruit for which your soul longed has gone from you, and all your delicacies and your splendors are lost to you, never to be found again!" ¹⁵ The merchants of these wares, who gained wealth from her, will stand far off, in fear of her torment, weeping and mourning aloud, ¹⁶"Alas, alas, for the great city that was clothed in fine linen, in purple and scarlet, adorned with gold, with jewels, and with pearls! ¹⁷ For in a single hour all this wealth has been laid waste." And all shipmasters and seafaring men, sailors and all whose trade is on the sea, stood far off ¹⁸ and cried out as they saw the smoke of her burning, "What city was like the great city?" ¹⁹ And they threw dust on their heads as they wept and mourned, crying out, "Alas, alas, for the great city where all who had ships at sea grew rich by her wealth! For in a single hour she has been laid waste. ²⁰ Rejoice over her, O heaven, and you saints and apostles and prophets, for God has given judgment for you against her!" ²¹ Then a mighty angel took up a stone like a great millstone and threw it into the sea, saying, "So will Babylon the great city be thrown down with violence, and will be found no more; ²² and the sound of harpists and musicians, of flute players and trumpeters, will be heard in you no more, and a craftsman of any craft will be found in you no more, and the sound of the mill will be heard in you no more, ²³ and the light of a lamp will shine in you no more, and the voice of bridegroom and bride will be heard in you no more, for your merchants were the great ones of the earth, and all nations were deceived by your

sorcery. ²⁴ And in her was found the blood of prophets and of saints, and of all who have been slain on earth."
(Revelation 18:1-24)

In Revelation 18, we see the fall of Babylon; as discussed in Chapter 17, it is not a place but a perception or idea. Many consider that this Babylon will infect every nation of the world with her sensuality. Many people will turn their backs on God. Verse 3 says, *"all nations,"* meaning the entire earth.

"For all nations have drunk the wine of the passion of her sexual immorality, and the kings of the earth have committed immorality with her, and the merchants of the earth have grown rich from the power of her luxurious living." (Revelation 18:3)

Chapter 18 is a prophetic vision of the world to come, showing what happens to those who follow the harlot. Again, this should be a warning to the United States: if it lingers on its present trend, it will lose its power due to its fall from within. This will come about due to the increasing lack of faith in God, along with practicing all kinds of sexual immorality, following the ways of the harlot. Currently, the United States is the economic center of the world. Businessmen have come from all over the world to do business in America, which figuratively becomes part of the new Babylon due to its corruption in the later days.

As seen in Revelation 18:8, God destroys her: *"And she will be burned up with fire; for mighty is the Lord God who has judged her."* This destruction was also foretold in Chapter 17.

"And the ten horns that you saw, they and the beast will hate the prostitute. They will make her desolate and naked, and devour her flesh and burn her up with fire." (Revelation 17:16)

If the *"harlot"* is not a person but a system. What does this mean? It is believed that after the first half of the tribulation, all the nations and people who follow the harlot will be destroyed by God. This destruction is thought to be caused by natural disasters and wars, which will be the beginning of large-scale wars. This will lead to the destruction of all nations, which gave in to her behavior. This will be the end of the so-called peaceful half of the Tribulation and the start of the *"Great Tribulation,"* the world's downfall and destruction as God's judgments continue to fall upon the earth. Notice who weeps the loudest over the fall of Babylon the Great.

"And the kings of the earth, who committed sexual immorality and lived in luxury with her, will weep and wail over her when they see the smoke of her burning. They will stand far off, in fear of her torment, and say, "Alas! Alas! You great city, you mighty city, Babylon! For in a single hour your judgment has come. "And the merchants of the earth weep and mourn for her"
(Revelation 18:9-11).

The harlot is not just a false religious system but also a political system. With the removal of the Christians at the Rapture, the harlot will have a luxurious presence, which means she will have a great appeal to the sensual and political nature of men before she falls. This fall will bring on the greatest depression the world has ever seen. Greater than the market crash of 1929. In Revelation 18 we find out that this fall not only affects all the goods and commodities of the nations who gave in to the *"harlot"* but everyone who bought into her temptation.

[23] and the light of a lamp will shine in you no more, and the voice of bridegroom and bride will be heard in you no more, for your merchants were the great ones of the earth, and all nations were deceived by your sorcery. [24] And in her was found the blood of

prophets and of saints, and of all who have been slain on earth."
(Revelation 18:23-24)

The *"Harlot"* starts in Chapter 17 and is thought not to be a place but an occult religious system, which begins as an illicit relationship with the Antichrist, the eighth empire, enticing all nations to her. This relationship will only last the first half of the Tribulation when she turns the nations from God. Then, the Beast takes over the world and calls himself god.

REVELATION CHAPTER 19

Chapter 19 resumes the chronological narration of the end times at the point where it was left off, at the end of Chapter 16.

¹ After this I heard what seemed to be the loud voice of a great multitude in heaven, crying out, "Hallelujah! Salvation and glory and power belong to our God,² for his judgments are true and just; for he has judged the great prostitute who corrupted the earth with her immorality, and has avenged on her the blood of his servants." ³ Once more they cried out, "Hallelujah! The smoke from her goes up forever and ever." ⁴ And the twenty-four elders and the four living creatures fell down and worshiped God who was seated on the throne, saying, "Amen. Hallelujah!" ⁵ And from the throne came a voice saying, "Praise our God, all you his servants, you who fear him, small and great." ⁶ Then I heard what seemed to be the voice of a great multitude, like the roar of many waters and like the sound of mighty peals of thunder, crying out, "Hallelujah! For the Lord our God the Almighty reigns.
(Revelation 19:1-6)

At the start of Chapter 19 we look into Heaven, and it's like a pep rally for God. There are five thunderous, resounding hallelujah shouts sung in unison by angels, Old Testament saints,

Tribulation saints, and all the Church-age saints. Verse 2 states God's judgments are true and just. However, in the eyes of unbelieving man, God is never fair in his judgments. When men suffer impartial consequences for flaunting God's grace, rejecting His love, and despising His law, they continuously blame God. Men blaspheme and curse God, even though He has given warning after warning of impending judgment, trying to get men to turn to Him in faith and receive His grace.

⁷ Let us rejoice and exult and give him the glory, for the marriage of the Lamb has come, and his Bride has made herself ready;⁸ it was granted her to clothe herself with fine linen, bright and pure"- for the fine linen are the righteous deeds of the saints. ⁹ And the angel said to me, "Write this: Blessed are those who are invited to the marriage supper of the Lamb." And he said to me, "These are the true words of God." ¹⁰ Then I fell down at his feet to worship him, but he said to me, "You must not do that! I am a fellow servant with you and your brothers who hold to the testimony of Jesus. Worship God." For the testimony of Jesus is the spirit of prophecy. (Revelation 19:7-10)

The Church is known as the *Bride of Christ.* The Apostles describe this as a mystery, being the marriage of Church-Age believers to Jesus. In Ephesians Chapter 5, we are told that each person who believes in Jesus as Christ becomes a member of His body, flesh of His flesh, and blood of His blood. Paul writes in Ephesians 5:

"²⁵ Husbands, love your wives, as Christ loved the church and gave himself up for her, ²⁶ that he might sanctify her, having cleansed her by the washing of water with the word, ²⁷ so that he might present the church to himself in splendor, without spot or wrinkle or any such thing, that she might be holy and without blemish. ²⁸In the same way husbands should love their wives as their own

bodies. He who loves his wife loves himself. ²⁹ For no one ever hated his own flesh, but nourishes and cherishes it, just as Christ does the church, ³⁰ because we are members of his body. ³¹"Therefore, a man shall leave his father and mother and hold fast to his wife, and the two shall become one flesh." ³² This mystery is profound, and I am saying that it refers to Christ and the church." (Ephesians 5:25-32)

To better understand the marriage relationship with Christ, we have to examine the customs of the ancient world, the time in which Paul wrote. Although marriage customs vary, most have three steps, from the initial process to the marriage union.

First, a marriage contract was negotiated between the parents, usually when the children were still young before they were adults. This contract was a binding agreement. They were legally married even though they would have no sexual contact with each other for perhaps years. This condition was known as a *"betrothal"* but was a much stronger tie than our present-day engagement. It gave time for their relationship to grow before the actual marriage vows.

Second, the marriage vows took place when the couple reached a suitable age of maturity. The groom, accompanied by his friends, would go to the bride's home and escort her to the house he had prepared for them to live in.

Third and final, they would come to the consummating event, the wedding feast. For this occasion, he would invite many guests to share in celebrating the union of the happy bride and groom. Now, apply this picture of marriage to the *"Bride of Christ."* So, when a person accepts the gift of salvation provided by Jesus' death on the cross, he enters into a legal union contract with Jesus. The Holy Spirit gives new life to the dead human spirit, and a growing relationship develops between Christ and the new believer. This growth is known as maturing in your faith. Thus, when Christ returns at the Rapture for the Church, He is the

Bridegroom coming to take His beloved bride (the Church) to the home He has been preparing.

"In my Father's house are many rooms. If it were not so, would I have told you that I go to prepare a place for you? And if I go and prepare a place for you, I will come again and will take you to myself, that where I am you may be also." (John 14:2-3)

The final step in the marriage of Christ to the Church is the wedding feast. While it is not said when the time or place of this feast will be, we know from Matthew 26:29 that after the Last Supper, Jesus says:

"I tell you I will not drink again of this fruit of the vine until that day when I drink it new with you in my Father's kingdom." (Matthew 26:29)

His *"Father's Kingdom"* is the 1000-year reign of Christ on earth following the Tribulation and the Battle of Armageddon. The wedding feast of the Lamb and His bride is thought to occur on the new earth at the beginning of His Kingdom.

An instructive incident occurred when John, amazed by what the angel showed him, fell at the angel's feet and worshipped him.

"Then I fell down at his feet to worship him, but he said to me, 'You must not do that! I am a fellow servant with you and your brothers who hold to the testimony of Jesus. Worship God.' For the testimony of Jesus is the spirit of prophecy." (Revelation 19:10).

The angel that showed this to John is described in Revelation 18:1 as having great authority and illuminated the earth with his glory. *"After this I saw another angel coming down from heaven, having great authority, and the earth was made bright with his glory.*" Yet he told John when he fell at his feet in Revelation 19:10: *"I am a fellow servant with you and your brothers who hold to the testimony of Jesus. Worship God."* This mighty angel refused to accept worship, showing no creature created by God should be worshipped or prayed to. Only God is to be worshiped.

Another thing the angel in Revelation 19:10 told John is, "*...Jesus is the spirit of prophecy*." Why? This emphasizes that Jesus is the essence of all prophecy; all that John is being shown is true and will happen.

¹¹ Then I saw heaven opened, and behold, a white horse! The one sitting on it is called Faithful and True, and in righteousness he judges and makes war.¹² His eyes are like a flame of fire, and on his head are many diadems, and he has a name written that no one knows but himself.¹³ He is clothed in a robe dipped in blood, and the name by which he is called is The Word of God.¹⁴ And the armies of heaven, arrayed in fine linen, white and pure, were following him on white horses.¹⁵ From his mouth comes a sharp sword with which to strike down the nations, and he will rule them with a rod of iron. He will tread the winepress of the fury of the wrath of God the Almighty.¹⁶ On his robe and on his thigh, he has a name written, King of kings and Lord of lords.
(Revelation 19:11-16)

This is not the same white horse found in Revelation 6. This is not a member of the *"Four Horsemen of the Apocalypse."* The rider of the first white horse was the Anti-Christ. Now, the rider of this white horse is Jesus Christ. The description reveals Him as a warrior executing judgment. This is the moment when Jesus returns to earth as King of Kings and Lord of Lords. He establishes his kingdom of justice, equity, and peace, forever putting down those who oppose Him. Jesus will return where He ascended the

Mount of Olives. This was prophesied in Acts Chapter 1, stating He would return as He left.

"¹⁰ And while they were gazing into heaven as He went, behold, two men stood by them in white robes, ¹¹ and said, 'Men of Galilee, why do you stand looking into heaven? This Jesus, who was taken up from you into heaven, will come in the same way as you saw him go into heaven.'" (Acts 1:10-11)

The Prophet Zechariah predicted that 500 years before Jesus was born, Christ would come to earth at the Mount of Olives, in the End Times, at the time of a great battle.

Then the LORD will go out and fight against those nations as when he fights on a day of battle. On that day his feet shall stand on the Mount of Olives that lies before Jerusalem on the east, and the Mount of Olives shall be split in two from east to west by a very wide valley, so that one half of the Mount shall move northward, and the other half southward. And you shall flee to the valley of my mountains, for the valley of the mountains shall reach to Azal. And you shall flee as you fled from the earthquake in the days of Uzziah king of Judah. Then the LORD my God will come, and all the holy ones with him. On that day there shall be no light, cold, or frost. And there shall be a unique day, which is known to the LORD, neither day nor night, but at evening time there shall be light. On that day living waters shall flow out from Jerusalem, half of them to the eastern sea and half of them to the western sea. It shall continue in summer as in winter. And the LORD will be king over all the earth. On that day the LORD will be one and his name one. (Zechariah 14:3-9)

Revelation 19 Continues:

Revelation: A Line by Line Breakdown

¹⁷ Then I saw an angel standing in the sun, and with a loud voice he called to all the birds that fly directly overhead, "Come, gather for the great supper of God, ¹⁸ to eat the flesh of kings, the flesh of captains, the flesh of mighty men, the flesh of horses and their riders, and the flesh of all men, both free and slave, both small and great." ¹⁹ And I saw the beast and the kings of the earth with their armies gathered to make war against him who was sitting on the horse and against his army. ²⁰ And the beast was captured, and with it the false prophet who in its presence had done the signs by which he deceived those who had received the mark of the beast and those who worshiped its image. These two were thrown alive into the lake of fire that burns with sulfur. ²¹ And the rest were slain by the sword that came from the mouth of him who was sitting on the horse, and all the birds were gorged with their flesh. (Revelation 19:17-21)

    The hardness of men's hearts reaches its peak at the sight of Christ's return. The armies of the Antichrist, the False Prophet, and the other great armies join forces against their mutual enemy, Jesus. The False Prophet mesmerized unbelievers with his sorcery and miracles from Satan. The Antichrist, also known as the *"Beast,"* is now judged by King Jesus and cast into the Lake of Fire. Their judgment is unlike all the other unbelievers because they are sent directly to the place called in chapter 20, *"the second death."* Immediately after their disposal, Jesus will judge all those still alive on earth who rejected Him. As described in the Gospel of Matthew.

³¹"When the Son of Man comes in his glory, and all the angels with him, then he will sit on his glorious throne. ³² Before him will be gathered all the nations, and he will separate people one from another as a shepherd separates the sheep from the goats. ³³ And he will place the sheep on his right, but the goats on the left. ³⁴Then the King will say to those on his right, 'Come, you who are blessed by my Father, inherit the kingdom prepared for you from

the foundation of the world. ³⁵ For I was hungry and you gave me food, I was thirsty and you gave me drink, I was a stranger and you welcomed me, ³⁶I was naked and you clothed me, I was sick and you visited me, I was in prison and you came to me.' ³⁷ Then the righteous will answer him, saying, 'Lord, when did we see you hungry and feed you, or thirsty and give you drink? ³⁸ And when did we see you a stranger and welcome you, or naked and clothe you? ³⁹ And when did we see you sick or in prison and visit you?' ⁴⁰And the King will answer them, 'Truly, I say to you, as you did it to one of the least of these my brothers, you did it to me.' ⁴¹"Then he will say to those on his left, 'Depart from me, you cursed, into the eternal fire prepared for the devil and his angels.⁴² For I was hungry and you gave me no food, I was thirsty and you gave me no drink, ⁴³ I was a stranger and you did not welcome me, naked and you did not clothe me, sick and in prison and you did not visit me.'⁴⁴ Then they also will answer, saying, 'Lord, when did we see you hungry or thirsty or a stranger or naked or sick or in prison, and did not minister to you?'⁴⁵ Then he will answer them, saying, 'Truly, I say to you, as you did not do it to one of the least of these, you did not do it to me.'⁴⁶ And these will go away into eternal punishment, but the righteous into eternal life."
(Matthew 25:31-46)

In Matthew Chapter 25, Jesus stated, or foretold, that when He came the second time, He would come to Judge. He stated he would separate the sheep from the goats. The sheep are those who accepted Him as Savior. These are known as *"the righteous."* The goats are those who opposed Christ and rejected Him.

The carnage of this battle is so great that the birds are called to dine on that slain.

"And the rest were slain by the sword that came from the mouth of him who was sitting on the horse, and all the birds were gorged with their flesh." (Revelation 19:21)

A 75-Day Transitional Period

Most Biblical scholars of End Time prophecy believe there will be a 75-day interval period that separates the end of the Tribulation from the beginning of the Millennial Kingdom. During this brief interim, several significant events transpire. But how do we know it will be 75 days?

"And from the time that the regular burnt offering is taken away and the abomination that makes desolate is set up, there shall be 1,290 days. Blessed is he who waits and arrives at the 1,335 days." (Daniel 12:11-12)

The last half of the Tribulation will last 1260 days or three and a half years. Thus, the abomination that makes desolate is removed from the Jewish Temple thirty days after the Tribulation ends, and an additional forty-five days must also be added to the prophetic timetable; according to Daniel, 1335 days minus 1290 days equals 45 days so that 45+30 = 75 (days). Seventy-five days after the Tribulation is when the judgment of the nations takes place, along with the Jewish and Gentile survivors of the Tribulation period.

"When the Son of Man comes in his glory, and all the angels with him, then he will sit on his glorious throne. Before him will be gathered all the nations, and he will separate people one from another as a shepherd separates the sheep from the goats." (Matthew 25:31-32)

<u>Some key events take place during this interval. Some are:</u>

❖ The antichrist and the false prophet will be cast into the lake of fire.

- ❖ Satan will be bound from this point until the end of the Millennium.
- ❖ Old Testament saints will be resurrected from the dead.
- ❖ It is also feasible that the marriage feast of Christ, the divine Bridegroom, and His bride will take place during these 75 days.

REVELATION CHAPTER 20

[1] Then I saw an angel coming down from heaven, holding in his hand the key to the bottomless pit and a great chain.[2] And he seized the dragon, that ancient serpent, who is the devil and Satan, and bound him for a thousand years,[3] and threw him into the pit, and shut it and sealed it over him, so that he might not deceive the nations any longer, until the thousand years were ended. After that he must be released for a little while.[4] Then I saw thrones, and seated on them were those to whom the authority to judge was committed. Also I saw the souls of those who had been beheaded for the testimony of Jesus and for the word of God, and those who had not worshiped the beast or its image and had not received its mark on their foreheads or their hands. They came to life and reigned with Christ for a thousand years.[5] The rest of the dead did not come to life until the thousand years were ended. This is the first resurrection.[6] Blessed and holy is the one who shares in the first resurrection! Over such the second death has no power, but they will be priests of God and of Christ, and they will reign with him for a thousand years.[7] And when the thousand years are ended, Satan will be released from his prison[8] and will come out to deceive the nations that are at the four corners of the earth, Gog and Magog, to gather them for battle; their number is like the sand of the sea.[9] And they marched up over the broad plain of the earth and surrounded the camp of the saints and the beloved city, but fire came down from heaven and consumed them,[10] and the devil who had deceived them was

thrown into the lake of fire and sulfur where the beast and the false prophet were, and they will be tormented day and night forever and ever.[11] *Then I saw a great white throne and him who was seated on it. From his presence earth and sky fled away, and no place was found for them.*[12] *And I saw the dead, great and small, standing before the throne, and books were opened. Then another book was opened, which is the book of life. And the dead were judged by what was written in the books, according to what they had done.*[13] *And the sea gave up the dead who were in it, Death and Hades gave up the dead who were in them, and they were judged, each one of them, according to what they had done.*[14] *Then Death and Hades were thrown into the lake of fire. This is the second death, the lake of fire.*[15] *And if anyone's name was not found written in the book of life, he was thrown into the lake of fire.* (Revelation 20:1-15)

Chapter 20 continues in the chronological course of Jesus Christ's final judgments, immediately after His return.

"And the beast was captured, and with it the false prophet who in its presence had done the signs by which he deceived those who had received the mark of the beast and those who worshiped its image. These two were thrown alive into the lake of fire that burns with sulfur". (Revelation 19:20)

Now, in chapter 20, Satan is judged.

[2] *And he seized the dragon, that ancient serpent, who is the devil and Satan, and bound him for a thousand years,*[3] *and threw him into the pit, and shut it and sealed it over him, so that he might not deceive the nations any longer, until the thousand years were ended. After that he must be released for a little while.* (Revelation 20:2,3)

The 1000-year Millennial Kingdom starts as Satan is thrown into the pit. Most Christians have a predetermined notion, based on Scripture, about Jesus' Second Coming and final judgment. Jesus said He was coming back and how. There would be the Rapture, then the final judgment, based on Scripture. The Millennium, the 1000-year reign of Christ on the new earth, will follow again based on Scripture.

There is a certain amount of theological dispute over this chapter of Revelation. The issue is whether there will be a literal 1000-year period in which mortal and immortal man will live together on a new earth ruled by Jesus. This Kingdom on the new earth is referred to as the *Millennium*. The issue is whether God ever promised such an earthly 1000-year Kingdom. The Millennium is mentioned five times in seven verses of Revelation Chapter Twenty.

There are more prophecies in the Bible about this Kingdom and its significance than any other theme of prophecy. The heart of the Old Testament prophetic message is the coming of the Messiah to set up an earthly kingdom. One in which Jesus will rule from the throne of David. The only thing the *Book of Revelation* adds to this Messianic Kingdom is its duration of 1000 years. Also, Revelation chapters 21 and 22 discuss this earthly Kingdom. The Kingdom of God after Christ returns to the earth to set his Kingdom is foretold in Daniel.

"the God of heaven will set up a kingdom that shall never be destroyed, nor shall the kingdom be left to another people. It shall break in pieces all these kingdoms and bring them to an end, and it shall stand forever." (Daniel 2:44)

What will the Millennium Be like?

It will be like it was in the Garden of Eden. All sin will be removed. God will walk among His creation. It is a time of peace, prosperity, and individual joy.

The Millennium Will Be A Time of PEACE.

¹ It shall come to pass in the latter days that the mountain of the house of the LORD shall be established as the highest of the mountains, and it shall be lifted up above the hills, and peoples shall flow to it, ² and many nations shall come, and say: "Come, let us go up to the mountain of the LORD, to the house of the God of Jacob, that he may teach us his ways and that we may walk in his paths." For out of Zion shall go forth the law, and the word of the LORD from Jerusalem. ³ He shall judge between many peoples, and shall decide for strong nations far away; and they shall beat their swords into plowshares, and their spears into pruning hooks; nation shall not lift up sword against nation, neither shall they learn war anymore; (Micah 4:1-3)

The Millennium Will Be A Time of PROSPERITY.

"Behold, the days are coming, declares the LORD, when the plowman shall overtake the reaper and the reaper of grapes him who sows the seed; the mountains shall drip sweet wine, and all the hills shall flow with it." (Amos 9:13)

The Millennium Will Be A Time of HOLINESS.

"And on that day, declares the LORD of hosts, I will cut off the names of the idols from the land, so that they shall be remembered no more. And also I will remove from the land the prophets and the spirit of uncleanness." (Zechariah 13:2)

The Millennium Will Be A Time of PERSONAL JOY.

⁵ The LORD has broken the staff of the wicked, the scepter of rulers,⁶ that struck the peoples in wrath with unceasing blows, that ruled the nations in anger with unrelenting persecution.⁷ The whole earth is at rest and quiet; they break forth into singing. (Isaiah 14:5-7)

Still, there is controversy about this 1000-year kingdom period. There are three main views: pre-Millennialism, post-Millennialism, and A-Millennialism. Most people have no idea about these Millennium views, so we will discuss them briefly now.

The first view is based on a literal interruption of Scripture. It is also the oldest, called **Pre-Millennialism**. This view holds that Christ will return to earth as the literal 1000-year Kingdom begins, and Jesus will rule, just as the Scriptures state. The *Book of Revelation* is all true, being the Word of God. It is a warning of things to come, plus a hope for all Christians. Jesus will set up His Kingdom after He destroys Satan, and He will reign from the throne of David. After the literal 1000 years, Jesus will turn His Kingdom over to His Father, at which point it will meld with God's Eternal Kingdom. Pre-millennialists also believe that God, who made many promises and covenants with Israel, will fulfill everything not yet fulfilled. Israel is His chosen people. God said He would fulfill everything that has not yet been fulfilled, which will happen during this literal 1000-year kingdom.

In Acts Chapter One, just before Jesus ascended into heaven, the disciples asked Him if now was the time to start His Kingdom and restore Israel.

⁶ So when they had come together, they asked him, "Lord, will you at this time restore the kingdom to Israel?" ⁷ He said to them, "It is not for you to know times or seasons that the Father has fixed by his own authority." (Acts 1:6-7).

Christ didn't tell them there wouldn't be an earthly Kingdom. He told His disciples that it was not for them to know when it would come to pass. Only the Father knows. In the Lord's Prayer, Jesus emphasized this anticipated earthly Kingdom when He told His followers to pray, **"Thy Kingdom come. Thy will be done on earth as it is in heaven."** God's will cannot be done on earth as it is in heaven until all of Christ's enemies have been put down, including Satan.

One of the major beliefs of Pre-Millennialists is that the earth is getting worse rather than better. The Kingdom Age can't begin until Christ returns to destroy those who led the world in its downward spiral (Satan). Revelation chapter 20:2-3 states:

[2] And he seized the dragon, that ancient serpent, who is the devil and Satan, <u>and bound him for a thousand years</u> [3] so that he might not deceive the nations any longer, <u>until the thousand years were ended</u>. (Revelation 20:2-3)

What are these 1000 years? Revelation states:

"Blessed and holy is the one who shares in the first resurrection! Over such the second death has no power, but they will be priests of God and of Christ, and <u>they will reign with him for a thousand years</u>." (Revelation 20:6)

Pre-millennialism is the strongest and clearest interruption of the 1000 years, as recorded in Revelation chapter 20. It tells of the kingdom. One must use a literal interruption of the Scriptures about the coming kingdom. It also works as a logical conclusion based on all Old Testament prophecies about the coming kingdom. Likewise, it supports the fact that God keeps all His promises.

The second view is *Post-Millennialism,* which teaches that there will not be a literal 1000-year kingdom on earth as Scripture records. This school of thought proclaims that the Millennium is only symbolic. Jesus will claim His Kingdom only after the Millennium has passed, which started when Christ came to this world in the first century. Post-millennialists believe that the world is getting better and better through the spread of the gospel.

The Millennial Age will be ongoing with the time many call the *Church Age*. Those who hold this view believe that the Church will Christianize the world. This will be the Millennial Age; it will bring on the second coming whenever it ends. Thus, Jesus comes after the Millennial Age or Post-Millennial. This is not supported by any Scripture in the Old or New Testaments.

Then, after the Millennium, Christ will take His believers to heaven and condemn those who reject Him. Post-millennialism holds that Jesus Christ established his kingdom on earth through His preaching and redemptive work in the first century. He equips his church with the gospel, empowers the church with the Holy Spirit, and charges the church with the Great Commission.

[19] Go therefore and make disciples of all nations, baptizing them in the name of the Father and of the Son and the Holy Spirit, [20] teaching them to observe all that I have commanded you. And behold, I am with you always, to the end of the age."
(Matthew 28:19-20)

Post-millennialism teaching was common in the 1850s, spread by American Protestants who promoted reform movements and the Social Gospel. Post-millennialism has become one of the key views of a movement known as *Christian Reconstructionism*. Christian reconstructionisms advocate the restoration of specific biblical laws that are said to have continuing applicability. These include the death penalty not only for murder but also for idolatry, open homosexuality, adultery, witchcraft, and blasphemy. It has been an attempt to immanentize the eschaton. Immanentize the eschaton is a somber term referring to efforts to bring about utopian conditions and successfully create heaven on earth.

Post-millennialism assumes that the vast majority of people living will eventually be saved. This will increase the gospel's success, gradually producing a time in history before Christ's return in which faith, righteousness, peace, and prosperity will prevail. However, this idea has several flaws, such as Jesus died on the cross over 2000 years ago, and in that time, there have been several wars, depressions, and plagues.

Since 1900, there have been two world wars and several 'police' actions, or other wars, plus the growing Muslim jihad. Many men appeared doing great evil, like Hitler, Stalin, and Mao, to name a few. Nations are always having another war. There have also been depressions and several plagues on the earth. The latest is COVID. The world is not getting better and better, even though the gospel has been spreading over the world for over 2000 years.

The third view is *A-Millennialism,* which also teaches that there will be no literal 1000-year reign of Christ on earth and no earthly Kingdom of God. They tend to view the Millennial Kingdom as being fulfilled in eternity. A-Millennialists deduce that the thousand years figuratively refer to a temporary bliss of souls in heaven before the Second Coming or to the infinite joy of the righteous.

This view of *eschatology* (end-times theology) does not hold that Jesus Christ will physically reign on the earth for exactly 1,000 years, as written in prophecy. A-Millennialists reject the view that Jesus Christ will physically reign on the Earth for exactly one thousand years. There will not be the Rapture. The Church Age ends with Jesus' Second Coming. The A-Millennial view regards the *thousand years* as symbolic, not literal. They hold that Jesus Christ established His kingdom on earth through His preaching and redemptive work in the first century. He equips his church with the gospel and empowers the church with the Holy Spirit.

According to this view, when Jesus returns, He will take all the believers with Him, condemn all the unbelievers, and eternity will begin right then. Like post-millennialists' views, this view tends to allegorize all the prophecies in the Old and New Testament and about the promised Kingdom. They tend to forget that the Book of Revelation is a prophecy, warning, and hope. Why reject it as a prophecy of things to come?

Additionally, Post and A-Millennialists believe that the prophecies about the End Times in the Old and New Testament, including everything in Revelation, have occurred. Revelation is not a prophecy but history. This encourages Christians to ignore the Bible prophecy being fulfilled today. Post and A-Millennial are Preterists who teach that the *Book of Revelation* occurred in the first century. The church fulfilled all of God's promises to Israel. Therefore, Israel has no significance today (Replacement Theology).

The Tribulation was fulfilled by the destruction of Jerusalem in AD 70. Preterists contend that Nero reigned from 54 AD until his death by suicide in 68 AD. The *Great Tribulation* resulted in the fall of Jerusalem in AD 70, two years after Nero's death. None of this is backed by Scripture, history, or what is written in any Biblical prophecy or the *Book of Revelation*.

The description of the antichrist DOES NOT fit Nero. Another interesting point that Preterism can't answer is if Revelation is history, why doesn't John name the Antichrist and False Prophet? It had been twenty-five years since Jerusalem was destroyed, but Revelation has no names in it. Why? Because it is prophecy, just as it says in Revelation 1:3, **"Blessed is the one who reads aloud <u>the words of this prophecy</u>."**

Some of the Characteristics of the Antichrist as Written in the Scriptures:

- ❖ He Will Blaspheme God;
- ❖ The number of the antichrist is 666 (Nero had no known number);

- ❖ He claims to be God and worshiped; (Nero did believe he was a god.)
- ❖ He Will Display Miraculous Powers (Nero never did);
- ❖ He appears to come back to life from a mortal head wound (Never happened to Nero);
- ❖ He rules the earth in full authority (Rome ruled most of the known world.)
- ❖ He will control the world's economy (Rome controlled part of the world economy);
- ❖ He defiles God's temple in Jerusalem, known as the *"abomination of desolation"*; (Nero never went to Jerusalem to sit on the Temple throne. Nero died in 68 AD).
- ❖ He has the fight against Christ at Armageddon (Nero never fought Jesus).

Additionally, most Biblical scholars assume John wrote the Book of Revelation about AD 95. Even the unanimous teachings of early church fathers, like Ireneaeus, Clement of Alexandria, Origen, Victorinus, Jerome, and Eusebius, fix the date as the mid-90s. The question to be asked is why John would write a book of prophecy over 25 years after the event. He wouldn't!

"Blessed is the one who reads aloud <u>the words of this prophecy</u>, and blessed are those who hear, and who keep what is written in it, for the time is near." (Revelation 1:3)

God also warns us not to alter the words of His prophecy.

[18] I warn everyone who hears the words of the prophecy of this book: if anyone adds to them, God will add to him the plagues described in this book, [19] and if anyone takes away from the words of the book of this prophecy, God will take away his share in the tree of life and in the holy city, which are described in this book. (Revelation 22:18,19).

Post and A-Millennialists are practitioners of Preterism theology. They want people to believe that Revelation is a history, not prophecy, primarily because of one verse taken out of context and wrongly interrupted: the passage about *"this generation will not pass away."*

"Truly, I say to you, this generation will not pass away until all these things take place." (Matthew 24:34)

The Preterists interpret Jesus' prophecy as meaning that this applies to the generation of people living at the time of Jesus in the first century. However, Jesus is referring to those who see the *'birth pains'* or *'signs of the times.'* Do not take a text out of context! Study the text before:

[32] From the fig tree learn its lesson: as soon as its branch becomes tender and puts out its leaves, you know that summer is near. [33] So also, when you see all these things, you know that he is near, at the very gates. [34] Truly, I say to you, this generation will not pass away until all these things take place. (Matthew 24:32-34).

Jesus commands us to learn from the *Parable of the Fig Tree* to understand better when the general time of His second coming is near. The one primary point of this parable is also stated in Mark Chapter 13.

[28] From the fig tree learn its lesson: as soon as its branch becomes tender and puts out its leaves, you know that summer is near. [29] So also, when you see these things taking place, you know that he is near, at the very gates. (Mark 13:28,29)

Now look at the whole passage from Luke Chapter 21.

²⁵ And there will be signs in sun and moon and stars, and on the earth distress of nations in perplexity because of the roaring of the sea and the waves, ²⁶ people fainting with fear and with foreboding of what is coming on the world. For the powers of the heavens will be shaken.²⁷ And then they will see the Son of Man coming in a cloud with power and great glory. ²⁸ Now when these things begin to take place, straighten up and raise your heads, because your redemption is drawing near. ²⁹ And he told them a parable: 'Look at the fig tree and all the trees. ³⁰ As soon as they come out in leaf, you see for yourselves and know that the summer is already near. ³¹ So also, when you see these things taking place, you know that the kingdom of God is near. ³² Truly, I say to you, this generation will not pass away until all has taken place.'" (Luke 21:25-32).

Preterists, Post, and A-Millennialists teach that Israel forfeited all of God's promises and covenants because Israel rejected Jesus (*Replacement Theology*). This is not based on anything in the Bible. Believing this makes God out to be a liar, and contradicts clear statements in the New Testament, which shows all covenants are still a force. Jesus said in Matthew Chapter 5:

¹⁷ Do not think that I have come to abolish the Law or the Prophets; I have not come to abolish them but to fulfill them. ¹⁸ For truly, I say to you, until heaven and earth pass away, not an iota, not a dot, will pass from the Law until all is accomplished. (Matthew 5:17-18)

"Now the LORD said to Abram, Go from your country and your kindred and your father's house to the land that I will show you. And I will make of you a great nation, and I will bless you and make your name great, so that you will be a blessing. I will bless those who bless you, and him who dishonors you I will curse, and

in you all the families of the earth shall be blessed."
(Genesis 12:1-3)

    From this, God made a blood covenant with Abram. It is the equivalent of a signed contract today, but it was more. If someone breaks a contract today, they can be sued; however, in a blood covenant, as in Abram's day, it was binding forever, and if anyone tried to break it, they were killed. After Pentecost, the world was divided into three groups, where previously there had only been two, Jew and Gentile. Paul writes in 1 Corinthians 10:32, **"Give no offense to Jews or to Greeks or to the church of God."**
    A-Millennialists believe that the Church is the fulfillment of the millennial Kingdom and that Christ presently reigns through the Church in peace and righteousness. Like Post-Millennialists, A-Millennialists believe that all the prophecies of the book of Revelation have been fulfilled; everything after Christ's assentation is only symbolism. Do not fall for this deception.
    If this is true, consider a few of the prophecies: When did the meteor hit the earth and destroy a third of the freshwater, killing many people because of tainted water? When did everything in the sea die? And when did angels fly over the world preaching the Gospel? History would have recorded such significant events, especially angels preaching the word of God.

The third angel blew his trumpet, and a great star fell from heaven, blazing like a torch, and it fell on a third of the rivers and on the springs of water. The name of the star is Wormwood. A third of the waters became wormwood, and many people died from the water because it had been made bitter.
(Revelation 8:10-11)

"The second angel poured out his bowl into the sea, and it became like the blood of a corpse, and every living thing died that was in the sea." (Revelation 16:3)

"Then I saw another angel flying directly overhead, with an eternal gospel to proclaim to those who dwell on earth, to every nation and tribe and language and people." (Revelation 14:6)

Similarly, if you take all the people who are to die on earth during the seven-year Tribulation period, as recorded in Revelation, approximately 70% of the world's population perishes. When did that happen? What are these examples if everything in Revelation already happened, as some believe (called Preterism)? When did all of this happen? There are several examples like this in God's prophecy. Revelation is a warning of things to come. It offers hope to everyone who believes in Jesus that they will avoid God's judgments, the Tribulation, by what is known as the Rapture.

A-Millennialists also teach that Christ bound Satan in his first coming, so now, each time a believer has a victory over temptation, it's due to Satan being bound. This goes against what is written in the Scriptures. Likewise, God's Word says 1000 years; everywhere else in the Bible, when God gives a timeline, He means precisely that. The number He says is that number, literally. So why is it in Revelation, when God says 1000 years, it is not literal? Is God lying? He can't. Remember, back in chapter 17, we noted an important point when God stated Israel would be the slaves of Egypt, and for 400 years, they were.

"Then the LORD said to Abram, 'Know for certain that your offspring will be sojourners in a land that is not theirs and will be servants there, and they will be afflicted for four hundred years.'" (Genesis 15:13).

God stated 400 years, and Jewish slavery was 400 years. When God gives us a number, that number is literal, absolute. There are numerous examples in the Bible of God using exact numbers. One thousand years means one thousand years, not over two thousand years.

Revelation: A Line by Line Breakdown

Before the fifth century, pre-millennialism dominated the Church. Most of the early church fathers strongly believed in a literal future 1000-year reign of Jesus, with the onset of A-Millennialism promoted by Augustine in the late fourth and early fifth century.

Augustine was a theologian, philosopher, and bishop of Hippo Regius in Numidia, Roman North Africa. His writings influenced the development of Western philosophy and Western Christianity. His influence, which developed into what now is Post- and A-Millennialism, profoundly changed the church. It altered the church's view of Scripture and prophecy and damaged the Church's doctrine of future prophetic events, which continues to this day.

Augustine derived his views by combining scripture with the opinions of Plato, an ancient Greek philosopher who regarded material things as insignificant or evil and thus placed a greater value on perceived spiritual realities. Augustine disagreed with much of what Plato taught; nevertheless, he incorporated Plato's pagan scheme of existence into his theology. While Augustine regarded Christianity as an improvement on Plato's thinking, he accepted Plato's worldview, which placed the immaterial above the physical.

This combining biblical prophecy with Platonism, called *Christoplantonism,* continues today. Theologian Randy Alcorn said this about it: *"Christoplantonism has had a devastating effect on our ability to understand what Scripture says about Heaven, particularly about the eternal Heaven, the New Earth. ... "Christoplantonism has closed our minds to the possibility that the present Heaven may be a physical realm. As a result, many today believe that it's 'unspiritual' to think of spending eternity in resurrected and immortal bodies even though this is clearly taught in Scripture."*(Randy Alcorn, from his book Heaven, 2004).

All the teachings of Post and A-Millennialism, Christoplantonism, Preterism, and Replacement Theology, NONE of these are based on ANY Scripture. There is no support for any of these in the Bible ANYWHERE. When questioned, the believers in these teachings constantly give unsubstantiated answers or text out of context. Along with saying, these teachings have been around for centuries. However, it's all smoke and mirrors. Just as the math word problem which states:

Three men check into a motel room for $30. Each pays $10 (10 x 3 = 30). The motel manager tells the desk clerk the room is on sale for $26 (30 – 4 = 26). The desk clerk gives $4 to the bellhop to give back to the men. The bellhop figures four cannot go into three evenly, so keep $1 and give each man back $1. Now, each man has paid $9 (10 – 1 = 9). Thus, 9 x 3 = 27 plus the one from the bellhop equals 28 (27 + 1 =28). Where are the other 2? Therefore 28 = 30.

We know this is not true, but it sounds correct. Just as Post and A-Millennialism, Christoplantonism, Preterism, and Replacement Theology are not based on scripture; however, some think it sounds right. Don't fall for their fuzzy math. Remember, Scripture interrupts Scripture. Never take the text out of context. Read it for yourself.

"For as the lightning comes from the east and shines as far as the west, so will be the coming of the Son of Man Scripture has several warnings against false prophets and teachers. Jesus himself warned of this." (Matthew 24:27)

Unfortunately, the long-term impact of denying a literal 1000-year Kingdom has also opened doors to abundant false teachings, even opinions that reject the beliefs of historic Christianity. The denial of all Old Testament prophecies relating to Israel causes Post and A-Millennialists to overlook the signs of many fulfilled prophecies in our current world. The very existence of Israel today is a miraculous fulfillment of biblical prophecy. Go back and read Ezekiel Chapter 37, because it is a key prophecy about the end times.

Once again, look at the opening of the *Book of Revelation,* written after Jesus' death, resurrection, assentation, and the destruction of Jerusalem and God's Temple.

₁"The revelation of Jesus Christ, which God gave him to show to his servants the things that must soon take place. He made it known by sending his angel to his servant John, ² who bore witness to the word of God and the testimony of Jesus Christ, even to all that he saw.³ Blessed is the one who reads aloud the words of this prophecy, and blessed are those who hear, and who keep what is written in it, for the time is near. (Revelation 1:1-3)

These are only the basics of the three views, and there are countless variations to Post- and A-Millennialist positions. If you consider God's Word to be always true, then all scriptures must be true, so everything in Revelation must also be absolutely true as the Word of God. Therefore, pre-millennialism is the only one that must be fact.

Saying Revelation should be taken nonliterally has no foundation. How can one interpret *End-Time prophecy as nonliteral when no evidence supports that assumption anywhere in the Bible?* Look at Jesus's words concerning the End Times. How do these unbelievers in Revelation's *End-Time* prophecy explain Christ's words, which many believe are about the Rapture?

⁴⁰"Then, two men will be in the field; one will be taken and one left. ⁴¹ Two women will be grinding at the mill; one will be taken and one left. ⁴² Therefore, stay awake, for you do not know on what day your Lord is coming. ⁴³ But know this, that if the master of the house had known in what part of the night the thief was coming, he would have stayed awake and would not have let his house be broken into. ⁴⁴ Therefore you also must be ready, for the Son of Man is coming at an hour you do not expect."
(Matthew 24:40-44)

Continuing in Revelation Chapter 20 there are four important parts or phases to the Millennium.

Phase One – Satan is Bound and Jailed

"Then I saw an angel coming down from heaven, holding in his hand the key to the bottomless pit and a great chain. And he seized the dragon, that ancient serpent, who is the devil and Satan, and bound him for a thousand years, and threw him into the pit, and shut it and sealed it over him, so that he might not deceive the nations any longer, until the thousand years were ended. After that he must be released for a little while." (Revelation 20:1-3)

John tells us here of a mighty angel (many believe it is Michael) who comes down from heaven with a key to the bottomless pit and a chain. He goes to Satan and does six things to him: (1) he lays hold of him; (2) ties him up for 1000 years; (3) he casts Satan bound into a pit or abyss; (4) he locks or seals him up in the pit; (5) the angel sets a seal on him that keeps Satan from continuing to deceive the nations; Also Revelation states Satan will be released after the 1000-year Kingdom is over, for a short time.

Why does God finally put Satan under lock and key? This is so Satan cannot continue deceiving the nations during the 1000-year Kingdom. Since the beginning of time, Satan has deceived the nations of the world. It influences them to think they can build a better world without God and Jesus Christ. The Messianic Kingdom promised throughout the Old Testament is a period of universal righteousness and peace. This wouldn't be possible if Satan was free to provoke a man. Even with Satan's bond, there will still be a certain amount of sin during the Millennium due to the sinful nature of man. The believers who survived the Tribulation will still have their physical bodies, and they will have children who can choose God or sin. Some will choose sin.

Phase Two – The First Resurrection

⁴ Then I saw thrones, and seated on them were those to whom the authority to judge was committed. Also I saw the souls of those who had been beheaded for the testimony of Jesus and for the word of God, and those who had not worshiped the beast or its image and had not received its mark on their foreheads or their hands. They came to life and reigned with Christ for a thousand years. ⁵ The rest of the dead did not come to life until the thousand years were ended. This is the first resurrection. ⁶ Blessed and holy is the one who shares in the first resurrection! Over such the second death has no power, but they will be priests of God and of Christ, and they will reign with him for a thousand years. (Revelation 20:4-6)

While many religions promise a resurrection, they generally refer to a spiritual resurrection that lets the spirit live on in some way. But a spiritual resurrection leaves the body to decay, returning to dust never to live again. This is not so with Judeo-Christian teaching. The Old and New Testaments speak of a bodily resurrection of the righteous and unrighteous who are deceased.

In Revelation, Chapter 20, a first and second resurrection is mentioned. Jesus' resurrection was the first phase. Christ was the first man to permanently be raised from the dead with a new body that would never see death, destruction, disease, or decay. The second phase of the first resurrection occurs when the Church, the living and the dead, are caught up at the Rapture. In this stage, all the deceased in Christ and all living believers who trust in Christ, from the cross until the day of the Rapture, will be taken into heaven.

Old Testament believers, however, will not be bodily resurrected until the third phase of the resurrection. This phase will occur after the Tribulation when Christ returns to the earth. At this point, all the Old Testament saints will have their bodies brought out of the grave and united with their souls and spirits. They will receive immortal, eternal bodies and go right into the Kingdom.

The fourth phase of the first resurrection will be all the mortal believers who live through the 1000-year millennial Kingdom. These will be the final ones to receive eternal bodies. The believers who survived the Tribulation and lived through the Millennium will not die, even though there will be an immediate judgment of death for unbelievers on Christ's return.

In Revelation 20:4, John states he saw thrones with an unidentified group of people sitting on them; they will have the authority to dispense or allot justice.

"Then I saw thrones, and seated on them were those to whom the authority to judge was committed. Also I saw the souls of those who had been beheaded for the testimony of Jesus and for the word of God, and those who had not worshiped the beast or its image and had not received its mark on their foreheads or their hands. They came to life and reigned with Christ for a thousand years." (Revelation 20:4)

We're not told here specifically who these rulers could be, but other places in the Bible say that believers will rule over even angels during the Millennium.

"Or do you not know that the saints will judge the world? And if the world is to be judged by you, are you incompetent to try trivial cases? Do you not know that we are to judge angels? How much more, then, matters pertaining to this life!" (1 Corinthians 6;2,3)

John also states in Revelation 20:4 that the souls of the martyred Tribulation saints are elevated to a ruling role with Jesus for his 1000-year reign. A question often pondered is, whom will these believers rule over? We can't be sure, but in some way, believers will help Christ govern the universe through all its diverse creation. It will be a rule based on Jesus' love. There will be an incredible number of people on earth, and they will need some direction.

Phase Three – Satan is Unbound and Judged

⁷ And when the thousand years are ended, Satan will be released from his prison ⁸ and will come out to deceive the nations that are at the four corners of the earth, Gog and Magog, to gather them for battle; their number is like the sand of the sea.⁹ And they marched up over the broad plain of the earth and surrounded the camp of the saints and the beloved city, but fire came down from heaven and consumed them,¹⁰ and the devil who had deceived them was thrown into the lake of fire and sulfur where the beast and the false prophet were, and they will be tormented day and night forever and ever. (Revelation 20:7-10)

The biggest question is why Satan is released after 1000 years of imprisonment. We know that the Millennial Kingdom will begin with believers; look at Matthew 24:31-46. Christ says in Matthew:

"When the Son of Man comes in his glory, and all the angels with him, then he will sit on his glorious throne. Before him will be gathered all the nations, and he will separate people one from another as a shepherd separates the sheep from the goats. And he will place the sheep on his right, but the goats on the left. Then the King will say to those on his right, 'Come, you who are blessed by my Father, inherit the kingdom prepared for you from the foundation of the world." (Matthew 25:31-34).

Then, in Matthew 25:41, He says: *"Then he will say to those on his left, 'Depart from me, you cursed, into the eternal fire prepared for the devil and his angels.' "And these will go away into eternal punishment, but the righteous into eternal life."* (Matthew 25:46).

Many of these believers who were alive after the Tribulation in the Millennium will have children born during this period. However, many of these children will not believe in Jesus as their Savior. Satan will deceive them after he is let loose and follow him. Even though during the Millennium, there will be great security, equality, prosperity, peace, perfect ecology, and government, many will reject Christ. This proves what the Prophet Jeremiah said about man:

"The heart is deceitful above all things, and desperately sick; who can understand it? I the LORD search the heart and test the mind, to give every man according to his ways, according to the fruit of his deeds." (Jeremiah 17:9-10)

The first thing Satan does when released is to organize a war with Gog and Magog, who were the enemies of Israel in the Old Testament. This army must be made from their descendants born during the Millennium. But this rebellion doesn't even get off the ground before God ends it before it starts, with fire from heaven. This event ends Satan forever, and God cast him into the Lake of Fire with the False Prophet and the Antichrist for all of eternity.

Phase Four – The Final Judgment

[11] Then I saw a great white throne and him who was seated on it. From his presence earth and sky fled away, and no place was found for them. [12] And I saw the dead, great and small, standing before the throne, and books were opened. Then another book was opened, which is the book of life. And the dead were judged by what was written in the books, according to what they had done. [13] And the sea gave up the dead who were in it, Death and

Hades gave up the dead who were in them, and they were judged, each one of them, according to what they had done. [14] Then Death and Hades were thrown into the lake of fire. This is the second death, the lake of fire. [15] And if anyone's name was not found written in the book of Life, he was thrown into the lake of fire. (Revelation 20:11-15)

The greatest misunderstanding is that mankind will find out their final status for eternity at the final judgment. This misconception also teaches that at this judgment, one's good deeds will be weighed against one's evil deeds. This will decide whether a person is worthy of being in heaven or going to hell. Some people believe that they may be cast into a temporary place of torment called *Purgatory*. This idea is not found anywhere in the Bible. You can only accept Jesus as the Messiah before death. After that, you spend eternity separated from God.

The place of the dead in the Old Testament is called Death, or Sheol; in the New Testament, it is called *Hades,* or *Hell*. Many mistakenly have the idea that hell is strictly a place of punishment. This is not the case. The fact is that *Sheol* and *Hades* are the same place, the place where all departed dead spirits went before Jesus' resurrection, both good and bad. Hades or Hell had two compartments: *Paradise* (Abraham's Bosom), where those who had faith in God and His sacrifice for sin went, and *Torments*, where all unbelievers went and still are.

The first and most important judgment took place at the cross. It is where God dealt with the sins of mankind. This is why God became man and thereby took on the nature of man, to take on the sins of the world. Jesus was born of a human mother, but God was the father, which is why Jesus was called the Son of God. Jesus was born of a virgin, without a human father. Jesus was without inherited sin, called original sin. Many hold that it was an Immaculate Conception, meaning that God chose Mary to be the

Messiah's mother and was free of original sin from the moment of her conception by God the Father.

"And Mary said to the angel, 'How will this be since I am a virgin?' And the angel answered her, 'The Holy Spirit will come upon you, and the power of the Most High will overshadow you; therefore the child to be born will be called holy.-the Son of God.'"
(Luke 1:34-35)

The greatest judgment was when Jesus, the Messiah, willingly took on all mankind's sins and then bore the full measure of God's judgment on the cross. By His death in our place, we received a pardon. Jesus was all mankind's sacrificial lamb. Therefore, since our judgment has already taken place, all who accept Jesus as their Savior will never stand at a judgment of condemnation because we have already been judged and pardoned at the cross.

"For our sake He made Him to be sin who knew no sin, so that in Him we might become the righteousness of God."
(2 Corinthians 5:21)

We're told that when Jesus Christ died on the cross, He descended into hell (Hades). It is certain that He went into the Paradise side and announced that the promised redemption of the faithful was now completed. When Jesus rose from the grave, He took to heaven with Him all those who were in Paradise.

"Therefore it says, When he ascended on high he led a host of captives, and he gave gifts to men. In saying, 'He ascended,' what does it mean but that he had also descended into the lower regions, the earth? He who descended is the one who also ascended far above all the heavens, that he might fill all things."
(Ephesians 4:8-10)

Revelation: A Line by Line Breakdown

"And if anyone's name was not found written in the book of life, he was thrown into the lake of fire." (Revelation 20:15)

The reason eternal hell-fire is so hard for many to believe is that it seems out of character for God, who is all-loving. Hell was never made for man but for Satan and his demons. The only people sent there will reject God's Savior's grace and provision for a pardon.

"Whoever believes in him is not condemned, but whoever does not believe is condemned already, because he has not believed in the name of the only Son of God. And this is the judgment: the light has come into the world, and people loved the darkness rather than the light because their works were evil. For everyone who does wicked things hates the light and does not come to the light, lest his works should be exposed." (John 3:18-20)

The books that were opened are thought to be (1) *The Book of God's Law*; (2) *The Books of Works*; and (3) *The Book of Life*.

The **Book of God's Law** is mentioned in numerous verses in the Bible as the written Word of God's law. We're told that anyone who's had exposure to God's Word is responsible for living according to it, and if he doesn't, he's condemned by God. No doubt, there will be many who come before God who can plead they never heard God's law in their lifetime. However, God inspired Paul to write that those who have not heard the law have had it written instinctively in them by God called their consciences. Their consciences will be the standard by which they are condemned because they haven't lived up to what their consciences showed them.

¹² For all who have sinned without the law will also perish without the law, and all who have sinned under the law will be judged by the law. ¹³ For it is not the hearers of the law who are righteous before God, but the doers of the law who will be justified. ¹⁴ For when Gentiles, who do not have the law, by nature do what the law requires, they are a law to themselves, even though they do not have the law. ¹⁵ They show that the work of the law is written on their hearts, while their conscience also bears witness, and their conflicting thoughts accuse or even excuse them ¹⁶ on that day when, according to my gospel, God judges the secrets of men by Christ Jesus. (Romans 2:12-16)

"For all who rely on works of the law are under a curse; for it is written, Cursed be everyone who does not abide by all things written in the Book of the Law, and do them. Now it is evident that no one is justified before God by the law, for The righteous shall live by faith." (Galatians 3:10-11)

The second book is the **Book of Works**. Each person is thought to have a recording angel writing down all their deeds. So that every time a person has an opportunity to receive Jesus Christ as their Savior and turns it down, it's recorded in the book. Every bad deed done, as well as every good deed, is recorded.

"For God will bring every deed into judgment, with every secret thing, whether good or evil." (Ecclesiastes 12:14)

However, if you've received God's grace by accepting Jesus for the forgiveness of your sins, then God has already judged all the wrong things you have done. This is because Jesus has already taken God's wrath on your behalf. You don't have to worry that God will keep a list of all your deeds. Our list was nailed to the cross, and Jesus buried it in His grave.

"And you, who were dead in your trespasses and the uncircumcision of your flesh, God made alive together with him, having forgiven us all our trespasses by canceling the record of

debt that stood against us with its legal demands. This he set aside, nailing it to the cross". (Colossians 2:13-14)

Last is the **Book of Life**; the New Testament refers to this book eight times. The Old Testament doesn't call it by that name. However, the Old Testament refers three times to a book in which names are written. This book contains the name of every person born. If by the time any person dies and has not received God's saving grace, their name is blotted out. When God opens this book, at the *Great White Throne Judgment*, the only names left are those who believed in Jesus as their Savior and Lord. That's why the book's title is also called *The Lamb's Book of Life*.

[4] But God, being rich in mercy, because of the great love with which he loved us, [5] even when we were dead in our trespasses, made us alive together with Christ-by grace you have been saved- [6] and raised us up with him and seated us with him in the heavenly places in Christ Jesus,[7] so that in the coming ages he might show the immeasurable riches of his grace in kindness toward us in Christ Jesus.[8] For by grace you have been saved through faith. And this is not your own doing; it is the gift of God,[9] not a result of works, so that no one may boast. (Ephesians 2:4-9)

REVELATION CHAPTER 21

Revelation chapters 21 and 22 are a view of the New Earth and New Jerusalem and are very literal and easy to understand, so we will discuss these two chapters together as if they were one. The Kingdom of God after Christ returns to the earth to set his Kingdom was written about in Daniel.

[1] Then I saw a new heaven and a new earth, for the first heaven and the first earth had passed away, and the sea was no more. [2] And I saw the holy city, new Jerusalem, coming down out of

Revelation: A Line by Line Breakdown

heaven from God, prepared as a bride adorned for her husband. ³And I heard a loud voice from the throne saying, "Behold, the dwelling place of God is with man. He will dwell with them, and they will be his people, and God himself will be with them as their God. ⁴ He will wipe away every tear from their eyes, and death shall be no more, neither shall there be mourning, nor crying, nor pain anymore, for the former things have passed away." ⁵ And he who was seated on the throne said, "Behold, I am making all things new." Also, he said, "Write this down, for these words are trustworthy and true." ⁶ And he said to me, "It is done! I am the Alpha and the Omega, the beginning and the end. To the thirsty I will give from the spring of the water of life without payment. ⁷The one who conquers will have this heritage, and I will be his God and he will be my son. ⁸ But as for the cowardly, the faithless, the detestable, as for murderers, the sexually immoral, sorcerers, idolaters, and all liars, their portion will be in the lake that burns with fire and sulfur, which is the second death." ⁹ Then came one of the seven angels who had the seven bowls full of the seven last plagues and spoke to me, saying, "Come, I will show you the Bride, the wife of the Lamb." ¹⁰ And he carried me away in the Spirit to a great, high mountain, and showed me the holy city Jerusalem coming down out of heaven from God, ¹¹ having the glory of God, its radiance like a most rare jewel, like a jasper, clear as crystal. ¹²It had a great, high wall, with twelve gates, and at the gates twelve angels, and on the gates the names of the twelve tribes of the sons of Israel were inscribed ¹³ on the east three gates, on the north three gates, on the south three gates, and on the west three gates. ¹⁴ And the wall of the city had twelve foundations, and on them were the twelve names of the twelve apostles of the Lamb. ¹⁵ And the one who spoke with me had a measuring rod of gold to measure the city and its gates and walls. ¹⁶ The city lies foursquare, its length the same as its width. And he measured the city with his rod, 12,000 stadia. Its length and width and height are equal. ¹⁷ He also measured its wall, 144 cubits by human *measurement, which is also an angel's measurement. ¹⁸ The wall was built of jasper, while the city was pure gold, clear as glass. ¹⁹The foundations of the wall of the city were adorned with every kind of jewel. The first was jasper, the second sapphire, the third agate, the fourth emerald, ²⁰ the fifth onyx, the sixth carnelian, the seventh chrysolite, the eighth beryl, the ninth topaz, the tenth chrysoprase, the eleventh jacinth, the twelfth amethyst. ²¹ And the twelve gates were twelve pearls, each of the gates made of a single pearl, and the street of the city was pure gold, transparent as glass. ²² And I saw no temple in the city, for its temple is the Lord God the Almighty and the Lamb. ²³ And the city has no need of sun or moon to shine on it, for the glory of God gives it light, and its lamp is the Lamb. ²⁴ By its light will the nations walk, and the kings of the earth will bring their glory into it, ²⁵ and its gates will never be shut by day-and there will be no night there. ²⁶ They will bring into it the glory and the honor of the nations. ²⁷ But nothing unclean will ever enter it, nor anyone who does what is detestable or false, but only those who are written in the Lamb's book of life.* (Revelation 21:1-27).

In Revelation chapter 21, John tells us about the new heaven and earth. They will not be separate from each other but together as one. Verse 5 states, *"And he who was seated on the throne said, "Behold, I am making all things new."* The new earth is for all the saints, in their glorified, resurrected bodies. The old world will have passed away along with all its corruption and troubles. God recreates the earth as it was at the time of the Garden of Eden. Verse 3 states, *"Behold, the dwelling place of God is with man. He will dwell with them, and they will be his people, and God himself will be with them as their God."*

The new earth will have freedom from conflicting passions, temptations, troubles, changes, and whatever can divide or disturb the confidence of saints. Verse 4 states, *"He will wipe away every tear from their eyes, and death shall be no more, neither shall there be mourning, nor crying, nor pain anymore, for the former things have passed away."*

The new Jerusalem will be the church of God in its new and perfect state, the church triumphant. Its holiness comes from God.

[10] And he carried me away in the Spirit to a great, high mountain, and showed me the holy city Jerusalem coming down out of heaven from God, [11] having the glory of God, its radiance like a most rare jewel, like a jasper, clear as crystal. [12] It had a great, high wall, with twelve gates, and at the gates twelve angels, and on the gates the names of the twelve tribes of the sons of Israel were inscribed [13] on the east three gates, on the north three gates, on the south three gates, and on the west three gates. [14] And the wall of the city had twelve foundations, and on them were the twelve names of the twelve apostles of the Lamb."
(Revelation 21:10-14)

The presence of God will be with his people; He will dwell with them continually. The saints will have no remembrance of former sorrows. Christ makes all things new. God states He is the Alpha and Omega, the Beginning and the End, as a pledge.

[6] And he said to me, "It is done! I am the Alpha and the Omega, the beginning and the end. To the thirsty I will give from the spring of the water of life without payment. [7] The one who conquers will have this heritage, and I will be his God and he will be my son.
(Revelation 21:6,7).

Man will have a magnificent association with Christ. This shows that the happiness of heaven consists of interaction with God. Revelation 20 tells of only taking general ideas of heaven. The wall stands for security. Those who are there are separated and secured from all evils and enemies. This city is vast, meaning there is room for all the people of God. The foundation of the wall shows the promise and power of God. These are strong foundations. These foundations are set forth by doctrines of the gospel, the graces of the Holy Spirit, and the personal qualities of the Lord Jesus Christ.

Heaven has gates, but there is free admission to all that is holy. None of God's people shall be shut out. These gates are made of pearls. Christ is the Pearl of great price, and He is our Way to God. The Messiah, the Redeemer, the Son of God.

"But nothing unclean will ever enter it, nor anyone who does what is detestable or false, but only those who are written in the Lamb's book of life." (Revelation 21:27).

What is there in heaven that supplies its light? The glory of God lightens that city and the Lamb, which is the true Light. There is no night; therefore, no need to shut the gates. All is at peace and secure.

[23] And the city has no need of sun or moon to shine on it, for the glory of God gives it light, and its lamp is the Lamb. [24] By its light will the nations walk, and the kings of the earth will bring their glory into it, [25] and its gates will never be shut by day-and there will be no night there. (Revelation 21:23-25).

This shows us we should think of heaven as filled with the glory of God and enlightened by the presence of the Lord Jesus. Nothing sinful or unclean can enter.

REVELATION CHAPTER 22

[1] Then the angel showed me the river of the water of life, bright as crystal, flowing from the throne of God and of the Lamb [2] through the middle of the street of the city; also, on either side of the river, the tree of life with its twelve kinds of fruit, yielding its

fruit each month. The leaves of the tree were for the healing of the nations. ³ No longer will there be anything accursed, but the throne of God and of the Lamb will be in it, and his servants will worship him.⁴ They will see his face, and his name will be on their foreheads. ⁵ And night will be no more. They will need no light of lamp or sun, for the Lord God will be their light, and they will reign forever and ever. ⁶ And he said to me, "These words are trustworthy and true. And the Lord, the God of the spirits of the prophets, has sent his angel to show his servants what must soon take place." ⁷"And behold, I am coming soon. Blessed is the one who keeps the words of the prophecy of this book." ⁸ I, John, am the one who heard and saw these things. And when I heard and saw them, I fell down to worship at the feet of the angel who showed them to me,⁹ but he said to me, "You must not do that! I am a fellow servant with you and your brothers the prophets, and with those who keep the words of this book. Worship God." ¹⁰ And he said to me, "Do not seal up the words of the prophecy of this book, for the time is near. ¹¹ Let the evildoer still do evil, and the filthy still be filthy, and the righteous still do right, and the holy still be holy." ¹²"Behold, I am coming soon, bringing my recompense with me, to repay everyone for what he has done. ¹³I am the Alpha and the Omega, the first and the last, the beginning and the end." ¹⁴ Blessed are those who wash their robes, so that they may have the right to the Tree of Life and that they may enter the city by the gates. ¹⁵ Outside are the dogs and sorcerers and the sexually immoral and murderers and idolaters, and everyone who loves and practices falsehood. ¹⁶"I, Jesus, have sent my angel to testify to you about these things for the churches. I am the root and the descendant of David, the bright morning star." ¹⁷ The Spirit and the Bride say, "Come." And let the one who hears say, "Come." And let the one who is thirsty come; let the one who desires take the water of life without price. ¹⁸I warn everyone who hears the words of the prophecy of this book: if anyone adds to them, God will add to him the plagues described in this book,

[19]and if anyone takes away from the words of the book of this prophecy, God will take away his share in the tree of life and in the holy city, which are described in this book. [20] He who testifies to these things says, "Surely I am coming soon." Amen. Come, Lord Jesus! [21] The grace of the Lord Jesus be with all. Amen. (Revelation 22:1-21)

Most people refer to the place they go to after death as heaven as their eternal home, but this is a misnomer. Anyone who dies before the Rapture will go to be with Christ in a place called heaven, but that's not where believers are going to spend eternity with God. Between the heaven that exists now and the eternal home with God is the 1000-year kingdom on earth.

The final dwelling place of all believers will be the re-created earth called the *New Earth,* and a virtually indescribable city called the *New Jerusalem*. We get a dazzling look at this home for all eternity. Isaiah wrote of this New Heaven and a New Earth hundreds of years before Christ or Revelation.

[17]"For behold, I create new heavens and a new earth, and the former things shall not be remembered or come into mind. [18] But be glad and rejoice forever in that which I create; for behold, I create Jerusalem to be a joy, and her people to be a gladness. [19]I will rejoice in Jerusalem and be glad in my people; no more shall be heard in it the sound of weeping and the cry of distress. [20] No more shall there be in it an infant who lives but a few days, or an old man who does not fill out his days, for the young man shall die a hundred years old, and the sinner a hundred years old shall be accursed.[21] They shall build houses and inhabit them; they shall plant vineyards and eat their fruit. [22] They shall not build and another inhabit; they shall not plant and another eat; for like the days of a tree shall the days of my people be, and my chosen shall long enjoy the work of their hands. (Isaiah 65:17-22)

Revelation: A Line by Line Breakdown

In this new earth and New Jerusalem, we will be able to talk to God as Adam did in our new immortal bodies, enjoying fellowship with Jesus forever. This is the greatest thing about it. Some say heaven is *"a state of mind, a fantasy, a dream,"* however, Jesus Himself called heaven a real place.

"Let not your hearts be troubled. Believe in God; believe also in me. In my Father's house are many rooms. If it were not so, would I have told you that I go to prepare a place for you? And if I go and prepare a place for you, I will come again and will take you to myself, that where I am you may be also." (John 14:1-3)

The size of the New Jerusalem is described as:

"The city lies foursquare, its length the same as its width. And he measured the city with his rod, 12,000 stadia. Its length and width and height are equal. He also measured its wall, 144 cubits by human measurement, which is also an angel's measurement." (Revelation 21:16,17).

When put on a map of the United States, on the east, it would be from the farthest point of northeast Maine to the southern tip of Florida and from the Atlantic Ocean to the western side of the Rocky Mountains. The levels rise one mile up with streets of gold.

The angel showed John a river that came down the middle of the street of the heavenly city and was lined on both sides with the trees of life that bore a different kind of fruit, which it yielded every month. The source of this river was the throne of God and the Lamb, called the *River of Life*.

[1] Then the angel showed me the river of the water of life, bright as crystal, flowing from the throne of God and of the Lamb [2] through the middle of the street of the city; also, on either side of

the river, the tree of life with its twelve kinds of fruit, yielding its fruit each month. The leaves of the tree were for the healing of the nations. (Revelation 22:1,2).

This tree was an emblem of Christ and of all the blessings of his salvation, and the leaves for the healing of the nations, mean that his favor and presence supply all good to the inhabitants of that blessed world. The devil has no power there. He cannot draw the saints from serving God, nor can he disturb them in the service of God. God and the Lamb are spoken of as one. It is believed that this river represents the outpouring of the Holy Spirit. Jesus, on speaking of the Holy Spirit, said in the Book of John:

"If anyone thirsts, let him come to me and drink. Whoever believes in me, as the Scripture has said, 'Out of his heart will flow rivers of living water." (John 7:37-38)

God also warns us not to change the words of Revelation, HIS prophecy.

"I warn everyone who hears the words of the prophecy of this book: if anyone adds to them, God will add to him the plagues described in this book, and if anyone takes away from the words of the book of this prophecy, God will take away his share in the tree of life and in the holy city, which are described in this book." (Revelation 22:18,19)

"the God of heaven will set up a kingdom that shall never be destroyed, nor shall the kingdom be left to another people. It shall break in pieces all these kingdoms and bring them to an end, and it shall stand forever." (Daniel 2:44)

Some of the promises of the Millennial Kingdom all will enjoy:

- ❖ Great numbers will be saved in the Tribulation (Revelation 7:9-17).
- ❖ Those believers who survive the Tribulation enter the Millennial Kingdom (Revelation 20:4-6; Daniel 12:1-3).
- ❖ The curse on nature and the animal kingdom will be removed (Isaiah 11:6-8; 65:17-25).
- ❖ The whole earth will be filled with the knowledge of the Lord (Isaiah 11:9).
- ❖ Jesus, the Messiah, will reign over all the earth from Jerusalem (Zechariah 14:9-21; Ezekiel 37:24-28; Jeremiah 33:14-16).
- ❖ Those still alive when entering the Millennial Kingdom will have a greatly extended life (Isaiah 65:20-22).
- ❖ There will be world peace (Micah 4:3)
- ❖ There will be justice for all (Isaiah 42:1-7; 11:3-5).
- ❖ There will be permanent prosperity for all (Isaiah 65:21-23).

CONCLUSION: BE READY

God knows the blindness of agnosticism. He understood that through the ages, men would read Revelation, His book of prophecy, and would be convinced that it is fantasy. However, a precise knowledge of Bible prophecy is vital, especially with *The Book of Revelation*. It's hard to argue that it's not prophecy, but it often happens. Revelation is about hope, showing things to come and a way out. It also foretells to unbelievers, what will happen to those who reject God's Messiah. Therefore, accept exactly what Scripture and Jesus say. Just as in the time of Lot and Noah, people will ignore the strong warnings of Scripture. Then, as now, people find themselves unprepared for future events. The most challenging time the world has ever seen is in the future, not the past. Be part of the Rapture, not the Tribulation.

All end-time events are foretold in the Bible. Especially in the Book of Revelation and Mount of Olives Disclosure. The Bible gives a big-picture view, not specific details, and is not always very clear. Such as many prophetic events will become clear as the time of their unfolding approaches. We must all be cautious not to speculate beyond what the Scriptures communicate. Do not make the Bible say what you want it to say. God knows all things, past, and future. He has a plan and knows how everything is going to end. He uses prophecy to tell us what to expect and as a warning. As is written in the *Book of Isaiah*:

"declaring the end from the beginning and from ancient times things not yet done, saying, 'My counsel shall stand, and I will accomplish all my purpose,' calling a bird of prey from the east, the man of my counsel from a far country. I have spoken, and I will bring it to pass; I have purposed, and I will do it.
(Isaiah 46:10-11)

The future has been decided and cannot be changed. Everything is God's sovereign plan. God told the prophet Daniel that many seemingly puzzling verses will become clear when the end is near. Undoubtedly, as the events prophesied are fulfilled more and more, the more apparent other signs will be.

As Daniel concluded his prophecy, in Daniel Chapter Twelve, he asked God to let him in on the timing of *End Time* events. God told Daniel in verse 12:4: **"But you, Daniel, shut up the words and seal the book, until the time of the end. Many shall run to and fro, and knowledge shall increase."** Then, in verse 12:10, God tells Daniel: **"Many shall purify themselves and make themselves white and be refined, but the wicked shall act wickedly. And none of the wicked shall understand, but those who are wise shall understand."** Notice that all End Times prophecies will become clearer when the end is close.

Revelation: A Line by Line Breakdown

Until the beginning of the twentieth century, *The Book of Revelation* remained largely unexplored. Most theologians considered it too complicated and didn't pertain to their time in the Church Age. They looked to other matters that the Church needed at that time. But at the dawn of the twentieth century, a revelation in Revelation began.

The study of Revelation began with an intensity unparalleled in Church history. In the last twenty years, more books on Revelation have been written than at any other time. However, most people have not even read Revelation or a single book on the subject. Plus, Revelation is the only book in the Bible that promises a special blessing to everyone who reads it and heeds its teachings.

Blessed is the one who reads aloud <u>the words of this prophecy</u>, and blessed are those who hear, and who keep what is written in it, for the time is near. Greeting to the Seven Churches.
(Revelation 1:3)

Sir Isaac Newton (1643-1727), a Theologian who, among many other accomplishments, made this statement about Bible prophecy: *"About the time of the end, a body of men will be raised up who will turn attention to the literal interpretation in the midst of much clamor and opposition."*

The Bible tells us that man will keep hardening his heart to God. Many will refuse God's grace and face the Tribulation.

"For by grace, you have been saved through faith. And this is not your own doing; it is the gift of God, not a result of works, so that no one may boast." (Ephesians 2:8-9)

There is no doubt that some great scholars have strong disagreements about what the correct interpretation of Revelation is. However, Christ is coming. Remember what Jesus said in the Parable of the Ten Virgins:

Revelation: A Line by Line Breakdown

"Then the kingdom of heaven will be like ten virgins who took their lamps and went to meet the bridegroom. Five of them were foolish, and five were wise. For when the foolish took their lamps, they took no oil with them, but the wise took flasks of oil with their lamps. As the bridegroom was delayed, they all became drowsy and slept. But at midnight there was a cry, 'Here is the bridegroom! Come out to meet him.' Then all those virgins rose and trimmed their lamps. And the foolish said to the wise, 'Give us some of your oil, for our lamps are going out.' But the wise answered, saying, 'Since there will not be enough for us and for you, go rather to the dealers and buy for yourselves.' And while they were going to buy, the bridegroom came, and those who were ready went in with him to the marriage feast, and the door was shut. Afterward the other virgins came also, saying, 'Lord, lord, open to us.' But he answered, 'Truly, I say to you, I do not know you.' Watch, therefore, for you know neither the day nor the hour. (Matthew 25:1-13)

Some say Revelation already happened; this is ill-advised thinking. Bible prophecy is God's Word. It is 100% accurate. If things were just examples of events that already happened, they wouldn't be prophecies. *The Book of Isaiah* was written about 800 years before Christ, and Isaiah chapter 53 perfectly describes Jesus. If you don't remember or know it, read it.

Jesus talks of the end times in several places in the New Testament, and many are quoted here. Are we saying Jesus is incorrect? NO! God is always right! So, what does Jesus mean when He speaks of the Rapture as literal and says:

"Then two men will be in the field; one will be taken and one left. Two women will be grinding at the mill; one will be taken and one left. Therefore, stay awake, for you do not know on what day your Lord is coming. But know this, that if the master of the house had known in what part of the night the thief was coming, he would

have stayed awake and would not have let his house be broken into. Therefore you also must be ready, for the Son of Man is coming at an hour you do not expect." (Matthew 24:38-44)

"Behold! I tell you a mystery. We shall not all sleep (die), but we shall all be changed" (1 Corinthians 15:51)

Revelation was written about AD 95 as most biblical scholars date the book. Documents by the early church fathers all fix the date as the mid-90s, in the latter part of Emperor Domitian's reign (AD 81-96). The unanimous teachings of early church fathers, like Polycarp, Ireneaeus, Clement of Alexandria, Origen, Victorinus, Jerome, and Eusebius, all fix the date as the mid-90s. Some mislead people by saying Revelation happened in AD 70 Nero as the Antichrist. However, Domitian was Emperor of Rome long after Nero's (AD 54-68) reign. Nero committed suicide in AD 68 before the destruction of Israel in AD 70.

Some believe all the prophecies about the *End Times* in the Old and New Testament, including everything in Revelation and *The Mount of Olives Disclosure,* are history. They state Revelation is not a prophecy but a history. This encourages Christians to ignore the Bible prophecy being fulfilled today. They teach that the *Book of Revelation* and *The Mount of Olives Disclosure* all took place in the first century. The Tribulation already happened in AD 70. None of this is backed by Scripture, history, or what is written in any Biblical prophecy. Believe what Jesus says in his Revelation to John. Hold close to the words of the opening of Revelation, which says:

"<u>The revelation of Jesus Christ</u>, which God gave him to show to his servants the <u>things that must soon take place</u>. <u>He made it known by sending his angel</u> to his servant John, who bore witness <u>to the word of God and to the testimony of Jesus Christ</u>, even to all that he saw. Blessed is the one who reads aloud <u>the words of this</u>

prophecy, and <u>blessed are those who</u> hear, and who <u>keep what is written in it</u>, for the time is near. (Revelation 1:1-3)

If you believe and understand the things shared with you here and grasp the fact that these things are categorically and literally going to happen, it is easy to see why one may be filled with dread. Revelation tells us that things will get really bad in the Tribulation. However, Revelation also tells us there is hope.

If you believe the Lord Jesus Christ is your savior, you are under His protection. He will remove (Rapture) His church before the Tribulation. No believer has to fear the Tribulation. If it takes the Rapture to make you a believer, remember you are still under God's protection during the Tribulation, but you will face many trials, even death. You are protected because God has always protected His people.

If you don't belong to Christ, there is no hope for you when God's judgments hits everyone on earth, as described in *The Book of Revelation*. And if you die before accepting Christ as your Savior, then your name will not be found in the *Book of Life*; you will spend eternity separated from God. However, there is good news for those who are not believers in Christ. Jesus has taken my broken and sinful self and made me whole forgiving me by his sacrifice and grace.

⁴But God, being rich in mercy, because of the great love with which he loved us,⁵even when we were dead in our trespasses, made us alive together with Christ-by grace you have been saved ⁶and raised us up with him and seated us with him in the heavenly places in Christ Jesus, ⁷so that in the coming ages he might show the immeasurable riches of his grace in kindness toward us in Christ Jesus. ⁸ For by grace, you have been saved through faith. And this is not your own doing; it is the gift of God, ⁹not a result of works, so that no one may boast. ¹⁰ For we are his

workmanship, created in Christ Jesus for good works, which God prepared beforehand, that we should walk in them.
(Ephesians 2:4-10)

So, how does one become a follower of Jesus? It's a leap of faith. The Scriptures say we must commit our lives to Jesus as our Lord and Savior. When we give our lives to Jesus, He forgives our sins and gives us eternal life.

"For God so loved the world, that he gave his only Son, that whoever believes in him should not perish but have eternal life. For God did not send his Son into the world to condemn the world, but in order that the world might be saved through him. Whoever believes in him is not condemned, but whoever does not believe is condemned already, because he has not believed in the name of the only Son of God." (John 3:16-18)

Deliverance from sin and death is possible through the sacrifice of Jesus as a sacrificial lamb for all who believe in him. This is a **FREE GIFT** from God. However, many say one must earn their way to heaven. To benefit from the sacrifice of Jesus, people not only must exercise faith in Jesus but must get baptized as a sign that they follow Jesus. However, those who say only a person's works or actions prove their faith, go against Scripture.

[8] For by grace, you have been saved through faith. And this is not your own doing; it is the gift of God, [9] not a result of works, so that no one may boast. [10] For we are his workmanship, created in Christ Jesus for good works, which God prepared beforehand, that we should walk in them." (Ephesians 2:8-10)

Whoever believes and is baptized will be saved, but whoever does not believe will be condemned. (Mark 16:16)

If you want Christ in your life, tell Him. God is not concerned with what words you use, only that your heart is in the right place and that you have faith in Jesus. All you have to do is ask Jesus to forgive your sins and have Him take control of your life. Then, your journey in Christ begins. Study His word and find others to have fellowship with. Faith is the key; from it, we learn to believe the promises of God and his prophecies.

Baptism and Holy Communion are two visible expressions of God's salvation. They are not something we do for God's salvation but something we do because of what God has done for us. The Lord commanded that we remember His salvation through practicing these sacraments until the end of the world. First, we believe in Christ, and then we get baptized as a sign of faith or a sign of a covenant with Jesus as one of his followers. We take the Lord's supper as a remembrance of what Christ did for us. Both are vital signs of life within the church. The Scriptures do not say that baptism is necessary for salvation. Nothing is necessary for salvation apart from repentance and faith in Jesus Christ.

"For by grace you have been saved through faith. And this is not your own doing; it is the gift of God, not a result of works, so that no one may boast." (Ephesians 2:8-9)

We were buried therefore with him by baptism into death, in order that, just as Christ was raised from the dead by the glory of the Father, we too might walk in newness of life. (Romans 6:4)

[26]Now as they were eating, Jesus took bread, and after blessing it broke it and gave it to the disciples, and said, "Take, eat; this is my body." [27]And he took a cup, and when he had given thanks he gave it to them, saying, "Drink of it, all of you, [28]for this is my blood of the covenant, which is poured out for many for the forgiveness of sins. [29] I tell you I will not drink again of this fruit of

the vine until that day when I drink it new with you in my Father's kingdom." (Matthew 26:26-29)

Here are a few things the Bible declares come through faith:

- ❖ We are born into eternal life through faith.
- ❖ We are declared righteous before God by faith.
- ❖ We are forgiven by faith.
- ❖ We understand God's word by faith.
- ❖ By faith, we understand things to come (prophecy)
- ❖ We are controlled and empowered by the Holy Spirit by faith

In closing, be honest with yourself about this study of *The Book of Revelation*. Look into the Word of God, and let the Holy Spirit guide you. Remember, the key point is Jesus Christ is Returning. Also, it's a warning of the End Times for those who do not have Christ in their life and a hope for those who are Christians. Study God's word. Prophecy scholars point to Acts 17:10-13 saying that studying this pertains to false teachings, as the Post and A-Millennialists and practitioners of Preterism and Replacement Theology layout. As stated in the Book of Acts:

[10] The brothers immediately sent Paul and Silas away by night to Berea, and when they arrived they went into the Jewish synagogue. [11]Now, these Jews were more noble than those in Thessalonica; they received the word with all eagerness, examining the Scriptures daily to see if these things were so. [12] Many of them therefore believed, with not a few Greek women of high standing as well as men. [13] But when the Jews from Thessalonica learned that the word of God was proclaimed by Paul at Berea also, they came there too, agitating and stirring up the crowds." (Acts17:10-13).

¹⁸ *I warn everyone who hears the words of the prophecy of this book: if anyone adds to them, God will add to him the plagues described in this book,* ¹⁹ *and if anyone takes away from the words of the book of this prophecy, God will take away his share in the tree of life and in the holy city, which are described in this book.* (Revelation 22:18,19)

²¹ *"Not everyone who says to me, 'Lord, Lord,' will enter the kingdom of heaven, but the one who does the will of my Father who is in heaven.* ²² *On that day many will say to me, 'Lord, Lord, did we not prophesy in your name, and cast out demons in your name, and do many mighty works in your name?'* ²³ *And then will I declare to them, 'I never knew you; depart from me, you workers of lawlessness.* (Matthew 7:21-23)

²⁸ *Pay careful attention to yourselves and to all the flock, in which the Holy Spirit has made you overseers, to care for the church of God, which he obtained with his own blood.* ²⁹ *I know that after my departure fierce wolves will come in among you, not sparing the flock;* ³⁰ *and from among your own selves will arise men speaking twisted things, to draw away the disciples after them.* (Acts 20:28-30)

"See that no one leads you astray. For many will come in my name, saying, 'I am the Christ,' and they will lead many astray." (Matthew 24:4-5)

"And if those days had not been cut short, no human being would be saved. But for the sake of the elect those days will be cut short. Then if anyone says to you, 'Look, here is the Christ!' or 'There he is!' do not believe it. For false christs and false prophets will arise and perform great signs and wonders, so as to lead astray, if possible, even the elect. See, I have told you beforehand. So, if they say to you, 'Look, he is in the wilderness,' do not go out. If

they say, 'Look, he is in the inner rooms,' do not believe it. For as the lightning comes from the east and shines as far as the west, so will be the coming of the Son of Man Scripture has several warnings against false prophets and teachers. Jesus himself warned of this." (Matthew 24:23-27)

The Book of Revelation should be taken literally of things to come. The key point is Jesus Christ is returning to set up his Kingdom on earth, and unbelievers will be judged. His return has nothing to do with anyone having faith in Him. Jesus will return because it is a sovereign act of God. No matter if you believe in God. Whether you believe the *Book of Revelation* and *the Mount of Olives Disclosure* are history or prophecy. If you believe in the Rapture or not, **THESE THINGS WILL HAPPEN**. These are sovereign acts of God, not dependent on faith.

Some conclusions that we can make from this study is: Israel will return to the promised land, and the prophecy was fulfilled in 1948. Jesus Christ will return to rapture His church before the Tribulation. There will be a rebuilding of the Temple in Jerusalem. The rise of a literal Antichrist and False Prophet who will launch the battle of Armageddon. This will be followed by Jesus' return to earth (the Second Coming) to set up a literal 1000-year kingdom.

We study God's Word to better understand His plan. We have to trust the Holy Spirit to lead us to know Him and His Word. John Milton put it this way: *"When we speak of knowing God, it must be understood with reference to man's limited powers of comprehension. God, as He really is, is far beyond man's imagination, let alone understanding. God has revealed only so much of Himself as our minds can conceive and the weakness of our nature can bear."*

[18] And Jesus came and said to them, "All authority in heaven and on earth has been given to me. [19] Go therefore and make disciples

of all nations, baptizing them in the name of the Father and of the Son and of the Holy Spirit, [20] teaching them to observe all that I have commanded you. And behold, I am with you always, to the end of the age." (Matthew 28:18-20)

As you study God's Word, remember the word **BREAD**.

BE STILL—Find a quiet space where you can be still and silent. Pray and ask God to speak to you, and let His Spirit guide you as you study His Word. Then...
READ - You might start by reading one chapter a day. If you are new to reading the Bible start in John. If you have read John, read Ephesians next. Read one chapter or one paragraph. And maybe write down what you see in the text. What questions do you have? What stands out? Then...
EXAMINE – What is going on in the text? Who wrote it? Why were they writing? And this is where a study Bible would be helpful.
APPLY – What is God asking you to know, or do in response? Then DO that. Is there a sin you need to confess? Is there an action you need to take? A command to obey? Then finally...
DEVOTE TO PRAYER – Ask God to do what he can to transform your life.

(From Clear Creek Community Church, League City, Texas)

BONUS STUDY ON THE MOUNT OF OLIVES DISCLOSURE

Introduction To The Mount of Olives Disclosure

The Mount of Olives Disclosure is called that because it happened on the Mount of Olives. It is a crucial *End Times* prophecy given directly by Jesus just a few days before He was crucified. Jesus was teaching His disciples from the Mount of Olives just outside Jerusalem. The circumstances for this prophecy are set in Matthew chapter 23. Jesus was leaving the temple after giving a pronouncement of judgment upon the nation of Israel and its religious leaders for their long history of unbelief in the prophets. This ended in their rejection of Him as the Messiah.

[27] Woe to you, scribes and Pharisees, hypocrites! For you are like whitewashed tombs, which outwardly appear beautiful, but within are full of dead people's bones and all uncleanness. [28] So you also outwardly appear righteous to others, but within you are full of hypocrisy and lawlessness. [29] Woe to you, scribes and Pharisees, hypocrites! For you build the tombs of the prophets and decorate the monuments of the righteous, [30] saying, "If we had lived in the days of our fathers, we would not have taken part with them in shedding the blood of the prophets." [31] Thus you witness against yourselves that you are sons of those who murdered the prophets. [32] Fill up, then, the measure of your fathers. [33] You serpents, you brood of vipers, how are you to escape being sentenced to hell? [34] Therefore I send you prophets and wise men and scribes, some of whom you will kill and crucify, and some you will flog in your synagogues and persecute from town to town, [35] so that on you may come all the righteous blood shed on earth, from the blood of innocent Abel to the blood of Zechariah the son of Barachiah, whom you murdered between the sanctuary and

the altar. ³⁶ Truly, I say to you, all these things will come upon this generation. Lament over Jerusalem ³⁷ O Jerusalem, Jerusalem, the city that kills the prophets and stones those who are sent to it! How often would I have gathered your children together as a hen gathers her brood under her wings, and you would not! ³⁸ See, your house is left to you desolate. ³⁹ For I tell you, you will not see me again, until you say, "Blessed is he who comes in the name of the Lord." (Matthew 23:27-39)

The Mount of Olives Disclosure is principally in Matthew chapters 24 and 25. However, it is also found in Mark 13, Luke 17, and 21. It is one of the most essential texts in the Bible because it provides Jesus' final address and His most extensive prophetic teaching. When taken with *The Book of Revelation,* we have some of the most in-depth prophecies on the *End Times*.

In the *Mount Olivet Discourse,* Jesus clarifies many Old Testament prophetic passages concerning Israel and the nations of the world. It serves as an inspired essential outline of end-time events. Furthermore, it explains God's final judgment on Israel and unbelievers called the *Tribulation*. It covers the last days of Satan, His promised restoration of the earth, and the establishment of His Kingdom at His Second Coming. It also tells of the events that describe the time immediately before Jesus' Second Coming.

Confusion about the Olivet Discourse has resulted from a failure to recognize that the Olivet Discourse involves Israel, not the church, and refers to the future Tribulation or God's judgments. This is because of a school of thought called *Replacement Theology or Supersessionism.* It claims that the Church has replaced Israel in God's plan, and the Church fulfills the promises and covenants God made to Israel. Replacement Theology is not based on any Scriptures or literal interpretation of the Bible. Additionally, it calls God a liar, which He can **NEVER BE**.

Jesus Himself said: *"¹⁷ **Do not think that I have come to abolish the Law or the Prophets; I have not come to abolish them but to fulfill them.** ¹⁸ **For truly, I say to you, until heaven and earth pass away, not an iota, not a dot, will pass from the Law until all is accomplished.**"* (Matthew 5:17-18)

"I ask, then, has God rejected his people? By no means! For I myself am an Israelite, a descendant of Abraham, a member of the tribe of Benjamin." (Romans 11:1)

For the gifts and the calling of God (promises and covenants) *are irrevocable.* (Romans 11:29)

Rome destroyed Israel in AD 70, and God brought it back as a nation in 1948. John, who wrote The Book of Revelation, knew that in God's plan, the Jews would return to the Promised Land as a nation. This makes 1948 significant from a prophetic understanding and destroys everything Replacement Theology tries to embody.

"And I will multiply people on you, the whole house of Israel, all of it. The cities shall be inhabited and the waste places rebuilt." (Ezekiel 36:10).

This prophecy did not find fulfillment until 1948. Ezekiel was written in 700 BC, and God knew that in AD 70, Israel would be destroyed and the people dispersed. He knew that in 1948, Israel would become a nation again. Ezekiel speaks of a future redemption, a restored Jerusalem, and a worldwide recognition of God and His Messiah.

Due to God's faithfulness to His Word through His covenants with Israel, He revived His people once more. He will always protect them. Israel will overwhelm all the forces and powers arrayed against them. Ezekiel's prophecy was fulfilled when

Israel was restored as a nation physically on the land God gave them at the time of Moses.

"Then he said to me, Son of man, these bones are the whole house of Israel. Behold, they say, Our bones are dried up, and our hope is lost; we are indeed cut off." (Ezekiel 37:11)

When Ezekiel uses the term *"they say"* in this verse, it is comparable to what the Replacement Theology practitioners teach. They say or teach that the Nation of Israel was finished in AD 70 and had no future as a distinct people or nation. However, God identifies the bones in Ezekiel as representing *"the whole house of Israel."* This prophecy is factually predicting the restoration and spiritual rebirth of the whole nation of Israel. The prophecy was fulfilled in 1948.

Replacement Theology means that the Christian church has replaced Israel in God's plan for mankind because the Jews rejected Jesus Christ as their Messiah. Because of this, Israel forfeited any claim to the covenants or Sovereign promises made to Abraham, Isaac, and Jacob, called the *Abrahamic Covenant* (Genesis 12, 13, 15, 17). As well as all covenants or Sovereign promises made to Moses in the *Land Covenant* (Deuteronomy 29, 30). Israel forfeited any claim to all covenants to David in the *Davidic Covenant* (2 Samuel 7). Moreover, all covenants made to Jeremiah in the *New Covenant* (Jeremiah 31). Thus making most of the Old Testament invalid and useless AND calling God a liar. Do not believe those who say Israel is dead. God knew there would be deceivers trying to change His words and prophecies. He knew there would be Replacement Theology practitioners.

"For the gifts and the calling of God (promises and covenants) ***are irrevocable."*** (Romans 11:29)

"Now the LORD said to Abram, Go from your country and your kindred and your father's house to the land that I will show you. And I will make of you a great nation, and I will bless you and make your name great, so that you will be a blessing. I will bless those who bless you, and him who dishonors you I will curse, and in you all the families of the earth shall be blessed."
(Genesis 12:1-3).

[17] For behold, I create new heavens and a new earth, and the former things shall not be remembered or come into mind. [18] But be glad and rejoice forever in that which I create; for behold, I create Jerusalem to be a joy, and her people to be a gladness.
(Isaiah 65:17,18)

[10] And he carried me away in the Spirit to a great, high mountain, and showed me the holy city Jerusalem coming down out of heaven from God, [11] having the glory of God, its radiance like a most rare jewel, like a jasper, clear as crystal. [12] It had a great, high wall, with twelve gates, and at the gates twelve angels, and on the gates the names of the twelve tribes of the sons of Israel were inscribed [13] on the east three gates, on the north three gates, on the south three gates, and on the west three gates. [14] And the wall of the city had twelve foundations, and on them were the twelve names of the twelve apostles of the Lamb."
(Revelation 21:10-14)

The misguided thinking of those who believe the deception of Replacement Theology contends that the church has not actually replaced Israel but rather that the church is simply the True Israel. All the promises made to Israel in the Old Testament were intended to be spiritually fulfilled by the church rather than literally by the Jews. However, God made unconditional and eternal covenants with His people, Israel. Was God Lying? **NEVER!**

Now, let us break down The Mount of Olives Disclosure. I take writing about the Scriptures very seriously, as I have now taken on the role of a teacher by writing about Biblical studies.

"Not many of you should become teachers, my brothers, for you know that we who teach will be judged with greater strictness." (James 3:1).

First, see what Jesus warned us to watch for concerning the coming *End Times*.

³ As he sat on the Mount of Olives, the disciples came to him privately, saying, "Tell us, when will these things be, and what will be the sign of your coming and of the close of the age?" ⁴ And Jesus answered them, "See that no one leads you astray. ⁵ For many will come in my name, saying, 'I am the Christ,' and they will lead many astray." (Matthew 24:3-5)

²³ Then if anyone says to you, 'Look, here is the Christ!' or 'There he is!' do not believe it. ²⁴ For false christs and false prophets will arise and perform great signs and wonders, so as to lead astray, if possible, even the elect. ²⁵ See, I have told you beforehand. (Matthew 24:23-25)

The only way to be sure no one deceives you is to know what God's Word says. Study the Bible. Ignorance of the Bible is what leads to deception. Deception is not telling an entire lie. It is a lie mixed with the truth. It begins with a truth, and then a lie is inserted so that the entire story sounds truthful. This makes it difficult for some to discern what is the truth and what is a lie. Thus, people fall for the lie and are deceived. The lie is spread after the deception is told because people think it is the truth. This is why we must stay knowledgeable of God's Word.

²¹"Not everyone who says to me, 'Lord, Lord,' will enter the kingdom of heaven, but the one who does the will of my Father who is in heaven. ²² On that day many will say to me, 'Lord, Lord, did we not prophesy in your name, and cast out demons in your name, and do many mighty works in your name?' ²³ And then will I declare to them, 'I never knew you; depart from me, you workers of lawlessness. (Matthew 7:21-23)

²⁸ Pay careful attention to yourselves and to all the flock, in which the Holy Spirit has made you overseers, to care for the church of God, which he obtained with his own blood. ²⁹ I know that after my departure fierce wolves will come in among you, not sparing the flock; ³⁰ and from among your own selves will arise men speaking twisted things, to draw away the disciples after them. (Acts 20:28-30)

We all should accept the word of God as written. Also, we need the guidance of the Holy Spirit. As the *End Times* grows closer, the understanding of *End Times* prophecies, which the *Mount of Olives Disclosure* and the *Book of Revelation* are, will get clearer. Jesus called these events just before the Tribulation and His Second Advent *"birth pains"* and *"signs of the times."* Are we entering that time? Many say **YES**. Some of these signs are recorded in 2 Timothy 3:1-8.

¹ But understand this, that in the last days there will come times of difficulty. ² For people will be lovers of self, lovers of money, proud, arrogant, abusive, disobedient to their parents, ungrateful, unholy, ³ heartless, unappeasable, slanderous, without self-control, brutal, not loving good, ⁴ treacherous, reckless, swollen with conceit, lovers of pleasure rather than lovers of God, ⁵ having the appearance of godliness, but denying its power. Avoid such people. ⁶ For among them are those who creep into households and capture weak women, burdened with sins and led astray by various passions, ⁷ always learning and never able to arrive at a knowledge of the truth. ⁸ Just as Jannes and Jambres opposed Moses, so these men also oppose the truth, men corrupted in mind and disqualified regarding the faith. (2 Timothy 3:1-8)

² For you yourselves are fully aware that the day of the Lord will come like a thief in the night. ³ While people are saying, "There is peace and security," then sudden destruction will come upon them as labor pains come upon a pregnant woman, and they will not escape. (1 Thessalonians 5:2-3)

Look around. Is this what is going on now? Is this prophecy of the last days being fulfilled? Are these signs of the times and birth pains happening now? Be honest with yourself, and compare what is happening in our time with what is recorded in 2 Timothy 3:1-8.

The Mount of Olives Disclosure and *The Book of Revelation* should be taken literally of things to come. Jesus Christ is returning to set up his earthly Kingdom, and the Tribulation will happen. Unbelievers will be judged. Jesus' return has nothing to do with anyone having faith in Him. Jesus will return because it is a sovereign act of God. No matter if you believe in God or His written Word. No matter if you believe the *Mount of Olives Disclosure* and the *Book of Revelation* are history or prophecy. No matter if you believe in the Rapture or not. **ALL THESE THINGS WILL HAPPEN**. These are sovereign acts of God not reliant on faith.

¹⁶ For we did not follow cleverly devised myths when we made known to you the power and coming of our Lord Jesus Christ, but we were eyewitnesses of his majesty. ¹⁷ For when he received honor and glory from God the Father, and the voice was borne to him by the Majestic Glory, "This is my beloved Son, with whom I am well pleased," ¹⁸ we ourselves heard this very voice borne from heaven, for we were with him on the holy mountain. [19] And we have something more sure, the prophetic word, to which you will do well to pay attention as to a lamp shining in a dark place, until the day dawns and the morning star rises in your hearts, [20]knowing this first of all, that no prophecy of Scripture comes from someone's own interpretation. [21] For no prophecy was ever produced by the will of man, but men spoke from God as they were carried along by the Holy Spirit. (2 Peter 1:16-21)

When studying prophecy, it is always best to use a literal approach. This means taking the text as used, not in a nonliteral or allegorical sense. Another way to define the literal meaning of Scripture is how it will hold in the everyday, common understanding of the terms. Words in Scripture should be given the meaning they usually have in everyday speech.

Remember that one passage may apply to more than one event. Prophetic Scripture may refer to two events separated by a significant period. These two events are found in the same passage but have different meanings in time, as in the prophecy on Jesus's first and second Advents.

As with history, to study Scripture, one must step out of modern times and become as if living in the time being studied. The Bible is set in ancient Israel, with Jewish customs. Also, some Roman customs and laws exist in the New Testament. Study those periods in history and learn the time's customs.

Pay close attention to context. Every word in the Bible is part of a sentence, every sentence is part of a paragraph, and every paragraph is part of a book. Books make up the Bible. Remember, when studying the Word of God, looking at the line before and after a noted verse or reading the whole paragraph or book to understand the meaning entirely is best. This prevents misinterpretation based on text out of context, often used to cause deception. Taking a verse out of context may give it a different meaning not intended. Remember also that Scripture interrupts Scripture.

The Mount of Olives Disclosure - Matthew 24

"Jesus left the temple and was going away, when his disciples came to point out to him the buildings of the temple." (Matthew 24:1)

As Jesus and the disciples left the temple, the disciples were awestruck by the temple's magnificence. It had become a source of Israeli pride. King Herod invested vast amounts of money into the temple to persuade the Jews to support him. The Jews hated Herod because he was a puppet administrator put in his position by the Romans. They hated Herod but loved the temple. Perhaps the disciples thought that the temple was invincible. Jesus' unexpected reply was that all the buildings they had shown Him would be torn down.

But he answered them, "You see all these, do you not? Truly, I say to you, there will not be left here one stone upon another that will not be thrown down." (Matthew 24:2)

No doubt, as the disciples thought on these words, they concluded that Jesus meant the final attack on Jerusalem that Zechariah predicted would come at the end of the age—the time when God will destroy the Gentile nations and establish Messianic rule, the Millennial Kingdom. The disciples believed these events were already in motion and would soon climax with Jesus' public disclosure and reign as Messiah.

[3] Then the LORD will go out and fight against those nations as when he fights on a day of battle. [4] On that day his feet shall stand on the Mount of Olives that lies before Jerusalem on the east, and

the Mount of Olives shall be split in two from east to west by a very wide valley, so that one-half of the Mount shall move northward, and the other half southward. [5] And you shall flee to the valley of my mountains, for the valley of the mountains shall reach to Azal. And you shall flee as you fled from the earthquake in the days of Uzziah king of Judah. Then the LORD my God will come, and all the holy ones with him. [6] On that day there shall be no light, cold, or frost. [7] And there shall be a unique day, which is known to the LORD, neither day nor night, but at evening time there shall be light. [8] On that day living waters shall flow out from Jerusalem, half of them to the eastern sea and half of them to the western sea. It shall continue in summer as in winter. [9] And the LORD will be king over all the earth. On that day the LORD will be one and his name one. (Zechariah 14:3–9).

However, as they walked with Jesus up the Mount of Olives, the disciples wanted clarification, especially concerning the issue of the Temple's destruction and Jesus' timetable for these events. Jesus responded by saying take a last look. This beautiful temple will be torn down. The disciples must have been excited to hear that. Why?

Because they knew the prophecies concerning the coming Messiah, they thought they were ending the 483 years from the Book of Daniel. They thought Jesus' First Coming and his Second Coming were in the same generation. They did not choose to remember one passage of prophecy that may apply to more than one event.

"As he sat on the Mount of Olives, the disciples came to him privately, saying, "Tell us, when will these things be, and what will be the sign of your coming and of the close of the age?"
(Matthew 24:3)

Disciples Three Questions

They are not asking Him, *"How will we know the End Times are here?"* The disciples are asking Jesus three questions in this verse:
1. What will be the sign of the end of the age?
2. What will be the sign of your coming?
3. When shall these things be?

Question 1: What will be the sign of the end of the age?

For the question, what will be the sign of the end of the age? We will look at Luke 21:20-28:

[20]"But when you see Jerusalem surrounded by armies, then know that its desolation has come near. [21] Then let those who are in Judea flee to the mountains, and let those who are inside the city depart, and let not those who are out in the country enter it, [22] for these are days of vengeance, to fulfill all that is written. [23] Alas for women who are pregnant and for those who are nursing infants in those days! For there will be great distress upon the earth and wrath against this people. [24] They will fall by the edge of the sword and be led captive among all nations, and Jerusalem will be trampled underfoot by the Gentiles, until the times of the Gentiles are fulfilled. The Coming of the Son of Man [25] And there will be signs in sun and moon and stars, and on the earth distress of nations in perplexity because of the roaring of the sea and the waves, [26] people fainting with fear and with foreboding of what is coming on the world. For the powers of the heavens will be shaken. [27] And then they will see the Son of Man coming in a cloud with power and great glory. [28] Now when these things begin to take place, straighten up and raise your heads, because your redemption is drawing near. (Luke 21:20-28)

In Luke 21:20, when Jesus said, "you," he was addressing the disciples. This is another reason practitioners of preterism theology want us to believe that the Olivet Discourse and Revelation are history, not prophecy. Preterism Theology teaches that all the Biblical prophecies, including the Olivet Discourse and the Book of Revelation, occurred in the first century. This means both are history, NOT prophecy. They do not believe Luke 21:21-28 applies to two different times. However, only verse 24 applies to the disciples' time.

²⁴ They will fall by the edge of the sword and be led captive among all nations, and Jerusalem will be trampled underfoot by the Gentiles, until the times of the Gentiles are fulfilled. The Coming of the Son of Man. (Luke 21:24)

Jesus told his disciples that Jerusalem would be invaded and destroyed in their lifetime. They should watch for Jerusalem to be surrounded by armies in their generation. However, this also applies to the End Times, Armageddon at the end of the age. All of this was predicted in the book of Daniel when Jerusalem would again be surrounded by armies just before Jesus' return.

In AD 70, the armies of Rome, under Roman general Titus, surrounded Jerusalem. The first thing he did was cut off all supplies to the city. No food, no water. Nothing got into Jerusalem while it was under siege by the Romans. The strategy of a siege is to weaken the enemy so they will lose their will to fight, even turn on each other. The Jews were no different from anyone else under siege. Inside the walls of Jerusalem, some of the most dreadful things took place. The people were starving, so their primary priority was not to starve to death. Children were no longer precious, but someone's next meal.

Roman-Jewish historian Flavius Josephus, who was there, recorded the siege events. He was a general in the Jewish army in Galilee until surrendering in AD 67 to the Roman army. Josephus entirely changed sides to the Romans and was given full Roman citizenship. He became a consultant and friend to Titus, serving as his translator when Titus led the siege of Jerusalem in AD 70. His records are considered some of the best history of the time. His works provide a valuable understanding of first-century Judaism and early Christianity. Josephus's writings are considered one the chief sources of the History of that time next to the Bible.

Josephus records that not only were the people inside Jerusalem eating their children, but the bodies of anyone who died, dogs, horses, rats, and anything they thought was eatable. This famous Roman historian as well as others recorded how desperate the situation was. After the Jews had become too weak to defend themselves, the Roman army entered the city and slew almost anyone they saw. The survivors who were taken captive were scattered throughout the Empire, the known world. Throughout the ages God has always left a remnant of His people on the promised land, the same happened here.

Jesus, acting as a prophet, was telling His disciples to flee Jerusalem when they saw armies begin to surround the city. Other Jews also knew this, trusting Daniel's prophecy. They fled when they saw the Romans building up armies around the city. When the Romans sacked Jerusalem and destroyed the temple, the fires melted the gold inside. It flowed down into the cracks of the temple floor. The Romans had to use pry bars to pry apart the temple to get at the gold. All of this was prophesized by Jesus and is recorded in history by Josephus.

This fulfilled Jesus' prophecy: *"You see all these, do you not? Truly, I say to you, there will not be left here one stone upon another that will not be thrown down."* (Matthew 24:2)

Again, Luke 21:24 says, [24]*They will fall by the edge of the sword and be led captive among all nations, and Jerusalem will be trampled underfoot by the Gentiles, until the times of the Gentiles are fulfilled.* The Gentiles referred to in the verse are the Romans, who in AD 70 destroyed Jerusalem and the entire temple. The Jews were either slain or led as captives all around the empire. Very few were left in Jerusalem and Israel.

The last part of the verse, *"until the times of the Gentiles are fulfilled,"* refers to two things. First is the Church Age which at this time was still a mystery. The Gentiles will control Jerusalem until the fulfillment of Christ's Church mission, *The Great Commission*. Second, once the times of the Gentiles, or the Church Age, are fulfilled, Jesus will return.

[18]And Jesus came and said to them, "All authority in heaven and on earth has been given to me. [19]Go therefore and make disciples of all nations, baptizing them in the name of the Father and of the Son and of the Holy Spirit, [20]teaching them to observe all that I have commanded you. And behold, I am with you always, to the end of the age." (Matthew 28:18-20)

How do we know when *the times of the Gentiles are fulfilled*? When is the end of the Church Age? Several prophecies are being fulfilled today in our lifetime. The Romans destroyed Israel in AD 70, and the people dispersed throughout the world. Those who fled Jerusalem before the siege also scattered around the world. Israel was destroyed; thus, they had no home. Israel returned to the Promised Land as a country in 1948 as was foretold in prophecy (see Ezekiel chapter 37). Prophecy fulfilled!

[11]Then he said to me, "Son of man, these bones are the whole house of Israel. Behold, they say, 'Our bones are dried up, and our hope is lost; we are indeed cut off.' [12]Therefore prophesy, and say to them, Thus says the Lord GOD: Behold, I will open your graves and raise you from your graves, O my people. And I will bring you into the land of Israel. (Ezekiel 37:11,12)

You should read all of Ezekiel's Chapters 36 and 37. These prophesies are key prophecies about the end times. No one other than God's power could have given life back to Israel. Ezekiel speaks of dry bones, representing Israel, receiving skin and flesh; the wind was told to blow upon them to restore them to life by the power of God. The wind is the sign of the Holy Spirit. This prophecy concerns Israel's restoration from their long-continued scattering over the centuries. It tells the Jews to look to Him (the Messiah), who will at last open graves, bringing people to judgment. The Messiah will deliver anyone from sin if they believe in Him. God will place his Spirit within us.

"For by grace, you have been saved through faith. And this is not your own doing; it is the gift of God, not a result of works, so that no one may boast." (Ephesians 2:8-9)

When John wrote the Book of Revelation in AD 95, Rome had already destroyed Israel. John knew it, he saw it, and he lived through it. However, John knew that in God's plan, the Jews must return as a nation to the Promised Land before Jesus' Second Coming. This did not happen until 1948. Per prophecy, Israel must be a viable political entity in the *End Times*, which it was not in AD 70. This makes the year 1948 significant from a prophetic understanding. There will also be a rebuilding of the Jewish Temple that will exist during the Tribulation period. This has not happened yet. Many believe this will happen after the Rapture.

Ancient Israel had been captured and put in bondage before. However, only to single nations, such as the Egyptians, the Assyrians, the Babylonians, and Persia. In each case, God delivered them. However, never in biblical history had the Israelites been delivered from all over the world for centuries. They were brought back together by the power of God in 1948. All of this was foretold in Ezekiel's prophecy and others.

⁶⁴And the LORD will scatter you among all peoples, from one end of the earth to the other, and there you shall serve other gods of wood and stone, which neither you nor your fathers have known. ⁶⁵And among these nations you shall find no respite, and there shall be no resting place for the sole of your foot, but the LORD will give you there a trembling heart and failing eyes and a languishing soul. ⁶⁶ Your life shall hang in doubt before you. Night and day you shall be in dread and have no assurance of your life. ⁶⁷ In the morning you shall say, 'If only it were evening!' and at evening you shall say, 'If only it were morning!' because of the dread that your heart shall feel, and the sights that your eyes shall see (Deuteronomy 28:64-67)

¹ And when all these things come upon you, the blessing and the curse, which I have set before you, and you call them to mind among all the nations where the LORD your God has driven you, ²and return to the LORD your God, you and your children, and obey his voice in all that I command you today, with all your heart and with all your soul, ³ then the LORD your God will restore your fortunes and have compassion on you, and he will gather you again from all the peoples where the LORD your God has scattered you (Deuteronomy 30:1-3)

As prophesized, God's program of restoring Israel was fulfilled in 1948, setting the stage for the future Tribulation and Christ's return. This one event disproves Replacement Theology.

- **1948**: Israel becomes a nation after being destroyed in AD 70. Prophecy fulfilled. *"I will take you from the nations and gather you from all the countries and bring you into your land."* (Ezekiel 36:24)
- **1967**: Israel captured Jerusalem and the West Bank during the Six-Day War after an Arab invasion of the new state of Israel. Prophecy fulfilled.

- **2017**: The US officially recognized Jerusalem as Israel's capital by President Donald Trump and opened the US Embassy there. Prophecy fulfilled.

Question 2: What Will Be The Sign of Your Coming?

The coming the disciples are referring to is Jesus' Second Coming. They did not know about the church age, it was still a mystery.

⁶ And you will hear of wars and rumors of wars. See that you are not alarmed, for this must take place, but the end is not yet. ⁷ For nation will rise against nation, and kingdom against kingdom, and there will be famines and earthquakes in various places. ⁸ All these are but the beginning of the birth pains. ⁹ "Then they will deliver you up to tribulation and put you to death, and you will be hated by all nations for my name's sake. ¹⁰ And then many will fall away and betray one another and hate one another. ¹¹ And many false prophets will arise and lead many astray. ¹² And because lawlessness will be increased, the love of many will grow cold. (Matthew 24:6-12)

²⁷ For as the lightning comes from the east and shines as far as the west, so will be the coming of the Son of Man. ²⁸ Wherever the corpse is, there the vultures will gather. The Coming of the Son of Man ²⁹ Immediately after the tribulation of those days the sun will be darkened, and the moon will not give its light, and the stars will fall from heaven, and the powers of the heavens will be shaken. ³⁰ Then will appear in heaven the sign of the Son of Man, and then all the tribes of the earth will mourn, and they will see the Son of Man coming on the clouds of heaven with power and great glory. ³¹ And he will send out his angels with a loud trumpet call, and they will gather his elect from the four winds, from one end of heaven to the other. (Matthew 24:27-31)

Believers in Preterism Theology say this already happened in AD 70. Supposedly, Jesus came in the clouds for the WHOLE WORLD to see him and mourn Him for the crucifixion. It is hard for them to explain it; NO history anywhere in the world records it, but they say it occurred. Just as everything in Revelation already occurred regardless of what history records. NONE of the judgments noted in *The Book of Revelation* are recorded in any historical source.

Question 3: When Shall These Things Be?

³⁶ "But concerning that day and hour no one knows, not even the angels of heaven, nor the Son, but the Father only. ³⁷ For as were the days of Noah, so will be the coming of the Son of Man. ³⁸ For as in those days before the flood they were eating and drinking, marrying and giving in marriage, until the day when Noah entered the ark, ³⁹ and they were unaware until the flood came and swept them all away, so will be the coming of the Son of Man. (Matthew 24:36-39)

The Mount of Olives Disclosure Continues:

And you will hear of wars and rumors of wars. See that you are not alarmed, for this must take place, but the end is not yet. (Matthew 24:6)

The wars going on today are a *"sign of the times"* leading up to the Battle of Armageddon. Jesus mentions two types of wars: **"wars and rumors of wars."** Wars are those wars that are actually happening. Rumors of wars are cold wars. The verse also says: **"this must take place"**. What Jesus is telling us is that the world will never know peace until the Prince of Peace returns and Satan is cast into the abyss.

Jesus is telling us not to be disturbed by wars and rumors of war. However, practitioners of Preterism Theology want you to believe that Christ bound Satan in his first coming, so now we can achieve peace on earth. This goes against what is written in the Scriptures. All we have to do is look at history and what is around us today and see that Satan is not bound.

⁷ For nation will rise against nation, and kingdom against kingdom, and there will be famines and earthquakes in various places. ⁸ All these are but the beginning of the birth pains. (Matthew 24:7,8)

There is a difference between nations and kingdoms. Nations are actual countries, while kingdoms are religions. An example of kingdoms would be the Muslims attacking the Jews. Jesus also states that there will be famines and earthquakes in various places. We have seen an increase in famines, and earthquake numbers are increasing. There are even earthquakes in areas that never had earthquakes before. Look at the statistics yourself. (https://earthquake.usgs.gov/)

"All these are but the beginning of the birth pains." Birth pains announce new life, so these birth pains are to announce the Second Coming of Jesus. We will see more birth pains and signs of the times as the coming of Christ gets closer. The difference between the two is that *birth pains* are of the earth and in the sky. *Signs of the times* are man-made, such as wars, the occult, corruption, and pestilence. Just as when birth pains in women get closer together, the baby is due, as these signs get closer together or happen more frequently, Jesus is due.

⁹ "Then they will deliver you up to tribulation and put you to death, and you will be hated by all nations for my name's sake.

¹⁰*And then many will fall away and betray one another and hate one another.* (Matthew 24:9,10)

In the time of Tribulation, which occurs after the Rapture, many of the NEW believers in Christ will be persecuted, some even killed. Remember that all of Christ's believers are taken at the Rapture, which ends the Church Age. These new post-rapture Christians are persecuted because they are followers of Jesus. Plus, in that time, many who profess to be Christians will betray other Christians to the enemy to save themselves. This is what happened to Jews when the Nazis persecuted them. Some Jews were pressured to betray others. During the Tribulation, the same thing will occur.

"And many false prophets will arise and lead many astray." (Matthew 24:11)

This tells us that in the end times, many will be deceived because of false prophets and teachings. As mentioned previously, ignorance of the Scripture leads to deception.

"And because lawlessness will be increased, the love of many will grow cold." (Matthew 24:12)

Today, we see the rise of lawlessness. This is a *sign of the times*. We see increased riots, drug abuse, sex trafficking, homosexuality, pedophiles, and much more. All of these things are increasing exponentially. These things are portrayed as normal in movies and television and should be accepted.

The word *love* used in this verse is distinct from erotic love or emotional affection. In Greek, the word used was *agape*. This is the highest form of love, the love of God for man and of man for God. It embraces a profound sacrificial love that continues regardless of condition.

This verse refers to those who become believers during the Tribulation. It warns that unless followers of Jesus stay in the Word of God, they will grow cold to God. This is because the world around them pulls them into lawlessness.

"But the one who endures to the end will be saved."
(Matthew 24:13)

When Jesus states that *the one who endures to the end,* He refers to the end of the Tribulation; the Christians who became born again during the Tribulation, after the Rapture, will only make it to the end or endure, by believing in Christ and knowing the Word of God. This does not mean you will not be saved if you do not make it to the end of the Tribulation. This verse states that the Christians who stand on the Word of God to the end of the Tribulation will be with Him in His Millennial Kingdom. Many Christians will suffer martyrdom during the Tribulation. These are known as the *Tribulation Saints*.

"And this gospel of the kingdom will be proclaimed throughout the whole world as a testimony to all nations, and then the end will come." (Matthew 24:14)

This verse says that the end will come after the gospel is preached throughout the world, which is Jesus' Second Coming to set up his kingdom. This verse is not to the Christians of the Church Age. The Church was still a mystery at the time Jesus spoke this. God saved the Church Age followers in Christ from the Tribulation through the Rapture. The church was Christ's witness until the Rapture. To make sure all nations hear the Gospel, Revelation tells us two things. One will be the 144,000 Jewish evangelists chosen by God. Second, the Angels will preach the gospel to all the nations.

Revelation: A Line by Line Breakdown

"And I heard the number of the sealed, 144,000, sealed from every tribe of the sons of Israel" (Revelation 7:4)

Who will these 144,000 be? Revelation 7:4-8 tells us exactly.

⁴And I heard the number of the sealed, 144,000, sealed from every tribe of the sons of Israel: ⁵12,000 from the tribe of Judah were sealed, 12,000 from the tribe of Reuben, 12,000 from the tribe of Gad, ⁶12,000 from the tribe of Asher, 12,000 from the tribe of Naphtali, 12,000 from the tribe of Manasseh, ⁷12,000 from the tribe of Simeon, 12,000 from the tribe of Levi, 12,000 from the tribe of Issachar, ⁸12,000 from the tribe of Zebulun, 12,000 from the tribe of Joseph, 12,000 from the tribe of Benjamin were sealed. (Revelation 7:4-8)

God never allows Himself to be without evangelists to proclaim His Word—a way to receive forgiveness through grace. After the Rapture, a spiritual void or emptiness will be left on the earth. This will be due to the removal of all true believers. The Rapture removed the church. These 144,000 new believers will fill the void and proclaim the way to salvation through Jesus.

Many say this has to be a symbol; it cannot mean what it says, and nonetheless, it does. God spelled it all out: who these 144,000 will be. Do not fall into Preterism Theology, which means everything in Revelation has already happened and is only symbolic. God's word is always accurate. God redeems 144,000 literal Jews and ordains them as His evangelists for the seven years of the Tribulation. Twelve thousand from each tribe of Israel, this is the word of God.

Also, in the Tribulation, a phenomenon never seen before in the history of the world, **ANGELS WILL PREACH THE GOSPEL TO THE PEOPLE OF THE WORLD!** God offers one last offer to unbelievers for grace through Jesus before the final judgment.

Angels will fly through the air proclaiming the gospel. God makes sure everyone around the world has the opportunity to hear the Good News.

"Then I saw another angel flying directly overhead, with an eternal gospel to proclaim to those who dwell on earth, to every nation and tribe and language and people." (Revelation 14:6)

¹⁵ So when you see the abomination of desolation spoken of by the prophet Daniel, standing in the holy place (let the reader understand), ¹⁶ then let those who are in Judea flee to the mountains. ¹⁷ Let the one who is on the housetop not go down to take what is in his house, ¹⁸ and let the one who is in the field not turn back to take his cloak. (Matthew 24:15-18).

      The abomination of desolation, according to Daniel, is when the Antichrist goes into the temple and sits on the throne, demanding to be worshiped. According to Preterism, this happened in AD 70. However, Nero, their chosen antichrist, was never in Jerusalem in AD 70, having committed suicide in AD 68. Daniel also said the abomination of desolation will occur in the middle of the week or three and half years into the Tribulation. The siege of Jerusalem did not last three and a half years or the predicted seven years the Tribulation is supposed to last, as recorded in Daniel. History records it lasted 4 months, 3 weeks, and 4 days.

      Another interesting point that Preterism cannot answer is if Revelation is history, why doesn't John name the Antichrist or the False Prophet? It had been twenty-five years since Jerusalem was destroyed, but Revelation does not mention their names. Why? Because it is prophecy, just as it says in Revelation 1:3, *"Blessed is the one who reads aloud the words of this <u>prophecy</u>."*

      When the middle of the Tribulation arrives, as indicated by the abomination of desolation, Jewish believers are to flee. God will protect them if they flee to the mountains. If they stay in Jerusalem, they will be killed. They are told not to take time to get anything from their homes. They are to leave as quickly as possible.

These Jewish believers are to go to the mountain ranges surrounded by the Dead Sea: Edom, Moab, and Ammon. God will protect them here. How do these Jewish newborn believers in Christ know this? By studying God's word.

19 And alas for women who are pregnant and for those who are nursing infants in those days! 20 Pray that your flight may not be in winter or on a Sabbath. (Matthew 24:19-20).

This is to warn those fleeing that it will be difficult, but worse for those who are pregnant. Traveling to the mountains in winter offers more significant hardship. If on the Sabbath, it will be worse because all the shops will be closed, and thus, there will be no way to get provisions.

"For then there will be great tribulation, such as has not been from the beginning of the world until now, no, and never will be." (Matthew 24:21).

The second half of the Tribulation is called the *Great Tribulation,* which starts with the abomination of desolation. This will be the worst time ever in world history. The second half of the Tribulation will be worse because Satan is cast out of heaven at that time. He will no longer be allowed there. Satan, called the accuser, will finally be removed from Heaven and will no longer be able to accuse anyone before God.

When Satan is cast out and thrown onto the earth, he realizes his end is near. He will unleash all his fury on man. The moment Satan is cast from heaven, there will be increased wrath, anguish, carnage, and slaughter, along with great upheavals in nature. Many believe that Satan may even possess the antichrist. It will be through his antichrist who will demand everyone has to worship him, and all Jews be killed. Especially Christian Jews. Those who know the Word of God will flee to the mountains for God's protection.

⁹ And the great dragon was thrown down, that ancient serpent, who is called the devil and Satan, the deceiver of the whole world- he was thrown down to the earth, and his angels were thrown down with him. ¹⁰ And I heard a loud voice in heaven, saying, "Now the salvation and the power and the kingdom of our God and the authority of his Christ have come, for the accuser of our brothers has been thrown down, who accuses them day and night before our God. ¹¹ And they have conquered him by the blood of the Lamb and by the word of their testimony, for they loved not their lives even unto death. ¹² Therefore, rejoice, O heavens and you who dwell in them! But woe to you, O earth and sea, for the devil has come down to you in great wrath because he knows that his time is short!" ¹³ And when the dragon saw that he had been thrown down to the earth, he pursued the woman who had given birth to the male child. (Revelation 12:9-13)

"And if those days had not been cut short, no human being would be saved. However, for the sake of the elect those days will be cut short." (Matthew 24:22).

If Jesus does not return at the end of the Tribulation's seven years, no one on earth will remain alive. However, due to those who were saved during the Tribulation, Christ returns for their sake.

²³ Then if anyone says to you, 'Look, here is the Christ!' or 'There he is!' do not believe it. ²⁴ For false christs and false prophets will arise and perform great signs and wonders, so as to lead astray, if possible, even the elect. ²⁵ See, I have told you beforehand. ²⁶ So, if they say to you, 'Look, he is in the wilderness,' do not go out. If they say, 'Look, he is in the inner rooms,' do not believe it. (Matthew 24:23-26).

The Antichrist will try to lure the new Christians away from Jesus. He will also try to lure the Jews out of the mountains to kill them. He will say, *"Look, here is the Christ"* or *"There he is,"* Christ is warning His followers not to believe it. Satan will perform crafty signs and wonders to deceive God's believers, which is why they must know the Word of God. Scripture describes Jesus' return and where he will return, study the Word of God.

"For as the lightning comes from the east and shines as far as the west, so will be the coming of the Son of Man." (Matthew 24:27).

Jesus will come back like a flash of lightning from the East to the West. This is not about the church's rapture but the Second Coming of Christ, which will be at the Mount of Olives.

[10] And while they were gazing into heaven as he went, behold, two men stood by them in white robes, [11] and said, "Men of Galilee, why do you stand looking into heaven? This Jesus, who was taken up from you into heaven, will come in the same way as you saw him go into heaven." (Acts 1:10,11)

"Wherever the corpse is, there the vultures will gather." (Matthew 24:28)

This verse describes vultures circling a dead carcass. Israel, where the Battle of Armageddon is to take place just before Jesus' return, is that corpse. The vultures circling are all the nations of the world, led by the Antichrist approaching to destroy Israel. This was foretold in Zechariah chapters ten to fourteen and Joel chapters two and three.

Armageddon or Harmagedon is from the Hebrew *Har Megiddo*, the Mount of Megiddo. The King James Bible called it Armageddon, and this name is found in Revelation 16:16.

"And they assembled them at the place that in Hebrew is called Armageddon." (Revelation 16:16)

Armageddon is described as the rallying place of all the kings of the world. They will be led by the Beast or Antichrist and controlled by Satan. They will assemble here for the final war against God. This did not happen in AD 70. It will appear as a repeat of what happened in AD 70 when the Romans sacked Jerusalem. However, the Battle of Armageddon will be different because, as prophecy declares, all the kings of the earth will assemble there to fight Jerusalem, after the seven years of the Tribulation. Jesus will return to end the battle, destroying all armies against God. He will liberate Jerusalem and Israel. This is the world's great hope, the Second Advent of Jesus. The great hope of the Church Age was the Rapture.

The Coming of the Son of Man [29] Immediately after the tribulation of those days the sun will be darkened, and the moon will not give its light, and the stars will fall from heaven, and the powers of the heavens will be shaken. [30] Then will appear in heaven the sign of the Son of Man, and then all the tribes of the earth will mourn, and they will see the Son of Man coming on the clouds of heaven with power and great glory. (Matthew 24:29-30).

When Jesus returns at the Second Coming, there will be signs in the heavens showing the coming of the Lord. This will not happen at the Rapture when Jesus returns to His Church. At the Rapture, the sun will keep shining, the moon will be bright, and the stars will fill the night air. At the Rapture, only Christians will see Jesus and rise to meet Him in the sky. All the unbelievers in the world will only know that believers in Christ were here one minute and gone the next.

¹⁶ For the Lord himself will descend from heaven with a cry of command, with the voice of an archangel, and with the sound of the trumpet of God. And the dead in Christ will rise first. ¹⁷ Then we who are alive, who are left, will be caught up together with them in the clouds to meet the Lord in the air, and so we will always be with the Lord. ¹⁸ Therefore encourage one another with these words. (1 Thessalonians 4:16-18)

⁵¹ Behold! I tell you a mystery. We shall not all sleep, but we shall all be changed, ⁵² in a moment, in the twinkling of an eye, at the last trumpet. For the trumpet will sound, and the dead will be raised imperishable, and we shall be changed.
(1 Corinthians 15:51-52).

"And he will send out his angels with a loud trumpet call, and they will gather his elect from the four winds, from one end of heaven to the other." (Matthew 24:31)

The elect are those who become believers after the Rapture. They will be gathered together for protection by the angels from God's wrath, the Tribulation. His wrath will be poured out on the earth on all unbelievers. After Jesus' return, it will be the opposite of the Rapture, where believers were removed from the earth in the Rapture; after the Second Coming, unbelievers are removed.

Parable of the Fig Tree

³² From the fig tree learn its lesson: as soon as its branch becomes tender and puts out its leaves, you know that summer is near. ³³So also, when you see all these things, you know that he is near, at the very gates. ³⁴ Truly, I say to you, this generation will not pass away until all these things take place. ³⁵ Heaven and earth will pass away, but my words will not pass away. ³⁶ But concerning that day and hour no one knows, not even the angels of heaven, nor the Son, but the Father only. ³⁷ For as were the days of Noah, so will be the coming of the Son of Man. (Matthew 24:32-37).

Practitioners of Preterism Theology want you to believe that *Mount of Olives Disclosure* and *The Book of Revelation* are history, not prophecy. This is primarily because of one verse from the *Mount of Olives Disclosure*. It is taken out of context and wrongly interrupted by them. It is Matthew 24:34, which says, *"this generation will not pass away."*

"Truly, I say to you, this generation will not pass away until all these things take place." (Matthew 24:34)

The Preterists like to use text out of context. Always pay close attention to context. Do not take Matthew 24:34 by itself; read the whole passage to comprehend the meaning entirely. This prevents misinterpretation based on text out of context. Matthew 24:34 is taken from Jesus teaching the *Parable of the Fig Tree.* The verse does not apply to the generation of people living at the time of Jesus in the first century but to the generation who sees the 'birth pains' and 'signs of the times.'

Jesus commands us to learn from the *Parable of the Fig Tree* to understand better when the general time of His second coming is near. The one primary point of this parable is also stated in Mark chapter 13.

²⁸ From the fig tree learn its lesson: as soon as its branch becomes tender and puts out its leaves, you know that summer is near. ²⁹So also, when you see these things taking place, you know that he is near, at the very gates. (Mark 13:28,29)

Now look at the whole passage from Luke Chapter 21:

²⁵ And there will be signs in sun and moon and stars, and on the earth distress of nations in perplexity because of the roaring of the sea and the waves, ²⁶ people fainting with fear and with foreboding of what is coming on the world. For the powers of the heavens will be shaken. ²⁷ And then they will see the Son of Man coming in a cloud with power and great glory. ²⁸ Now when these things begin to take place, straighten up and raise your heads, because your redemption is drawing near. ²⁹ And he told them a parable: "Look at the fig tree and all the trees. ³⁰ As soon as they come out in leaf, you see for yourselves and know that the summer is already near. ³¹ So also, when you see these things taking place, you know that the kingdom of God is near. ³² Truly, I say to you, this generation will not pass away until all has taken place." (Luke 21:25-32).

³⁶ "But concerning that day and hour no one knows, not even the angels of heaven, nor the Son, but the Father only. ³⁷ For as were the days of Noah, so will be the coming of the Son of Man. (Matthew 24:36,37)

Verse 36 uses the word *"day,"* which refers to the Second Coming of Christ. Plus, it states that only the Father knows the day. Verse 37 still refers to the Second Advent by stating, **"For as were the days of Noah,"** God protects His people—first the Rapture for His church, then the Tribulation. After the Second Coming, the angels will gather His Tribulation converts.

³⁸ For as in those days before the flood they were eating and drinking, marrying and giving in marriage, until the day when Noah entered the ark, ³⁹ and they were unaware until the flood came and swept them all away, so will be the coming of the Son of Man. (Matthew 24:38,39)

Those who were *"eating and drinking, marrying and giving in marriage, until the day when Noah entered the ark"* were unbelievers in God. However, none of these activities were sins. Just like during the Tribulation, people will be living everyday lives. They only rejected the Word of God and believed in the gospel. In Noah's time, the unbelievers ignored his preaching and prophecies. They laughed at Noah building the ark. When the flood came, they wanted in his ark, but the door was shut, it was too late.

During the Tribulation, people will act similarly, trying to live an everyday life while God pours out His wrath on the earth. There will be earthquakes, floods, famine, and multitudes of deaths. The Antichrist will rule the world and force people to take the mark of the beast. Nevertheless, people will still try to live a normal life. When Christ comes in glory, no opportunity to receive Him will remain. It'll be too late. The door will have been shut. The Bible tells us that man will keep hardening his heart to God. Many will refuse God's grace and face the Tribulation.

"For by grace, you have been saved through faith. And this is not your own doing; it is the gift of God, not a result of works, so that no one may boast." (Ephesians 2:8-9)

Additionally, these verses are an example of the Rapture. At the Rapture, the believer in Christ is taken, and the one left will face the Tribulation.

40 Then two men will be in the field; one will be taken and one left. 41 Two women will be grinding at the mill; one will be taken and one left. (Matthew 24:40,41)

42 Therefore, stay awake, for you do not know on what day your Lord is coming. 43 But know this, that if the master of the house had known in what part of the night the thief was coming, he would have stayed awake and would not have let his house be

broken into. ⁴⁴ Therefore you also must be ready, for the Son of Man is coming at an hour you do not expect. (Matthew 24:42-44)

Once again, these verses are about two events: the Rapture and the Second Coming of Jesus. They are a warning to people to be alert for His coming. The signs of times and birth pains will point to the general period, like leaves sprouting on a fig tree. Everyone must be ready for Christ's coming. You would watch for him just like if you knew when a thief was coming. You should always be ready even after the Rapture, as millions will refuse His grace.

⁴⁵ "Who then is the faithful and wise servant, whom his master has set over his household, to give them their food at the proper time? ⁴⁶ Blessed is that servant whom his master will find so doing when he comes. ⁴⁷ Truly, I say to you, he will set him over all his possessions. ⁴⁸ But if that wicked servant says to himself, 'My master is delayed,' ⁴⁹ and begins to beat his fellow servants and eats and drinks with drunkards, ⁵⁰ the master of that servant will come on a day when he does not expect him and at an hour he does not know ⁵¹ and will cut him in pieces and put him with the hypocrites. In that place there will be weeping and gnashing of teeth. (Matthew 24:48-51)

At the time Jesus returns, there will be believers and unbelievers. After the Second Coming, believers will go into the Millennium. They also will be rewards for those who come through the Tribulation and endure to the end. Once again, people will try to live a normal life as was in the time of Noah. Not accepting God's grace. The unbelievers will think, *"I'll wait to decide,"* after all, **"My master is delayed."** They will be put in that place, where there will be weeping and gnashing of teeth.

Matthew Chapter 25 *The Mount of Olives Disclosure* Continues

The *Mount of Olives Disclosure* continues in Matthew chapter 25. This is a continuation of what Jesus was saying in chapter 24. A separation was unnecessary; chapter 25 continues the same sermon. The first word is *"Then."* The word *then* is used to continue a thought. The use of *"then"* here is speaking of the Second Coming of Jesus.

Parable Of The Ten Virgins

¹"Then the kingdom of heaven will be like ten virgins who took their lamps and went to meet the bridegroom. ² Five of them were foolish, and five were wise. ³ For when the foolish took their lamps, they took no oil with them, ⁴ but the wise took flasks of oil with their lamps. ⁵ As the bridegroom was delayed, they all became drowsy and slept. ⁶ But at midnight there was a cry, 'Here is the bridegroom! Come out to meet him.' ⁷ Then all those virgins rose and trimmed their lamps. ⁸ And the foolish said to the wise, 'Give us some of your oil, for our lamps are going out.' ⁹ But the wise answered, saying, 'Since there will not be enough for us and for you, go rather to the dealers and buy for yourselves.' ¹⁰ And while they were going to buy, the bridegroom came, and those who were ready went in with him to the marriage feast, and the door was shut. ¹¹ Afterward the other virgins came also, saying, 'Lord, lord, open to us.' ¹² But he answered, 'Truly, I say to you, I do not know you.' ¹³ Watch, therefore, for you know neither the day nor the hour. (Matthew 25:1-13)

When Jesus told this parable, everyone listening understood the customs of a wedding at that time. However, that was 2000 years ago. At that time, a marriage was more like a business deal, and a contract was made between the girl's father and the groom. It started with a discussion of how much the dowry would be. A dowry is a *"gift"* from the bride's family to the groom's family as a gesture for taking her into their home.

Through the centuries, dowry has been used politically between families and countries to unite through blood, avoiding wars or feuds. Some people even used it to rid themselves of a daughter. Once an agreement on the dowry and wedding terms was made, a wedding date was set.

Once the marriage date was decided upon, the wedding feast or celebration plans were made. The wedding party, or feast, began after the wedding. All the family and friends of the bride and groom were invited. This celebration started at the home of the groom. The bride was at home, preparing for her future husband. The groom would then go with those to attend the wedding feast to her home to claim his bride. Once there, the bride's father would turn her over to her new husband. The groom, with his new bride, would lead everyone to the place he had prepared for them, their new home. In the ancient world, there was no ceremony. The marriage contract was sealed by the couple having sex, called consummating the marriage.

The celebration began once the bride and groom got to the place he had prepared for her. At some point during the party, the bride and groom would go and consummate the marriage. These feasts could last several days to weeks, up to a month. During that time, the new husband and wife would periodically celebrate with their guests, eating and drinking.

²In my Father's house are many rooms. If it were not so, would I have told you that I go to prepare a place for you? ³And if I go and prepare a place for you, I will come again and will take you to myself, that where I am you may be also. (John 14:2,3)

The Church is called the *Bride of Christ*. We who are believers, those Born Again, will have the wedding feast with Christ in His millennial kingdom. No one knows when that celebration will be other than after the Rapture. Some think it will be during the seven-year Tribulation. Jesus talked of this at the Last Supper. Jesus said he would not drink wine until he was in His Kingdom.

[26] Now as they were eating, Jesus took bread, and after blessing it broke it and gave it to the disciples, and said, "Take, eat; this is my body." [27] And he took a cup, and when he had given thanks he gave it to them, saying, "Drink of it, all of you, [28] for this is my blood of the covenant, which is poured out for many for the forgiveness of sins. [29] I tell you I will not drink again of this fruit of the vine until that day when I drink it new with you in my Father's kingdom." (Matthew 26:26-29)

"And the angel said to me, "Write this: Blessed are those who are invited to the marriage supper of the Lamb." And he said to me, "These are the true words of God." (Revelation 19:9)

The parable begins with ten virgins, all of whom know the bridegroom (Jesus) is coming soon. Five of them are foolish, and five are wise. The foolish represents the unsaved, those not Born Again. They are like those who know Christ is coming but put off accepting His grace. The wise characterizes believers in Christ expecting Jesus' Second Coming even though they do not know when but have faith in Him. They accepted His salvation by grace as a gift from God.

"For by grace, you have been saved through faith. And this is not your own doing; it is the gift of God, not a result of works, so that no one may boast." (Ephesians 2:8-9)

[5] As the bridegroom was delayed, they all became drowsy and slept. [6] But at midnight there was a cry, 'Here is the bridegroom! Come out to meet him.' [7] Then all those virgins rose and trimmed

their lamps. ⁸ And the foolish said to the wise, 'Give us some of your oil, for our lamps are going out.' ⁹ But the wise answered, saying, 'Since there will not be enough for us and for you, go rather to the dealers and buy for yourselves.' (Matthew 25:5-9)

The wise are believers in Christ, those waiting to meet the groom. They are waiting for Him to claim his bride, the church, which will be the Rapture. They tell the unwise, who are nonbelievers, to accept Christ. Only Jesus can give you salvation. They cannot do it. They were prepared for His coming.

¹⁰ And while they were going to buy, the bridegroom came, and those who were ready went in with him to the marriage feast, and the door was shut. ¹¹ Afterward the other virgins came also, saying, 'Lord, lord, open to us.' ¹² But he answered, 'Truly, I say to you, I do not know you.' ¹³ Watch, therefore, for you know neither the day nor the hour. (Matthew 25:10-13)

The door was shut, as it was in the time of Noah when he closed the door of the ark. The unwise virgins who were not *"Born Again"* were shut out of heaven. They lost their chance at salvation. Once the door is shut, meaning when you die, there is no longer a chance for salvation.

Some say that 2000 years is a long wait for Christ's return. Let's look at 2 Peter 3:3-10:

³ knowing this first of all, that scoffers will come in the last days with scoffing, following their own sinful desires. ⁴ They will say, "Where is the promise of his coming? For ever since the fathers fell asleep, all things are continuing as they were from the beginning of creation." ⁵ For they deliberately overlook this fact, that the heavens existed long ago, and the earth was formed out of water and through water by the word of God, ⁶ and that by means of these the world that then existed was deluged with water and perished. *⁷ But by the same word the heavens and earth that now exist are stored up for fire, being kept until the day of judgment and destruction of the ungodly. ⁸ But do not overlook this one fact, beloved, that with the Lord one day is as a thousand years, and a thousand years as one day. ⁹ The Lord is not slow to fulfill his promise as some count slowness, but is patient toward you, not wishing that any should perish, but that all should reach repentance. ¹⁰ But the day of the Lord will come like a thief, and then the heavens will pass away with a roar, and the heavenly bodies will be burned up and dissolved, and the earth and the works that are done on it will be exposed.* (2 Peter 3:3-10)

The Parable of the Talents

¹⁴ "For it will be like a man going on a journey, who called his servants and entrusted to them his property. ¹⁵ To one he gave five talents, to another two, to another one, to each according to his ability. Then he went away. ¹⁶ He who had received the five talents went at once and traded with them, and he made five talents more. ¹⁷ So also he who had the two talents made two talents more. ¹⁸ But he who had received the one talent went and dug in the ground and hid his master's money. ¹⁹ Now after a long time the master of those servants came and settled accounts with them. ²⁰ And he who had received the five talents came forward, bringing five talents more, saying, 'Master, you delivered to me five talents; here I have made five talents more.' ²¹ His master said to him, 'Well done, good and faithful servant. You have been faithful over a little; I will set you over much. Enter into the joy of your master.' ²² And he also who had the two talents came forward, saying, 'Master, you delivered to me two talents; here I have made two talents more.' ²³ His master said to him, 'Well done, good and faithful servant. You have been faithful over a little; I will set you over much. Enter into the joy of your master.' ²⁴ He also who had received the one talent came forward, saying,

'Master, I knew you to be a hard man, reaping where you did not sow, and gathering where you scattered no seed, ²⁵ so I was afraid, and I went and hid your talent in the ground. Here you have what is yours.' ²⁶ But his master answered him, 'You wicked and slothful servant! You knew that I reap where I have not sown and gather where I scattered no seed? ²⁷ Then you ought to have invested my money with the bankers, and at my coming I should have received what was my own with interest. ²⁸ So take the talent from him and give it to him who has the ten talents. ²⁹For to everyone who has will more be given, and he will have an abundance. But from the one who has not, even what he has will be taken away. ³⁰ And cast the worthless servant into the outer darkness. In that place there will be weeping and gnashing of teeth.' (Matthew 25:14-30)

In Biblical times, a talent represented either an amount of silver or gold. A talent was a large round ball of ~75 pounds. The talents given to each servant in the parable represent the Word of God, the Gospel. Each servant was given talents according to their capability. Everyone is unique and has different abilities. God gives people only what they can deal with. You are never given more than you can handle.

The servant given one talent represents the unbelievers who hear the gospel but do not receive it. Instead, he buried the *Word of God*. The other two servants heard the Word and accepted Jesus. They then went out spreading the gospel, bringing others to Christ.

Verse 25:19 speaks of the Lord returning: **"Now after a long time the master of those servants came and settled accounts with them."** This verse does not directly address the Rapture or the Second Coming of Jesus. Many say this verse has two meanings. Before the Rapture, those who accept Jesus are taken, and the ones who did not are left behind to go through the Tribulation. At Jesus's

Second Coming, those who believe in Christ will be with Him in His Kingdom. Those who reject Him and are not Born Again will not.

"Enter into the joy of your master" in verse 25:23 refers to those taken at the Rapture. These are all true believers born again after the Tribulation who will enter His Millennial Kingdom. Also, because they have done as He asked, Christ will reward them.

Note that the servant given one talent did not invest it but buried it. This represents those who hear the Gospel and bury it or reject the word of God. When Christ returns, the unbeliever tells Jesus he heard He was a harsh ruler.

"Master, I knew you to be a hard man, reaping where you did not sow, and gathering where you scattered no seed, so I was afraid, and I went and hid your talent in the ground." (Matthew 25:24).

Jesus responds by saying the least you could have done is ask for salvation through faith and by His Grace. However, you buried the Gospel. In the end, Jesus tells His angels,

"Cast the worthless servant into the outer darkness. In that place there will be weeping and gnashing of teeth." (Mathew 25:30)

All of these parables warn that you must be right with God. You need to accept Jesus as your Lord and Savior, what is called being *Born Again*. There are people today, even in the church, who act like *Born Again* Christians but have never taken the leap of faith. When the Rapture comes, they will be left behind. It is our prayer that, at that time, they truly accept Christ as they endure the Tribulation.

[1] Now there was a man of the Pharisees named Nicodemus, a ruler of the Jews. [2] This man came to Jesus by night and said to him, "Rabbi, we know that you are a teacher come from God, for no one can do these signs that you do unless God is with him." [3] Jesus

answered him, "Truly, truly, I say to you, unless one is born again he cannot see the kingdom of God." [4] Nicodemus said to him, "How can a man be born when he is old? Can he enter a second time into his mother's womb and be born?" [5] Jesus answered, "Truly, truly, I say to you, unless one is born of water and the Spirit, he cannot enter the kingdom of God. [6] That which is born of the flesh is flesh, and that which is born of the Spirit is spirit. [7] Do not marvel that I said to you, 'You must be born again.' [8] The wind blows where it wishes, and you hear its sound, but you do not know where it comes from or where it goes. So it is with everyone who is born of the Spirit." [9] Nicodemus said to him, "How can these things be?" [10] Jesus answered him, "Are you the teacher of Israel and yet you do not understand these things? [11] Truly, truly, I say to you, we speak of what we know, and bear witness to what we have seen, but you do not receive our testimony. [12] If I have told you earthly things and you do not believe, how can you believe if I tell you heavenly things? [13] No one has ascended into heaven except he who descended from heaven, the Son of Man. [14] And as Moses lifted up the serpent in the wilderness, so must the Son of Man be lifted up, [15] that whoever believes in him may have eternal life. [16] "For God so loved the world, that he gave his only Son, that whoever believes in him should not perish but have eternal life. [17] For God did not send his Son into the world to condemn the world, but in order that the world might be saved through him. [18] Whoever believes in him is not condemned, but whoever does not believe is condemned already, because he has not believed in the name of the only Son of God. [19] And this is the judgment: the light has come into the world, and people loved the darkness rather than the light because their works were evil. [20] For everyone who does wicked things hates the light and does not come to the light, lest his works should be exposed. [21] But whoever does what is true comes to the light, so that it may be clearly seen that his works have been carried out in God." (John 3:1-21)

The Parable of the Sheep and Goats

[31] *"When the Son of Man comes in his glory, and all the angels with him, then he will sit on his glorious throne. [32] Before him will be gathered all the nations, and he will separate people one from another as a shepherd separates the sheep from the goats. [33] And he will place the sheep on his right, but the goats on the left. [34] Then the King will say to those on his right, 'Come, you who are blessed by my Father, inherit the kingdom prepared for you from the foundation of the world. [35] For I was hungry and you gave me food, I was thirsty and you gave me drink, I was a stranger and you welcomed me, [36] I was naked and you clothed me, I was sick and you visited me, I was in prison and you came to me.' [37] Then the righteous will answer him, saying, 'Lord, when did we see you hungry and feed you, or thirsty and give you drink? [38] And when did we see you a stranger and welcome you, or naked and clothe you? [39] And when did we see you sick or in prison and visit you?' [40] And the King will answer them, 'Truly, I say to you, as you did it to one of the least of these my brothers, you did it to me.' [41] "Then he will say to those on his left, 'Depart from me, you cursed, into the eternal fire prepared for the devil and his angels. [42] For I was hungry and you gave me no food, I was thirsty and you gave me no drink, [43] I was a stranger and you did not welcome me, naked and you did not clothe me, sick and in prison and you did not visit me.' [44] Then they also will answer, saying, 'Lord, when did we see you hungry or thirsty or a stranger or naked or sick or in prison, and did not minister to you?' [45] Then he will answer them, saying, 'Truly, I say to you, as you did not do it to one of the least of these, you did not do it to me.' [46] And these will go away into eternal punishment, but the righteous into eternal life."*
(Matthew 25:31-46)

This parable is about what will happen at Jesus's Second Coming, which occurs to end the Battle of Armageddon. This is when Jesus defeats Satan, his antichrist and false prophet. He then begins His Millennial Kingdom. Jesus then gathers all those from the Tribulation. The *"sheep"* represents the believers, while the *"goats"* are the unbelievers.

This parable is about establishing the Millennial Kingdom, which will occur just after Jesus returns. This millennial kingdom has been prophesied throughout the Old and New Testaments throughout the Bible. The sheep are the followers of Christ who became believers during the Tribulation.

This parable discusses the righteous (sheep) and the unrighteous (goats). The sheep who are righteous following God spend eternity with Him. The unrighteous (goats) are sent to a place of eternal fire prepared for Satan and his fallen angels.

The Mount of Olives Disclosure Found in Mark 13 is shorter. The explanation is the same.

Conclusion For The Olivet Discourse

Jesus Christ gives *the Olivet Discourse* on the Mount of Olives. His subject is the *End Times, one* of the Bible's most significant texts since it is Jesus' final address before His crucifixion. It is also His most extensive prophetic teaching. It is essential to know that Jesus' teaching is about Israel and not the Church, which was still a mystery at that time. Christ was talking of God's future plan for Israel. Extensive confusion has been caused by a failure to recognize that the Olivet Discourse involves Israel, not the church, and refers to a future age, not the past. God's plan for the Church Age concludes with the Rapture.

[51] Behold! I tell you a mystery. We shall not all sleep, but we shall all be changed, [52] in a moment, in the twinkling of an eye, at the

last trumpet. For the trumpet will sound, and the dead will be raised imperishable, and we shall be changed.
(1Corinthians 15:51-52)

Jesus warns us to watch for deception. There will be those who will try to deceive Jesus' believers. The practitioners of Preterism Theology want to fool you into believing that everything Jesus says in the *Mount of Olives Disclosure* and everything in the *Book of Revelation* already happened in the first century. The teachers of Replacement Theology want to deceive you into believing that the Church has replaced the Jews – Israel. Even though in both cases, there is no biblical or historical proof for either premise. Believe in Christ and TRUST God's Word; do not be deceived.

Jesus gave the Olivet Discourse to correct any misunderstanding about his Second Coming. He also wanted to protect the disciples from becoming deceived due to the events that would take place in their generation. Jesus wanted them to know He would not bodily return to restore Israel and establish the Messianic Kingdom immediately after Rome destroyed the Temple. All these things only the Father knows.

"But concerning that day and hour no one knows, not even the angels of heaven, nor the Son, but the Father only."
(Matthew 24:36)

Therefore, Jesus began His discourse with a warning to see that no one deceives you. Failing to recognize this warning, those who teach Replacement Theology and Preterists have been led astray; those who say things different from what's in the Bible, like Mormons, Muslims, Buddhists, and Hindus, to name a few. Do not let them deceive you. This is part of the warning from Jesus to watch for deception. Study God's Word to prevent deception.

Revelation: A Line by Line Breakdown

[19] And we have something more sure, the prophetic word, to which you will do well to pay attention as to a lamp shining in a dark place, until the day dawns and the morning star rises in your hearts, [20] knowing this first of all, that no prophecy of Scripture comes from someone's own interpretation. [21] For no prophecy was ever produced by the will of man, but men spoke from God as they were carried along by the Holy Spirit. (2 Peter 1:19-21)

As Jesus left the temple, the disciples called His attention to the magnificent buildings on the temple mount. Jesus then tells the disciples, "*Not one stone here will be left on another.*" This prophecy was fulfilled in AD 70 when the Romans destroyed Jerusalem. The temple was burned, and the temple gold melted in the fire and ran down into the cracks between the stones. As the Romans later searched for the gold, they toppled every stone from its place. This destruction of Jerusalem was but a foreshadowing of things yet to come: the Tribulation.

"As he sat on the Mount of Olives, the disciples came to him privately, saying, 'Tell us, when will these things be, and what will be the sign of your coming and of the close of the age?'" (Matthew 24:3).

What follows in the *Mount of Olives Disclosure* in Matthew chapters 24 and 25 refers to the future. The seven-year Tribulation period before the second coming of Christ. During that time, God will complete His punishment and cleansing of Israel and unbelievers in His Christ. He will judge the whole world, as the Book of Revelation outlines. Matthew 24:15-26 gives further details concerning the tribulation. Jesus refers to an abomination and desolation of a future not yet built temple.

In Matthew 24:21, Jesus warns that the great tribulation will be the worst time ever seen on earth.

Revelation: A Line by Line Breakdown

"For then there will be great tribulation, such as has not been from the beginning of the world until now, no, and never will be." (Matthew 24:21)

If Christ's return had not been cut short in those days, no one would have survived. In Matthew 24, Jesus again warns us of false prophets in the last days.

²² "And if those days had not been cut short, no human being would be saved. But for the sake of the elect those days will be cut short. ²³ Then if anyone says to you, 'Look, here is the Christ!' or 'There he is!' do not believe it. ²⁴ For false christs and false prophets will arise and perform great signs and wonders so as to lead astray, if possible, even the elect. ²⁵ See, I have told you beforehand. ²⁶ So, if they say to you, 'Look, he is in the wilderness,' do not go out. If they say, 'Look, he is in the inner rooms,' do not believe it. ²⁷ For as the lightning comes from the east and shines as far as the west, so will be the coming of the Son of Man. (Matthew 24:22-27).

At the end of the tribulation, there will be astronomical upheaval, and the world's nations will see Christ *"coming on the clouds of the sky, with power and great glory."*

²⁹ "Immediately after the tribulation of those days the sun will be darkened, and the moon will not give its light, and the stars will fall from heaven, and the powers of the heavens will be shaken. ³⁰ Then will appear in heaven the sign of the Son of Man, and then all the tribes of the earth will mourn, and they will see the Son of Man coming on the clouds of heaven with power and great glory. (Matthew 24:29-30).

³¹And he will send out his angels with a loud trumpet call, and they will gather his elect from the four winds, from one end of heaven to the other. ³²*"From the fig tree learn its lesson: as soon as its branch becomes tender and puts out its leaves, you know that summer is near.* ³³ *So also, when you see all these things, you know that he is near, at the very gates.* ³⁴ *Truly, I say to you, this generation will not pass away until all these things take place.* ³⁵ *Heaven and earth will pass away, but my words will not pass away.* (Matthew 24:31-35)

Those who were saved during the tribulation will be gathered by the angels. Jesus emphasizes that there will be signs leading up to the day of judgment and that His Word is sure. Jesus also says that no one knows the timing of these events and that those upon whom judgment is coming will be unaware. He says to be ready for the Rapture always in Matthew 24:36-44.

³⁶ *But concerning that day and hour no one knows, not even the angels of heaven, nor the Son, but the Father only.* ³⁷ *For as were the days of Noah, so will be the coming of the Son of Man.* ³⁸*For as in those days before the flood they were eating and drinking, marrying and giving in marriage, until the day when Noah entered the ark,* ³⁹ *and they were unaware until the flood came and swept them all away, so will be the coming of the Son of Man.* ⁴⁰ *Then two men will be in the field; one will be taken and one left.* ⁴¹ *Two women will be grinding at the mill; one will be taken and one left.* ⁴² *Therefore, stay awake, for you do not know on what day your Lord is coming.* ⁴³ *But know this, that if the master of the house had known in what part of the night the thief was coming, he would have stayed awake and would not have let his house be broken into.* ⁴⁴ *Therefore you also must be ready, for the Son of Man is coming at an hour you do not expect.* (Matthew 24:36-44)

In the Olivet Discourse, Jesus tells parables about the *End Times*. The first one is **The Parable of the Fig Tree** (Matthew 24:32-35) concerning when his coming is near. The next, the **Parable of**

the Ten Virgins (Matthew 25:1-13), encourages readiness and watchfulness. The third parable is **The Parable of the Talents** (Matthew 25:14-30). Relating the story of three servants and their use (or misuse) of finances teaches faithfulness because God's servants must give an account of themselves one day. Jesus ends His discourse by telling of The Final Judgment (Matthew 25:31-46) in the **Parable of the Sheep and Goats.** This speaks of dividing the saved from the unsaved at the end of the tribulation, before the start of Christ's millennial reign.

Christ is coming to judge the world, which the phrase implies, and *then the end will come*. For this goal, this global evangel cannot be restricted to the first-century Roman Empire only. Nor could the spread of the Gospel around the world have been accomplished within 25 to 30 years of Christ's ascension and fulfill the Great Commission (Mark 16) by AD 70, as the Preterists contend.

³⁰ The times of ignorance God overlooked, but now he commands all people everywhere to repent, ³¹ because he has fixed a day on which he will judge the world in righteousness by a man whom he has appointed; and of this he has given assurance to all by raising him from the dead. (Acts 17:30,31)

¹⁵ And he said to them, "Go into all the world and proclaim the gospel to the whole creation. ¹⁶ Whoever believes and is baptized will be saved, but whoever does not believe will be condemned." (Mark 16:15,16)

After the Olivet Discourse, Jesus was betrayed and crucified. Jesus will return in glory to judge the world, but first, He had to provide the way of salvation, the Church Age, for all who would trust in Him. We study God's Word to understand His plan better. We must trust the Holy Spirit to lead us to know Him and His Word. Pray for the Holy Spirit's help.

John Milton said, "*When we speak of knowing God, it must be understood with reference to man's limited powers of comprehension. God, as He really is, is far beyond man's imagination, let alone understanding. God has revealed only so much of Himself as our minds can conceive and the weakness of our nature can bear."*

No matter if you believe in God or not. Whether you believe *the Mount of Olives Disclosure* and the *Book of Revelation* are history or prophecy. If you believe in the Rapture or not, **THESE THINGS WILL HAPPEN**. These are sovereign acts of God, not dependent on faith. If you are just a seeker wanting to know what Christ is about, do not wait. Accept Jesus NOW.

"For by grace, you have been saved through faith. And this is not your own doing; it is the gift of God, not a result of works, so that no one may boast." (Ephesians 2:8-9)

Revelation: A Line by Line Breakdown

FURTHER READING AND SOURCES

#1 is The Holy Bible

After The Rapture (2019)
By Dr. David Jeremiah; About what happens if you're left behind.

Because the Time is Near (2007)
By: John MacArthur, a widely known popular author and conference speaker for his thorough, candid approach to teaching God's Word.

The Book of Revelation Decoded: Your Guide to Understanding the End Times Through the Eyes of the Hebrew Prophets (2017)
By: Rabbi K. A. Schneider, an international evangelist who serves as Lion of Judah World Outreach Center rabbi.

Charting the End Times: A Visual Guide to Understanding Bible Prophecy (2021)
By: Tim LaHaye is an internationally known author, teacher, and expert on Bible prophecy.

End of the Age: The Countdown Has Begun (2021)
By: John Hagee, founder and senior pastor of Cornerstone Church in San Antonio, Texas. He also broadcasts the Gospel on radio and television throughout America and the world.

Faith for Earth's Final Hour (2003)
By: Hal Lindsey who is considered one of the world's leading experts on Bible prophecy.

Revelation: A Line by Line Breakdown

From Daniel to Doomsday: The Countdown Has Begun (2000)
By: John Hagee; The author discusses the end of the world by paralleling the Scripture with world events from the time of Daniel through the twentieth century.

Heaven: A Comprehensive Guide (2004)
By: Randy Alcorn is an author, founder, and director of Eternal Perspective Ministries (EPM). Randy has written more than fifty books.

THE HOUR That Changes Everything (2021)
By: Richard Pearsonis, a 1977 Graduate of Oral Roberts University and a former missionary pilot.

Is There Death In The Pot? Replacement Theology Exposed (2012)
By: Rev. Frank Andrews: Replacement theology is a relatively new title used to describe a very old doctrinal belief. It suggests that the Church has replaced Israel.

Jerusalem Countdown (2007)
By: John Hagee skillfully unveils the reasons radical Islam and Israel cannot dwell peaceably together as he paints a convincing picture explaining why Christians must support the State of Israel.

Lost Prophecies Of The Future Of America (2020)
By: Michael Snyder, who is the author of four books. He has been a frequent guest on major radio and television shows nationwide, and his websites have been viewed more than 100 million times.

Military Guide to Armageddon: Battle-Tested Strategies to Prepare Your Life and Soul for the End Times (2021)
By: Col. David J. Giammona, a U.S. Army chaplain, retired in 2018 after 32 years. He is an end-times expert, scholar, author, writer, and speaker.

Popular Encyclopedia of Bible Prophecy (2004)
By Tim LaHaye and Ed Hindson, Bible prophecy can seem vague and mysterious. Find the clarity and answers in this comprehensive resource.

The Rapture: Truth or Consequences (1983)
By Hal Lindsey: As the world's attention turns to a battle beginning in Israel, prophecies foretell that living men and women will suddenly vanish; the Bible says, "into the clouds to meet the Lord in the air."

The Road to Holocaust (1990)
By: Hal Lindsey (about Pre, Post, and A Millennialism) Just as current events converge into the precise pattern the biblical prophets predicted would herald the return of Jesus Christ, a new movement has arisen that denies all the precise meaning of prophecy—this movement, commonly known as Dominion or Replacement Theology.

Spiritual Warfare in the End Time (2020)
By: Ron Rhodes, Th.D., teaches at Dallas Theological Seminary and several other seminaries.

The Three Heavens: Angels, Demons and What Lies Ahead (2015)
By John Hagee; this biblical excursion of the three heavens takes you inside the timeless clash between the Kingdom of Light and the Kingdom of Darkness and explains why that battle makes all the difference in this world and the world to come.

Understanding Bible Prophecy for Yourself (2002)
By: Tim LaHaye; Biblical Prophecy with charts, tips for interpreting difficult passages, and Bible history and customs summaries.

Vanished into Thin Air: The Hope of Every Believer (1999)
By: Hal Lindsey: If you thought you knew all there was to know about the end times and the rapture, learn how to analyze today's world for yourself to see prophecy coming alive.

Your Guide To The Jewish Holidays (2015)
By: Cantor Matt Axelrod: Most Christians know nothing of Jewish life, culture, and celebrations. This is an excellent book for a basic understanding of Jewish holidays.

Made in the USA
Columbia, SC
27 July 2024

9670ac23-d810-458f-866f-9ce3f37fa7b4R01